Children's Literature
Volume 20

Volume 20

*Annual of
The Modern Language Association
Division on Children's Literature
and The Children's Literature
Association*

Yale University Press

New Haven and London

1992

Children's Literature

Editor-in-chief: Francelia Butler
Guest Editor: Judith A. Plotz
Editor: Barbara Rosen
Editorial Associates: Christine Doyle Francis, Julie K. Pfeiffer, Anne K. Phillips
Intern: Samantha Jane Wilcox
Book Review Editor: John Cech
Advisory Board: Jan Alberghene (representing the ChLA), Margaret Higonnet, U. C. Knoepflmacher, Alison Lurie, Sam Pickering, Jr., Albert J. Solnit, M.D.
Consultants for Volume 20: Gillian Adams, Geoffrey Carter, Robert Combs, Margaret Garrett, Richard Gillin, Cynthia Leenerts, Jane Rabb, Joseph Sendry

The editors gratefully acknowledge support from the University of Connecticut.

Volume 21 is the last issue of *Children's Literature* that will be edited at the University of Connecticut. Beginning April 1, 1992, please submit all articles to:

The Editors, *Children's Literature*
Department of English
Hollins College
Roanoke, Virginia 24020

Manuscripts submitted should conform to the new MLA style. An original on non-erasable bond with two copies, a self-addressed envelope, and return postage are requested. Name should appear only on the original. Yale University Press does not accept dot-matrix printouts, and it requires double-spacing throughout text and notes. Unjustified margins are preferred.

Volumes 1–7 of *Children's Literature* can be obtained directly from John C. Wandell, The Children's Literature Foundation, Box 370, Windham Center, Connecticut 06280. Volumes 8–19 can be obtained from Yale University Press, 92A Yale Station, New Haven, Connecticut 06520, or from Yale University Press, 23 Pond Street, Hampstead, London NW3 2PN, England.

Library of Congress catalog card number: 79-66588
ISBN: 0-300-05173-5 (cloth); 0-300-05172-7 (paper)

Set in Baskerville type by Tseng Information Systems, Inc., Durham, N.C. Printed in the United States of America by Vail-Ballou Press, Binghamton, N.Y.

Published with the assistance of the Frederick W. Hilles Publication Fund of Yale University.

10   9   8   7   6   5   4   3   2   1

Contents

Why the Kipling Issue Was Made

Critics have often treated Kipling as if he were the Rhinoceros of his own fable. With "no manners then, and . . . no manners now," the Rhinoceros-Kipling has been portrayed from the 1890s to the present as a thick-skinned truculent hooligan and imperialist. With his self-righteous appropriation of the Parsee's goods, his geographic expansiveness in the "Exclusively Uninhabited Interior," his hypermasculine but ultimately futile posturings, and his myopic unawareness of his crumby inner self, the Rhinoceros-Kipling may seem an anachronism. Surely he can no longer reasonably be commended as a friend to the children of our multicultural postmodern era.

Yet judging by their pertinacity, Kipling's children's books are anything but anachronistic. As Brian Alderson's "Just-So Pictures" points out, Kipling's major works for children—*Just So Stories*, *The Jungle Books*, and *Kim*—have been continuously in print since their first publication and have gone through multiple editions, even in this postcolonial era.

The contributors to this volume acknowledge the always imperial and sometimes brutal quality of Kipling's vision. Indeed, three essays—John Murray's "The Law of *The Jungle Books*," Judith A. Plotz's "The Empire of Youth," and Carole Scott's "Kipling's Combat Zones"—stress his politicizing of children's texts, even when those texts offer the seeming sanctuary of what Scott calls "otherworlds." Murray demonstrates the ways in which imperial administrative law is replicated within Kipling's jungle; Plotz analyzes Kim's Janus identity—Perfect Friend and Perfect Spy—as an artifact of empire; and Scott claims Kipling's imaginary universes as antiutopian initiatory "combat zones" governed by incontrovertible codes of law.

Yet the contributors see Kipling less as a thick-skinned rhinoceros than as a boundlessly curious and perennially empathetic Elephant's Child who fills his texts "with his 'satiable curtiosities . . . about everything that he saw, or heard, or felt, or smelt, or touched." Learning, especially the physically exuberant learning of early childhood, is the recurrent concern of a number of these critics. Alderson, Howard R. Cell, U. C. Knoepflmacher, and D. H. Stewart all focus on Kipling's ability to "carry on the feelings of childhood into the powers of manhood," the power Coleridge identified as the mark of genius. Alderson's "Just-So Pictures" argues for the superiority of Kipling's illustrations to the *Just So Stories* over those of all other illustrators because of his ability to turn pictures into serious, uncondescending dialogues with the reading/listening child. In "The Socratic Pilgrimage of the Elephant's Child," Cell plays out the resemblances between Socrates, the dean of all philosophers, and the Elephant's Child, surrogate for all questioning children and for the insatiably curious Kipling as well. Knoepflmacher, in "Female Power and Male Self-Assertion," locates Kipling's great achievement precisely in his retentive grasp of the early childhood experience of male creativity nurtured and circumscribed by maternal power. Stewart's "*Stalky* and the Language of Education" highlights Kipling's keen awareness of the physicality of childhood language and learning. In "Puck & Co." Corinne McCutchan demonstrates how *Puck of Pook's Hill* and *Rewards and Fairies* operate within the sophisticated romance tradition. Juliet McMaster emphasizes Kipling's pedagogic manipulation of archetypes in "The Trinity Archetype in *The Jungle Books* and *The Wizard of Oz*."

If, despite his unsparing portrayal of its brutalities, Kipling's thick-skinned imperialism has not worn well, his resilient and joyous curiosity about how and what and why children explore and learn continues to engage both scholars and children. And that is why the Kipling issue was made.

JUDITH A. PLOTZ
Guest Editor

The Law of The Jungle Books

John Murray

There is broad critical agreement that the concept of law is vital and pervasive in Kipling's work, and the concept has been the subject of at least one book, Shamsul Islam's *Kipling's "Law"*. Islam devotes considerable space to a discussion of the law in *The Jungle Books*, asserting that "an exposition of the nature of the Law is one of Kipling's main aims in *The Jungle Books* in general and the Mowgli stories in particular" (122). He highlights their didactic purpose by stating that while they are "primarily children's books, [they] are secondarily educational manuals" and that Kipling is being "didactic as well as entertaining" (121). Bonamy Dobrée agrees with these sentiments, asserting that "what Kipling felt to be essential to the Law is made plain in *The Jungle Books*, where it . . . brings into play the virtues of loyalty, keeping your promises, courage, and respect for other people" and that the law in *The Jungle Books* "is intended to be far from what we often casually refer to as 'jungle law'" (67). Ironically, in the jungle, where popular usage finds no law at all, Kipling finds a detailed and pervasive, but morally neutral, code "that has arranged for almost every accident that may befall the Jungle-people" and ensures the preservation of jungle society ("How Fear Came," *Second JB* 3). In the village, however, he finds the disorder and improvidence that lead to its eventual destruction.

The Mowgli stories contain more than forty direct references to law,[1] and the first of the stories, "Mowgli's Brothers," contains fifteen such references, repeatedly adverting to the "Law of the Jungle, which never orders anything without a reason" (5), and "lays down very clearly" the rights of individual wolves (10) and the procedures for solving disputes (12). Yet many critics writing in the second half of this century react to such an obviously important matter with unease, evasion, or dislike. Islam feels constrained to comment on the primitive social setting of the law to excuse the vengeful violence that Kipling's "educational manuals" contain; violent revenge, he says, "need not trouble the reader too much" (129). Elliot L.

Children's Literature 20, ed. Francelia Butler, Barbara Rosen, and Judith A. Plotz (Yale University Press, © 1992 by The Children's Literature Foundation, Inc.).

Gilbert tries to counter misgivings about the ethical nature of the law in his article "Three Criticisms of *The Jungle Books*" by saying that the law in *The Jungle Books* is a "law of nature," thereby removing all legal and ethical content from it (7). A "law of nature" is not a law in the usual sense but rather a proposition concerning the working of the universe: one cannot, for example, claim that the First Law of Thermodynamics is good or evil, desirable or otherwise, and one cannot disobey or alter it. ("Natural law," by contrast, is law deduced from ideals of justice and human rights.) [2] C. S. Lewis, who cannot "understand how a man of taste could doubt that Kipling is a very great artist," can still "recoil" from Kipling's world because it is "unendurable—a heavy, glaring, suffocating monstrosity" (99). His reaction is partly caused by ethical considerations, and he puts his finger precisely on the reason for his reaction: much of the law is a code of group survival, and is "morally neutral—the obedient servant of valour and public spirit, but equally of cruelty, extortion, oppression, and dishonesty" (115–16).

This uneasy or hostile reaction of otherwise sympathetic critics stems from their assumption of a necessary connection between law and ethics. A crucial distinction may be made among all the different conceptions of law, however, and it hinges on a single issue: whether or not there is an ethical dimension to law. Proponents of the doctrine of natural law would say that there is. On the other hand, proponents of the "analytical positivism" associated with John Austin (1790–1859), and current in English jurisprudence at the time of the writing of *The Jungle Books*,[3] would say that there is not—as would adherents of today's "critical legal studies" movement.[4] In the light of legal theory, Dobrée's association of the law with virtue is not a necessary one, and Islam's hopeful assertion that the "end of both law and ethics is to make man good, teaching him to practise virtue and refrain from vice" (126) is both dubious and oversimple, though it is easy enough to see why both critics write as they do. Accepting Kipling's patently didactic purpose as being appropriate in books for children, they expect Kipling's law to embody ethics, and therefore have to assert that it does so despite its apparent ethical poverty. They also have to excuse the brutality and occasional arbitrariness in the application of the law.

Further, along with Lewis, whose objection to the moral neutrality of Kipling's law has already been noted, they are writing in the third quarter of the twentieth century, unavoidably aware of

such instances of arbitrary but legal violence as the Holocaust and
the Gulag Archipelago, and of "the testimony of those who have
descended into Hell, and, like Ulysses or Dante, brought back a
message for human beings. Only in this case Hell was not beneath
or beyond the earth but on it; it was a Hell created on earth by men
for other men" (Hart, "Positivism" 615–16). The Nuremberg and
Eichmann trials brought into high relief the conflict between invio-
lable human rights, as propounded by theories of natural law, and
the unlimited legality of the commands of a sovereign state, as propounded by theories of analytical positivism. Though both trials
were conducted under positive law, both raised the question, "Is
there a higher law which could render such acts [as the Holocaust]
punishable whatever might be the decrees of a particular state to
which the accused owed allegiance?" (Lloyd 88).[5] To a degree, such
an international statement of values as the Universal Declaration
of Human Rights sought in 1948 to supply such a higher law, and
though the "tendency of the present day is to formulate these values
in specifically positive-law terms, the natural-law origin of this mode
of approach still remains fairly apparent" (Lloyd 141). The experience of critics who lived through the Second World War and its
aftermath may well place them in the position described by Lon L.
Fuller: "[I]f you were raised with a generation that said 'law is law'
and meant it, you may feel the only way you can escape one law
is to set another off against it, and this perforce must be a 'higher
law'" (660).

   Though Kipling was no legal theorist, he was a child of his time
in his imperialism, in his trust in practical science, observation, and
experience, and in his distrust of metaphysics. It is not surprising
that his concept of law shows practicality and lacks idealism; it is
even less surprising, given his imperialist attitudes, that a theory
of law that Wolfgang Friedmann says "enabled the rising national
State to assert its authority undisturbed by juristic doubts" (*Legal
Theory* 378) should have appealed to him. When Kipling returned
to India in 1882 he was entering a country whose rulers were re-
treating from an "earlier emphasis on moral force and the influence
of the example of British character, to the less ambitious idea that
India was held simply by military power" (Hutchins 186). He encountered what one of India's leading officials called, in a letter to
The Times on March 1, 1883, "an absolute government, founded not
on consent, but on conquest" (8). The writer of that letter, Sir James

Fitzjames Stephen, was a "highly respected commentator" (Wurgaft 71) whose influence upon the Indian Civil Service, especially upon its legal codes, was considerable:

> He was its political philosopher and gave to its prejudices and emotions a reasoned and logical support. He showed how a man could consistently favour every aspect of a free society and yet deny the gift of political freedom itself. In this he was standing in the line of intellectual Liberals whose most distinguished representative had been John Austin, one of the fountain-heads of Stephen's philosophy of law. [Stokes 305]

Stephen infused Austinian legal theory into the Indian Civil Service. "I had charge of the Code [of Criminal Procedure] of 1872, and carried it through the Legislative Council," he wrote in the chapter on Indian criminal law in his *History of the Criminal Law of England* (3.345). Austin's opinion about "higher law" is unequivocal: "Now, to say that human laws which conflict with the Divine law are not binding, that is to say, are not laws, is to talk stark nonsense" (185). Further, says Austin, because the Roman notion of *ius gentium* is often associated with belief in a moral instinct or in innate practical principles, "it ought to be expelled, with the *natural law* of the moderns, from the sciences of jurisprudence and morality" (179). Stephen's description of Indian criminal law shows a similar distaste for "higher law":

> The Penal Code, the Code of Criminal Procedure, and the institutions which they regulate, are somewhat grim presents for one people to make to another, and are little calculated to excite affection; but they are eminently well calculated to protect peaceable men and to beat down wrongdoers, to extort respect, and to enforce obedience. [*History* 3.345]

Critics who consciously or unconsciously believe in a necessary connection between law and morality balk at analytical positivism, and by extension at its literary embodiment in works like the Mowgli stories in *The Jungle Books*, all the more so because they are children's stories. Nevertheless, though Kipling was writing for children in *The Jungle Books*, and though one might therefore expect him to inculcate ethics rather than expediency, the exposition of the law in Kipling's Mowgli stories follows the notions of analytical positivism closely. An explanation of how this is so requires a brief summary of the main tenets of analytical positivism and natural law.

In the second edition of *Legal Theory* Friedmann conveniently and lucidly sums up Austin's positivism in a set of propositions, of which the most important are:

> Positive law and ideal law (or ethics) must be kept strictly distinct. Law cannot be defined by reference to any ideal of justice.

> All positive law is deduced from a clearly determinable lawgiver as sovereign. . . . [This] may be an individual or a body or aggregate of individuals.

> The essence of all law is the command addressed by the sovereign to the subject, coupled with the threat of sanction if the command is disobeyed.

> The sovereign is not himself bound by any legal limitations. [145]

Against these propositions one may range those of natural law, which is inspired in its many forms by "two ideas, of a universal order governing all men, and of the inalienable rights of the individual" (Friedmann, *Legal Theory* 16). Using Friedmann's discussion of the French jurist François Gény (1861–1959), I have constructed a parallel set of propositions that clearly reveals the distinction between natural law theory and that of Austin:

> Positive and ideal law cannot be separated. Law must ultimately be defined by reference to an ideal of justice.

> Natural law is the basis of positive law and would include "the fundamental postulates of justice such as the sanctity of human life, the development of human faculties and . . . freedom of thought and inviolability of the person." [223]

> The essence of all law is the application of the "immutable and universal factors" [222] of natural law in terms of positive law.

> The sovereign is bound by legal limitations, and in the extreme case of "the oppression of despotic laws . . . natural law would legitimate rebellion." [224]

Application of these two sets of propositions to the Mowgli stories shows that Kipling assumes the analytical positivism of Austin, Stephen, and the Indian Civil Service, rather than natural law doctrine, as a basis of the Law of the Jungle.

In "How Fear Came" Kipling deduces the law "from a clearly determinable law-giver as sovereign" in the person of Tha, "the Lord of the Jungle" and "the First of the Elephants" (*Second JB* 20). The reason put forward for the imposition of law is not ethics but expediency. The establishment of a law that all must obey is required because the tiger's brutality and the ape's fecklessness have brought fear and shame to the jungle (20). The Mowgli stories also embody the Austinian proposition concerning the application of law, that the "essence of all law is a command addressed by the sovereign to the subject, coupled with the threat of sanction if the command is disobeyed." Hathi, the descendant of Tha, is sovereign; even Shere Khan knows "what every one else knows—that when the last comes to the last, Hathi is Master of the Jungle" (15–16). In "How Fear Came" Hathi condemns Shere Khan's boast of killing man by choice, and, supported by his sons, orders the tiger away from the river, but he does not deny the legality of Shere Khan's actions (15).

Kipling follows Austin's contention that law and ethics should "be kept strictly distinct." The rules of what Kipling calls law are not ethically based but are, rather, "positive laws" designed to ensure self-preservation or the preservation of society. In "The Law of the Jungle" verse at the end of "How Fear Came" (29–32) Kipling does not refer "to any ideal of justice" involved in obeying the law. Instead, he refers to the law in terms of self-interest and "the threat of sanction if the command is disobeyed": "*[T]he Wolf that shall keep it may prosper, but the Wolf that shall break it must die*" (line 2; Kipling's italics). In line after line, the verse inculcates utilitarian principles: cleanliness (5), adequacy of sleep (6), avoidance of danger from larger animals (9–10), avoidance of unnecessary conflict (11–12), limitation of internecine violence (13–14), construction of secure shelter (15–18), efficiency and avoidance of waste in hunting (19–21), avoidance of the retribution consequent upon killing man (22), sharing of food with other pack members, especially cubs and breeding females (23–32), and freedom of males to hunt solely for their own families (33–34). Apart from the injunctions to the young to be clean and polite, all of the remaining rules, including the prohibition against killing man, are designed to ensure that every member of the pack, strong or weak, has sufficient food to survive and does not run unnecessary risks of violence from within the pack, from other packs, or from "white men on elephants" ("Mowgli's Brothers," *JB* 5) who hunt down man-killers. Where there is no stated law, Kipling advocates Machiavellian guile and force: "Because of his age and his cunning, because of his gripe and his paw, / In all that the Law leaveth open, the word of the Head Wolf is Law" ("The Law of the Jungle" lines 35–36, *Second JB* 32). As a contrast to the law-abiding wolves, Kipling presents the monkeys as ineffectual, foolish outcasts because they do not submit their wills to law and to a leader in order to proceed toward goals in a disciplined fashion. He contrasts the effects of lawlessness and discipline. Lawlessness results in wolves "lame from traps . . . [limping] from shot-wounds . . . mangy from eating bad food" ("Tiger-Tiger!" *JB* 90–91). Discipline has the effect that "no stranger cared to break into the jungles . . . the young wolves grew fat and strong, and there were many cubs" ("Red Dog," *Second JB* 223). None of these outcomes, desirable or otherwise, is an ethical matter.

For Kipling, law is a matter of group cohesion and self-preservation rather than ethics, as Noel Annan notes in his essay "Kipling's Place in the History of Ideas." Nevertheless, Annan is as mistaken as Martin Seymour-Smith says he is (241) in trying to connect Kipling's concern for the survival of the group with the ideas of such social theorists as Emile Durkheim, Max Weber, and Vilfredo Pareto. Rather, Kipling acquired that concern in India, which was, in effect, an occupied country ruled on the basis of the Austinian proposition that the "essence of all law is the command addressed by the sovereign to the subject, coupled with the threat of sanction if the command is disobeyed." As Stephen argued in the 1883 letter to *The Times* already quoted:

> [I]t is impossible to imagine any policy more fearfully danger-
> ous and more certain, in the case of failure, to lead to results
> to which the Mutiny would be child's play than the policy of
> shifting the foundations on which the British Government of
> India rests. It is essentially an absolute Government, founded,
> not on consent, but on conquest, . . . and no anomaly can be
> more striking or so dangerous, as its administration by men,
> who being at the head of a Government founded upon con-
> quest, implying at every point the superiority of the conquering

race . . . and having no justification for its existence except that
superiority, shrink from the open, uncompromising, straightforward assertion of it. [8]

Kipling has no qualms about such an assertion, and shares Jeremy
Bentham's and Austin's liking for military efficiency: "The cohesion, discipline, and perfect subordination of a military body, which
worked almost in silence with the minimum of discussion and crisp
commands, appeared to such minds a thing of intellectual beauty"
(Stokes 309). In "Servants of the Queen" Kipling celebrates the
frightening power achieved by perfect obedience to the chain of
command stretching from the animals used by the army to the
empress (*JB* 208) and the effect of that power in maintaining the
empire: "And for that reason . . . your Amir whom you do not
obey must come here and take orders from our Viceroy" (*JB* 209).[6]
Kipling further stresses unquestioning obedience in "The Parade
Song of the Camp Animals" at the end of the story; even the men
who lead the animals "cannot tell why we or they / March and suffer
day by day" (*JB* 212).

Further, Kipling's law ensures that power is passed on to a sovereign able to enforce "the threat of sanction if the command is disobeyed." When "a leader of the pack has missed his kill, he is called
the Dead Wolf as long as he lives, which is not long" ("Mowgli's
Brothers," *JB* 26), and a new leader must "[fight] his way to the
leadership of the pack according to the Jungle Law" ("Red Dog,"
Second JB 280).[7] Kipling shares such social Darwinism with Stephen,
who proclaimed in another letter to *The Times* on January 4, 1878:

> I for one, feel no shame when I think of the great competitive
> examination which has lasted for just 100 years, and of which
> the first paper was set upon the field of Plassey, and the last
> (for the present) under the walls of Delhi and Lucknow. [3]

For Kipling and Stephen, effective rule based upon obedience, not
ethics, is of paramount importance.

Kipling places no limitations whatever upon obedience to the
law: "the head and the hoof of the Law and the haunch and the
hump is—Obey!" ("The Law of the Jungle," line 38, *Second JB* 32).
Nor does he sanction rebellion against "the oppression of despotic
laws." He demands complete obedience of Mowgli with respect to
human law when Mowgli leaves the jungle, even when such law is
unfair or outdated:

Keep the Law the man pack make—
For thy blind old Baloo's sake!
Clean or tainted, hot or stale,
Hold it as it were the trail,
Through the day and through the night,
Questing neither left nor right.

["The Outsong," lines 3–8, *Second JB* 296]

As a man, Mowgli is not subject to the Law of the Jungle, even though he knows its code thoroughly. This consideration explains Bagheera's comment that "there is more in the jungle now than Jungle Law, Baloo" when Mowgli refuses to give a reason for all that he chooses to do in "Letting in the Jungle" (*Second JB* 67), and it also explains Mowgli's treatment of Hathi in that story. Because Hathi is sovereign in the jungle, Mowgli cannot force Hathi to help him in obliterating the village. Mowgli can, however, form an alliance with Hathi on the basis of shared hatred of men who have trapped and scarred Hathi and who use the ankus to "teach [elephants] Man's Law" ("The King's Ankus," *Second JB* 166). Bagheera's "terror" and his exclamations to the effect that Mowgli is "Master of the jungle" ("Letting in the Jungle," *Second JB* 95) are not expressions of approbation of an act sanctioned by ethics or by previous law. Rather, Mowgli has become a human pack-leader of exceptional power who, in "Red Dog," uses his intelligence for unselfish ends to save the pack, but in "Letting in the Jungle" imposes his will upon the jungle animals through his human superiority and through an alliance with the sovereign of the jungle in order to exact personal revenge.

For a reader who subscribes to the theory of natural law, the case of revenge and exemplary destruction raises the matter of law and ethics inescapably. Kipling depicts Mowgli's revenge as a good thing; Mowgli enjoys having the "good conscience that comes from paying a just debt" ("Red Dog," *Second JB* 221). Yet in his "rage and hate" ("Letting in the Jungle," *Second JB* 95) Mowgli's indiscriminate destruction of the village lacks even the crude limitations of the *lex talionis:* "life for life, eye for eye, tooth for tooth, hand for hand . . . burn for burn" (Exodus 21:23–25). The victims of injustice are little better: Messua's husband intends to use English justice for revenge also, in "a lawsuit . . . as shall eat this village to the bone" ("Letting in the Jungle," *Second JB* 83). In Austin's eyes both of these actions are legitimate, simply because Mowgli, Hathi, and the English are able to enforce obedience. Kipling clearly demonstrates that the ultimate sanction ensuring such obedience and causing Bagheera's fear is the deliberate, premeditated, disciplined use of force. The same state of affairs held good in British India, though at the time of the writing of *The Jungle Books*, when the vast bulk of Indian society accepted British rule, the smug Austinian view that Stephen expressed in 1883 was not far from the truth:

> If it is asked how the system works in practice, I can only say that it enables a handful of foreigners (I am far from thinking that if they were more sympathetic they would be more efficient) to rule justly and firmly about 200,000,000 persons, of many races, languages, and creeds, and, in many parts of the country, bold, sturdy, and warlike. [*History* 3.344]

In the face of mounting nationalist resistance, however, the nakedness of the organized force behind British rule, like that behind the power of Mowgli and Hathi, manifested itself in law in the Rowlatt Acts, and in action in the Jallianwala Bagh massacre led by Brigadier General Reginald Dyer in April 1919—action that would probably have been classed as a "war crime" after 1945.

> Though the government of India vehemently dissociated itself from such a policy of intimidation, Dyer was expressing the general attitude of many of the civil and military in India. Dyer was removed from his command, but his actions (and presumably his motives) were supported by a large section of the British press as well as by members of parliament and others. A sum of £26,000 was subscribed as a testimonial for this gallant British soldier. [Edwardes 202]

Ten pounds of that *Morning Post* fund came from Rudyard Kipling (Draper 238).

Gandhi's use of nonviolent noncooperation repeatedly contested the moral neutrality of analytical positivism and showed again and again the ultimate brutality behind colonial rule. "Letting in the Jungle," more than any other story in *The Jungle Books*, depicts the organized force through which obedience is secured with a relish that readily explains C. S. Lewis's belief that Kipling could make the law the "servant . . . of cruelty [and] oppression." In Austinian terms, however, Kipling is doing no more than telling the unvarnished truth about the nature of law.

Proponents of natural law cannot avoid the issue of the nonethical nature of Kipling's law by arguing that it is not to be applied outside the jungle, because such an argument denies the clearly didactic purpose of the Mowgli stories, especially the explicit parallel between undisciplined monkeys and undisciplined humans in "Kaa's Hunting." As Mark Paffard points out, "there is an unmistakable similarity between the Bandar-Log . . . and the Yahoos of *Gulliver's Travels.* Both are species of monkeys, and both are portrayed as idle and senseless because they lack any organisation or any code of social conduct" (93). In addition, Mowgli's revenge applies outside the world of animals, and "The Outsong" at the end of *The Second Jungle Book* (296–99) enjoins upon Mowgli unswerving obedience to human law, no matter how defective or unpleasant.

Apart from the rules for self-preservation and the right of sovereigns, the law in the Mowgli stories contains only contracts: the curious, almost totemic injunction to Mowgli never to "kill . . . any cattle young or old" because of the "price of the bull's life" ("Mowgli's Brothers," *JB* 26); the contract under which Mowgli is entered into the pack and released from it; the contract under which Mowgli pays for a knife found "round the neck of a man who had been killed by a wild boar" ("Red Dog," *Second JB* 222) by killing the boar. Mowgli's undertaking to fight the dholes with the pack in "Red Dog," however, is based on Mowgli's love for Akela and his wolf parents and siblings, and is a personal agreement. In fact, as Kaa points out, Mowgli's undertaking is imprudent: "And thou hast tied thyself into a death-knot for the sake of the memory of dead wolves?" (232). There is love in the jungle, but it is not part of the law, just as there was, among some members of the Indian Civil Service, a genuine regard for the people they ruled that could never outweigh the need to maintain a clear separation between governors and governed.

An understanding of the disparity between Austin's theory of law and that of natural law explains the problems of some modern critics in reconciling the nonethical nature of the law in the Mowgli stories with their didacticism. Kipling's law, despite what sympathetic readers of the third quarter of this century would like it to be, is "morally neutral" just as British legal thinking of his day was morally neutral. By contrast, the standpoint of many twentieth-century readers and critics is that of the famous jurist Lauterpacht: "We would rather err in pursuit of a good life for all than glory in the secure infallibility of moral indifference" (136). Our conscious or unconscious assumption of a connection between law and ethics explains modern critical response to Kipling's exposition of law, ranging from unfounded approbation in Dobrée, to excuse in Islam, to evasion in Gilbert, to condemnation in Lewis. Despite what such critics might wish, Kipling's law was never intended to make his readers good. Rather, it was intended to make them safe citizens at home and effective rulers in the colonies.

Notes

1. The references in *The Jungle Book* are as follows: in "Mowgli's Brothers," 4, 5, 10, 12 (twice), 13 (twice), 14 (twice), 17, 19, 21, 25, 26, 27; in "Kaa's Hunting," 32 (twice), 33, 34, 36, 37, 51, 52, 63 (thrice); in "Tiger-Tiger!" 71. The references in *The Second Jungle Book* are as follows: "How Fear Came," 3, 7, 10, 11, 13, 16, 18, 20 (twice); the whole of "The Law of the Jungle" (29–32); "Letting in the Jungle," 67, 74 (twice), 82; "Red Dog," 223 (twice); "The Spring Running," 273 (twice), 292, 293; "The Outsong," 296, 297.

2. "Natural law" was adumbrated in classical Greece, developed in the *ius gentium* of Roman law, formed an essential part of the theological and philosophical system of Thomas Aquinas, and grew from the ideas of Hobbes and Locke into the declarations of rights and the constitutions promulgated during the American and French revolutions. Its most influential contemporary theorist is John Finnis (*Natural Law and Natural Rights*. Oxford: Clarendon, 1980).

3. "Analytical positivism" stems from the legal theory developed from Jeremy Bentham's utilitarian philosophy by John Austin (1790–1859). Though his writings were much admired by the Benthamite circle, they had little influence in his lifetime. With the posthumous publication in 1863 of the whole of his work, *The Province of Jurisprudence Determined* and *Lectures on Jurisprudence: Or, the Philosophy of Positive Law*, "his ideas came to dominate English jurisprudence, which for long remained analytical in character" (Hart, "Austin" 472). His theory had a direct influence on the Indian Civil Service through James Fitzjames Stephen (Stokes 305), and is still influential in the work of H. L. A. Hart and Ronald Dworkin.

4. The critical legal studies movement regards much legal theory as "the perennial effort to restate power and preconception as right" (Unger 674). "Its point of departure has been the thesis that law and legal doctrine reflect, confirm, and reshape the social divisions and hierarchies inherent in a type or stage of social organization such as 'capitalism' " (Unger 563n).

5. As Wolfgang Friedmann notes, the members of the Nuremberg Tribunal derived their jurisdiction from the Nuremberg Charter, "basing themselves on the binding force of the positive law imposed upon Germany by virtue of the Allied Military Government." At the Nuremberg and Tokyo trials, however, "there were indeed hints that individuals had legal duties higher than those of obedience to the positive law of their sovereign" (*Law in a Changing Society*, 41). Eichmann's trial was based upon a positive Israeli law passed retrospectively, "though many of its provisions, such as those dealing with 'crimes against humanity,' had a natural-law ring about them" (Lloyd 81).

6. A similar description occurs in another story about the necessity for unquestioning obedience, "The Conversion of Aurelian McGoggin," in *Plain Tales from the Hills* (98).

7. Kipling may possibly have had in mind the ritual killing of the priest of Nemi described in Frazer's *The Golden Bough*. As Nora Crook points out, Kipling met Frazer in 1921 when both men received honorary degrees from the Sorbonne, but Kipling may well have read Frazer long before. He "owned a volume of Frazer's *Folklore in the Old Testament* . . . and his annotated translation of Apollodorus (Bateman's). The 'Neminaka cafe' in 'Dayspring Mishandled,' which treats the literary world as a cut-throat priesthood, probably derives from Chapter 1 of *The Golden Bough*" (183n).

Works Cited

Annan, Noel. "Kipling's Place in the History of Ideas." In *Kipling's Mind and Art*, ed. Andrew Rutherford. London: Oliver and Boyd, 1964. 97–125.

Austin, John. *The Province of Jurisprudence Determined and The Uses of the Study of Jurisprudence*, ed. H. L. A. Hart. London: Weidenfeld and Nicolson, 1971.

Crook, Nora. *Kipling's Myths of Love and Death*. New York: St. Martin's Press, 1989.

Dobrée, Bonamy. *Rudyard Kipling: Realist and Fabulist*. London: Oxford University Press, 1967.

Draper, Alfred. *Amritsar: The Massacre That Ended the Raj*. London: Cassell, 1981.

Edwardes, Michael. *British India, 1772–1947: A Survey of the Nature and Effects of Alien Rule*. London: Sidgwick and Jackson, 1967.

Friedmann, Wolfgang. *Law in a Changing Society*. 2d ed. New York: Columbia University Press, 1972.

———. *Legal Theory*. 2nd ed. London: Stevens and Sons, 1949.

Fuller, Lon L. "Fidelity to Law—A Reply to Professor Hart." *Harvard Law Review* 71.4 (1958): 630–72.

Gilbert, Elliot L. "Three Criticisms of *The Jungle Books*." *The Kipling Journal* 33 (December 1966): 6–10.

Hart, H. L. A. "John Austin." In *International Encyclopaedia of the Social Sciences*, ed. David L. Sills. N.p.: Macmillan, 1968.

———. "Positivism and the Separation of Law and Morals." *Harvard Law Review* 71.4 (1958): 593–629.

Hutchins, Francis G. *The Illusion of Permanence: British Imperialism in India*. Princeton: Princeton University Press, 1967.

Islam, Shamsul. *Kipling's "Law": A Study of His Philosophy of Life*. London: Macmillan, 1975.

Kipling, Rudyard. *The Jungle Book*. London: Macmillan, 1894.

———. *Plain Tales from the Hills*. London: Macmillan, 1903.

———. *The Second Jungle Book*. London: Macmillan, 1908, rpt. 1963.

Lauterpacht, H. "Kelsen's Pure Science of Law." In *Modern Theories of Law*, preface by W. Ivor Jennings. London: Oxford University Press, 1933: 105–138.

Lewis, C. S. "Kipling's World." In *Kipling and the Critics*, ed. Elliot L. Gilbert. New York: New York University Press, 1965. 99–117.

Lloyd, Dennis. *The Idea of Law*. Harmondsworth: Penguin, 1973.

Paffard, Mark. *Kipling's Indian Fiction*. London: Macmillan, 1989.

Pound, Roscoe. *An Introduction to the Philosophy of Law*. Rev. ed. New Haven and London: Yale University Press, 1974.

Seymour-Smith, Martin. *Rudyard Kipling*. London: Queen Anne Press, 1989.

Stephen, James Fitzjames. *A History of the Criminal Law of England*. 3 vols. New York: Burt Franklin, 1883, rpt. 1973.

———. Letter. *The Times*. January 4, 1878: 3

———. Letter. *The Times*. March 1, 1883: 8.

Stokes, Eric. *The English Utilitarians and India*. Oxford: Oxford University Press, 1959.

Unger, Roberto Mangabeira. "The Critical Legal Studies Movement." *Harvard Law Review* 96.3 (1983): 561–675.

Wurgaft, Lewis D. *The Imperial Imagination: Magic and Myth in Kipling's India*. Middletown, Conn.: Wesleyan University Press, 1983.

Female Power and Male Self-Assertion: Kipling and the Maternal

U. C. Knoepflmacher

My first child and daughter was born in three foot of snow on the night of December 29th 1892. Her Mother's birthday being the 31st and mine the 30th of the same month, we congratulated her on her sense of the fitness of things, and she throve in her trunk-tray in the sunshine on the little plank verandah.

—Kipling, *Something of Myself*

Whether addressed to adults or children, Kipling's writings are preoccupied with female power—a power he persistently associates with a mother or a mother surrogate. The bluster and bravado of the barracks on which Kipling had built his early reputation owe much to a male assertiveness through which the young writer handled his uneasy relation to the feminine. That relation, however, underwent a significant change as soon as Kipling began to confront his childhood both in stories written for an adult audience such as the intensely emotional "Baa Baa, Black Sheep" and in the tales for children he began to compose during "the early days of his married life in Vermont, that halcyon time when Josephine was the summit of his delight—a young baby that was his own" (Wilson 128). Effie, his Best Beloved, reconciled Kipling to those two other beings he had once loved best, the mother by whom he had felt betrayed and the little boy whose sense of omnipotence had been severely bruised by that maternal betrayal.

Even in those fictions Kipling published prior to his becoming a family man, the emphasis on male bonding all too often conceals a boy's ambivalent perception of a matriarch's power. This ambivalence did not go unnoticed by some of Kipling's shrewder contemporaries. In a famous 1904 cartoon by Max Beerbohm, a hirsute Rudyard Kipling locks arms with "Britannia, 'is gurl," while tooting a tiny bugle. They have exchanged headgear. She is wearing his bowler, while he has donned her helmet. The caricature's

Children's Literature 20, ed. Francelia Butler, Barbara Rosen, and Judith A. Plotz (Yale University Press, © 1992 by The Children's Literature Foundation, Inc.).

target seems fairly obvious. As in Beerbohm's 1912 story entitled "P.C., X, 36," an excessive male assertiveness is mercilessly undercut. The strident imperialist; the ventriloquist able to give voice to the codes of masculinity bonding soldiers, seamen, and schoolboys; the misogynist who has a gruff speaker proclaim that a woman is only a woman but that a good cigar is a Smoke—these and other Kipling stereotypes are ostensibly being deflated.

And yet, as always, Beerbohm astutely catches something subtler. The Kipling narrator in "P.C., X, 36" becomes deeply hurt when the police constable whose masculinity he so admires brusquely tells him that it is time for him to be in bed since "Yer Ma'll be lookin' out for yer" (*A Christmas Garland* 11). The cartoon likewise treats Kipling as a mama's boy. The stately Britannia is twice as tall as the little reveler who has appropriated her helmet. This raucous bugler may regard the Pre-Raphaelite, Burne-Jones beauty who towers over him as " 'is gurl." Yet it is obvious that the grown woman who glances away from him with such a vacant and superior expression has been quite reluctantly drawn into the frenzied game of a child-man. And, as the interlocked arms strongly suggest, his power—or, rather, his pretense of power—depends on this grave matriarch's might.

Beerbohm's refusal to be taken in by such masculine posturings is even more strongly expressed in his sardonic "Kipling's Entire," a 1903 review of the dramatization by "George Fleming" (a female playwright called Julia Constance Fletcher) of *The Light That Failed* (1890), Kipling's first and last novel written for adults. As uninterested in Fletcher's play as in a decade of major children's books by Kipling, Beerbohm prefers to go back to the novel itself in order to expose the adolescent fantasies of an author he deems to be "permanently and joyously obsessed" with soldiers (246). Kipling's notions "of manhood, manliness, man" strike Beerbohm as being curiously "feminine," more feminine, in fact, than those of the woman who converted the novel into a play. Male writers who are secure in their masculine identity, Beerbohm suggests, can take the "virility" of their heroes for granted. But only "effeminate men" are overly eager in trying to avoid "a sudden soprano note in the bass" they try to sound (246). Reversing Henry James's dictum that George Sand may have impersonated a man but was "not a gentleman," Beerbohm contends that it might conversely be said "that Mr. Kipling, as revealed to us in his fiction, is no lady," though he is "not the less essentially feminine for that" (247).[1]

The cynical—and often downright misogynist—fictions the young Kipling wrote for adult readers differ markedly in their orientation toward female nurturance and female power from his stories for—and about—children. That difference can already be glimpsed if one contrasts two of the "adult" productions written in 1888, "The Man Who Would Be King" and *The Story of the Gadsbys*, to "Baa Baa, Black Sheep," also written in 1888 and the tale in which Kipling at last confronted the childhood trauma of parental desertion. All three fictions dramatize the damage inflicted by female figures on a male's aspirations toward power.

In "The Man Who Would Be King," Daniel Dravot and Peachy Carnehan agree not to look at "any Woman black, white, or brown" (56); and, indeed, had Dravot heeded his companion's injunction to "leave the women alone," he would have retained his kingship and have continued to be worshiped as "God or Devil" (83, 88). Instead, by choosing a wife, "a Queen to breed a King's son for the King" (84), Dravot precipitates his downfall. Bitten in the neck by the young woman who, "white as death," causes his hand to be "red with blood" (89), Dravot is crucified by the natives who lose faith in his omnipotence. The male bond that existed between him and Peachy is reduced to the "dried, withered head," still bearded and crowned, but eyeless, defaced, and "battered," that the crazed Carnehan carries in his horsehair bag (96).

The symbiotic relation between two males is similarly broken in *The Story of the Gadsbys*. But whereas the marriage between Dravot and the "strapping wench" whose bite proves so deadly is never consummated, the longer work sets out to document its misogynist epigraph, "That a young man married is a young man marred!" (*Gadsby* 220). Mothers are now targeted as destroyers. The novella begins by mocking "Poor Dear Mamma," the matron who soon engineers Captain Gadsby's marriage to her daughter Minnie, and it ends by mocking Minnie herself, in her own role as a domineering young mother. The infant boy she calls the "*Butcha*" becomes her instrument in her campaign to get Gadsby to break his bonds to the regiment and his lingering attachment to his brother-soldier, Captain Mafflin. The gruff soldier who had pleaded with Gadsby "to send the Wife Home . . . and come to Kashmir with me" (278) is as soundly defeated as Peachy Carnehan was in "The Man Who Would Be King." "Mrs. G." delivers her coup de grace when she encourages her baby to smash Captain Mafflin's watch. The male camaraderie which Beerbohm ridicules in his attack on Kipling's soldiers, "with their self-conscious blurtings of oaths and slang, their cheap cynicism about the female sex" ("Kipling's Entire" 247), is again in evidence. But it is the female who carries the day when Mrs. G. tells her baby that the dial and hands of Mafflin's broken watch have been "werry, werry feeble" (*Gadsby* 283)—too feeble, clearly, to withstand her temporal power. Domesticity has triumphed over what Beerbohm derisively calls "manlydom" (which, for him, is something more artificial and contrived than mere "manliness").

Having portrayed the young woman who refuses to "breed" a son for Dravot and the young mother whose baby son helps her to assert her superiority over adult males, Kipling was at last ready to adopt, in "Baa Baa, Black Sheep," the point of view of a boy in the most personal of his tales of male disempowerment. Significantly enough, Punch, the story's boy protagonist, and the adult narrator who supervises his disenchantment are far more complex than their counterparts in "The Man Who Would Be King" or *The Story of the Gadsbys*. And equally significant is the rich ambivalence that now marks Kipling's portrait of the "real, live, lovely Mamma" who returns to rescue the boy Punch, just as Alice Kipling returned to rescue her Ruddy in actual life.

"Baa Baa, Black Sheep," the story which critic-biographers from Edmund Wilson in 1941 to Angus Wilson in 1977 have rightly regarded as a turning point in Kipling's career as a writer, prepared him both for *The Light That Failed* (1890) and the children's stories he began to write in 1893. The tale's immense emotional force and its correspondence with Rudyard's and his sister Trix's accounts of their childhood deprivations certainly bear out Angus Wilson's contention that it remains unique among Kipling's fictions in its "closeness to biographical fact," or, as Wilson wisely qualifies his statement, "to biographical fact as he still remembered it as he came to write *Something of Myself* at the end of his life" (18). Still, Wilson misses, I think, the importance for Kipling's artistic development of the role played by the mother, whose absence leads Punch to hone his skills as a "little liar" ("Baa Baa, Black Sheep" 360). At the story's end, both Punch and his "Mother, dear" assume that their earlier symbiosis can be resumed "as if she had never gone" (368). Yet, as the narrator suggests in no uncertain terms, they are mistaken. Though not as severely ruptured, the bond between mother and son can no more remain intact than that which existed between Peachy and Dravot or between Mafflin and Gadsby. Integral yet displaced, adored yet resented, the mother cannot be fully reunited with one whose child's wits survived and developed without her supervision. Nor, as Kipling began to understand at this point in his career, could male bonding fully serve him as an emotionally satisfying replacement for that lost primal fusion. Instead, as his stories for children would show, the mother's power had to be adopted and incorporated by the grown-up male writer who learned how to reactivate his surviving child's wits.

The first thing to be noted about "Baa Baa, Black Sheep" is that the figure of Punch and Judy's Mamma is far more prominent than that of their father. She not only returns at the end of the story to take charge of her deserted children, but also acts as an interpreter-writer whose decisiveness and self-assurance counterpoint the implied author's ironic mode of indirection and understatement. Her final letter to the husband she addresses as "dear boy" exudes confidence, energy, and wit: although she looks forward to her mate's own return to the "home" country, she assures him that she has, in effect, already taken full charge. The family's future life "under one roof" again seems certain to the mother. The repair of the broken unit, she is convinced, will merely crown her ongoing efforts: "I shall win Punch to me before long." The mother thus feels perfectly "content." If her children will again come to know her, their former trust in her can be recaptured. She is sure that the "small deceptions" and "falsehood" that Punch adopted as his prime defense against betrayal and estrangement can soon fade away (367).

Yet if the mother's confidence still needs to be tested by Punch—only to be subverted by the narrator in the story's concluding paragraph—it is also true that the primacy she chooses to adopt seems rather belated. From the very start of "Baa Baa, Black Sheep," father and mother alike have, after all, been replaced by surrogates. And, what is more, the roles played by these surrogates have markedly differed for each parent. The father's two substitutes, the two Indian manservants and Uncle Harry, are associated with storytelling, as the father himself is. Later in the story, he complements Uncle Harry's nostalgic ballad about the battle of Navarino by sending his boy a gift "of 'Grimm's Fairy Tales' and a Hans Christian Andersen" (341). In actual life, little Rudyard was regaled with quite different fare: not just "Papa" but both parents are credited in *Something of Myself* with sending him "priceless volumes" which included a "bound copy of *Aunt Judy's Magazine* of the early 'seventies, in which appeared Mrs. Ewing's *Six to Sixteen*." The story of a girl transplanted from India to Yorkshire had, according to Kipling, a greater impact on his imagination than any other children's book: "I owe more in circuitous ways to that tale than I can tell. I knew it, as I know it still, almost by heart" (7).

The men in the story blend with each other: Meeta, the big Surti boy, acts as a substitute for a Papa who has not "come in" the nursery, as expected, to talk to Punch (324); later, just as the absent father will only send his child a parcel of books, so can the dying Uncle Harry at best pass on the battle song that Punch soon knows "through all its seventeen verses" (349). As mere transmitters of the tales of others, the male figures seem more passive than the women who shape Punch's character. The young mother who reappears to reclaim her children is the rival of the withered "Antirosa" (as Punch first thinks he is to call her). Yet beneath their opposition lie disturbing analogues. Both women, after all, clearly prefer little Judy over the difficult and obdurate boy whom his biological mother still "cannot quite understand" in her letter to her husband (367). And, as the story's opening makes clear, the child's Indian ayah proves to be more maternal than either Mamma or Aunty Rosa. In *The Jungle Books* the love that both Mother Wolf and Messua display for one who is not their own offspring helps to enhance the uniqueness of Mowgli. Similarly, in "Baa Baa, Black Sheep," the ayah's mother-love for Punch only reinforces his early sense of supremacy.

The ayah wants Punch to go to sleep, like the dozing Judy. But the boy refuses to be lulled without the compensation of a soothing fiction:

> "No," said Punch. "Punch-*baba* wants the story about the Ranee that turned into a tiger. Meeta must tell it, and the *hamal* shall hide behind the door and make tiger-noises at the proper time." [324]

The little sahib has his way. Male voices are required to impersonate the ranee who will become a fierce tiger. Meeta tells an oft-told tale; when the hamal makes "the tiger-noises in twenty different keys" the reassurance seems complete (324). The voice of the metamorphosed ranee appears to reconcile the opposites Kipling's fictions will try to tame: human and animal; male and female; adult and child; the power briefly wielded by an imperious little master who does not yet understand his limits and the games devised for him by complacent, because loving, subordinates. Like Bagheera in *The Jungle Books* or like Queen Balkis in the *Just So Stories*, these subordinates manage to teach one who would be king how best to exercise the imagination that must compensate him for his later loss of power.

By orchestrating the storytelling in the nursery, little Punch can revel in the illusion of his total control. Yet the reader who glimpses more than the child is made uneasy, sensing that the tale being acted out may well carry some undisclosed bearing on Punch's future. Hints abound. When the ayah sighs "softly," the narrator's voice intervenes only to explain that "the boy of the household was very dear to her heart" (324). When Punch wonders why Papa has not come, the ayah presents information that also remains half-glossed: "Punch-*baba* is going away. . . . In another week there will be no Punch-*baba* to pull my hair anymore" (324). Her self-pity seems to authenticate her love. But the little tyrant stays unshaken. He confidently assures her and Meeta that all of his retainers are bound to accompany him on a journey about which his parents have kept him uninformed. Lulled by the ayah's "interminable canticle," Punch falls asleep at last, secure, unaware that the oneness that makes him feel so potent and self-sufficient is about to be terminated (325). The actual words chanted by the ayah are inconsequential. It is the sound of her canticle which matters. Yet out of this unintelligible, reassuring "genotext," as Julia Kristeva would call it, Punch and the narrator, and Kipling behind them both, will have to carve out explanatory narratives, "phenotexts."

The scene is set for the entrance of Punch and Judy's actual parents. The allotted week has elapsed, and Papa and Mamma bend over the cots in the nursery late at night before the day of departure, on which the children will finally be told that Meeta and the ayah cannot accompany them on the journey across the ocean. In a story like "Hansel and Gretel" (which Punch will presumably read at the house of the witchlike Aunty Rosa), the abandonment of children by their parents is justified by poverty and hunger. Here, too, economic considerations are raised. Papa uneasily refers to the "moderate" price of the lodgings where he and his wife will leave Punch and Judy; but his rationalizations cannot overcome his obvious misgivings about the impending act of desertion. We expect

Mamma to give vent to emotions even more powerful than those
that the ayah was compelled to mask in front of Punch. Her children are asleep; she senses her husband's agitation. At first glance,
her pangs seem to resemble the ayah's: "'The worst of it is that the
children will grow up away from me,' thought Mamma, but she did
not say it aloud" (326). Is there a slight tinge of selfishness in her
melancholy? Is she concerned about her own deprivation as much
as that which her children might suffer away from home? She has
already relied on a surrogate to do her mothering in the past; small
wonder that Punch should soon view the new surrogate to whom
the children will be entrusted as simply "a new white *ayah*" (331).

Perhaps even more noteworthy is the mother's silence. Her reser-
vation cannot be heard by her husband. Only the narrator is privy
to it. And indeed, unexpectedly, a wary narratorial "I" emerges out
of nowhere to link the ayah (whom Punch himself had earlier heard
sighing "softly") to a mother who now may—or just as possibly may
not—be crying "softly" to herself: "[Both parents] were standing
over the cots in the nursery late at night, and *I think* that Mamma
was crying softly" (326; emphasis added). The very "obliqueness"
that Elliot Gilbert regards as the hallmark of Kipling's art of survival begins to shape this tale of a boy's psychological survival.
Henry James, who welcomed the young Kipling as a fellow crafts-
man, might well have appreciated the artful placing of that condi-
tional "I think."

But if the depth of the mother's sadness is only slightly under-
mined by the tentativeness of the narrator's "I think," her preference of Judy over Punch reverses the ayah's own priorities, as we
soon discover: "After Papa had gone away, she knelt down by Judy's
cot" (326). Just as she had screened her silent thoughts from her
husband so does the mother wait for him to leave the nursery before signifying her preference for "my Ju." Her action links the two
excluded males, son and father, anticipating the later links between
them and between Punch and Uncle Harry. But the mother's private ritual *is* observed by another witness besides the narrator, the
ayah, and that observer's point of view is now appropriated by the
narrator himself:

> The *ayah* saw her and put up a prayer that the Memsahib might
> never find the love of her children taken away from her and
> given to a stranger. [326]

There is no threat, obviously, that Punch will give his love to a tormentor like Aunty Rosa. Still, the ayah's fear that a stranger might disrupt the bonds that bind a mother to her child is nonetheless justified. For Punch, having learned to distrust and fear the hated Aunty Rosa, cannot but help identify this maternal replacement with the returning parent who wants to reclaim him as her own "darling boy" (364). She may be highly seductive, "young, frivolously young, and beautiful, with delicately flushed cheeks, eyes that shone like stars, and a voice that needed no appeal of outstretched arms to draw little ones to her" (364). But six years have elapsed, and Punch is no longer little. Only his smaller sister responds instinctively to those outstretched arms: "Judy ran straight to her, but Black Sheep hesitated" (364).

Judy's identification with her mother has remained intact, for the little girl was allowed "straight" access to Aunty Rosa's "heart" (336). But "the extra boy about the house" could only count on Uncle Harry for identification and support (336). Kipling deliberately places the children's joint mourning for their lost mother at the end of the first section of his story in direct apposition to the lonely Punch's horror on hearing the piercing scream "Uncle Harry is *dead!*" at the end of the second segment (335, 350). Renamed "Black Sheep" by Aunty Rosa, told "that he ought to be beaten by a man" (363) for sins her whippings cannot correct, Punch is at last given a reprieve by still another male figure, a visiting doctor from India who detects his near-blindness. In *Something of Myself*, significantly enough, there is the added diagnosis of some "sort of nervous break-down" (17); what is more, the diagnostician is an emissary from Rudyard's "beloved Aunt" Georgiana Burne-Jones, a kindly feminine presence who is never introduced in "Baa Baa, Black Sheep," even though she is credited in the autobiography as having provided, "for a month each year," a refuge from "the Woman" that became the "paradise which I verily believe saved me" (11).

Upon his mother's return, Punch remains understandably wary about the "beautiful woman" who treats him—the spurned miscreant and devil-child—"as though he were a small God" ("Baa Baa, Black Sheep" 366). In the last of the *Jungle Book* stories, "The Spring Running," Messua sinks to her feet before the naked adolescent who stands at the threshold of her cottage: "It is a godling of the woods! *Ahai!*" The narrator confirms her sense of awe: the "strong,

tall, and beautiful" male, he assures us, "might easily have been
mistaken for some wild god of a jungle legend" (316). In Kipling's
single "adult" Mowgli story, "In the Rukh," written before the *Jungle
Book* tales for children began to appear,[2] Mowgli seems even more
overtly identified with a deity like Krishna; the German Muller
(presumably named after Max Muller, the authority on comparative religion) awkwardly cites Swinburne to convey his own awe at
finding a reincarnated divinity in a rain forest that "is older dan der
gods" (216). But in "Baa Baa, Black Sheep," Punch cannot tap the
sense of omnipotence that he has lost in India upon his separation
from the worshipful ayah. Muller regards Mowgli as the product of
a throwback, "an anachronism, for he is before der Iron Age, and
der Stone Age" (216). To regain the primitive symbiosis that strikes
the displaced Punch as being just as anachronistic, the twelve-year-
old tries to infantilize himself. He regresses into an earlier mode of
behavior by soiling himself, as a small child would.

Punch's defiant act of regression allows him to test his mother's
tolerance. If his Mother is indeed the "sister, comforter, and friend"
she professes to be, she ought not to be angry at his reversion, but
will instead herself revert to the language of his Indian childhood
by lightheartedly calling him a "little *pagal*." He strides through
the ditch, deliberately "mires himself to the knees," and shouts:
"Mother, dear, . . . I'm just as dirty as I can pos-*sib*-ly be!" As Punch
proudly confirms to his little sister, Mamma has passed his test:

> "Then change your clothes as quickly as you pos-*sib*-ly can!"
> Mother's clear voice rings out from the house. "And don't be a
> little *pagal*!"
> "There! 'Told you so," says Punch. "It's all different now, and
> we are just as much mother's as if she had never gone." [368]

Yet if Punch is as much Mother's as ever, how much *is* that "much"?
The satisfied perspective of an adolescent who wants to reassume
his place as a child is immediately corrected by an adult narrator
who insists on the permanence of marks that no boyish bravado
can erase.

The narrator's qualification of Punch's point of view introduces
a sobering perspective similar to that which Kipling was to adopt,
two years later, in *The Light That Failed*:

> Not altogether, O Punch, for when young lips have drunk deep
> of the bitter waters of Hate, Suspicion, and Despair, all the

Love in the world will not wholly take away that knowledge;
though it may turn darkened eyes for a while to the light, and
teach Faith where no Faith was. [368]

In *The Light That Failed*, where this note of bitterness is extended,
childhood merely becomes a prolegomenon for the later crippling
of a failed artist and soldier. The blinded Dick Heldar cannot survive in an adult world where he must forsake his artistic ambitions
and act out, instead, a suicidal fantasy. The myopic Punch, however,
is at least given the opportunity to survive. And, what is more, he
may even have a chance to become someone like Kipling. The over-
confident child-voice and the narrator's more guarded utterance
in "Baa Baa, Black Sheep" would, after all, eventually be blended
in those stories for children that came to rely on a subtle traffic
between wishfulness and disenchantment.

"Baa Baa, Black Sheep" thus led Kipling to both *The Light That
Failed* and his subsequent fictions for children. In dramatizing the
damage caused by a warfare between masculine and feminine elements, Kipling's novel ostensibly returns to the quasi-adolescent
bonds between the soldier-brothers of the earlier stories. Destroyed
by the combined efforts of Maisie, Bessie, and the Red-Haired Girl,
the maimed Heldar, prematurely gray and with the tired "face of
an old man" (329), must gratefully expire in the arms of his male
friend Torpenhow. But in charting Dick Heldar's thwarted movement from childhood attachments to adult relationships, the novel
continues to pursue the close examination of a boy's psychology
first begun in "Baa Baa, Black Sheep" and later expanded in the
Mowgli stories and *Kim*.

In *The Light That Failed* Kipling accentuates the negative aspects
of a boy's development. Indeed, Dick's repeatedly unsuccessful con-
frontations with female power make him a far more pathetic figure
than Punch, whose name is that of the long-nosed puppet noted
for his sadistic wife-beating and aggressive "breaches of decorum"
(Cruikshank 24). Although Kipling's Punch is himself beaten as
severely as his puppet namesake, he also retains the *pulcinello*'s
angry energy. His aggressiveness and resourcefulness contrast with
the passivity of his little sister Judy (who, though seemingly exempt
from the anger directed at those who prefer her to Punch—Mother
and Aunty Rosa—nonetheless bears the name of the traditional victim of the Punch and Judy shows). By way of contrast, the very

beginning of *The Light That Failed* stresses Dick's subordination to the imperious little girl who nearly blinds him by shooting a pistol in his face. The fearless fellow orphan who is Dick's "companion in bondage" (4) to Mrs. Jennett (the Aunty Rosa figure now "incorrectly supposed to stand in place of a mother" [2] to both children) is by far the sturdier of the two. Whereas Dick deflects his need for nurturance on Maisie, she transfers her own need for a mother to the male goat she has endowed with the maternal name "Amomma." The goat easily survives swallowing "two loaded pin-fire cartridges" (7), but Dick cannot as easily digest female aggression, either as a boy or as a man.

The Light That Failed might well have been entitled "The Growth That Failed." For Dick Heldar remains an arrested adolescent, incapable of growing beyond the level at which Kipling will leave future boy heroes such as Mowgli or Kim, incapable even of Punch's tenuous reconciliation with the "sister, comforter, and friend" he needs to find in his mother. Yet despite its negativity and self-pity, the novel Kipling chose to dedicate to his mother also seems to display his understanding that creativity—his own as much as that of his artist hero—requires a reinstatement of powers first activated in a child's relation to its primary parent. In his important revaluation of the "thematics and poetics" of *The Light That Failed*, Robert Caserio shows how the novel subordinates a boyish ambition to "master the world" to an acceptance of the vulnerability and failure deeply feared by the male who wants to cling to his desire for domination (212, 208). Caserio thus considers Maisie's female friend, the nameless Impressionist who destroys her hurtful sketch of Dick "both to save him pain and to surrender her own defensive aggression," not just as Heldar's antagonist, but rather also as an artist figure who anticipates a role Kipling himself now knows he must adopt (208).

The hint of a possible synthesis between a childish desire for omnipotence and an adult acceptance of limits was already anticipated in "Baa Baa, Black Sheep" itself, where the chanting ayah indulged Punch's wishful belief in his power while trying to prepare him for his impending loss and alienation. Even the returning mother is, paradoxically enough, allowed to provide a bridge between innocence and experience. Her resolute voice provides an alternative to the final utterances of both Punch and the narrator by combining the cheerful faith of the one with the realism of the other. In mimicking the boy's speech with her own "pos-*sib*-ly," the mother turns into a game what could potentially have been construed as a defiance to her authority. But by also demanding an immediate change of clothes, she can at the same time insist on his need to submit to her superior awareness.

A similar combination of playfulness with authority would soon animate Kipling's stories for children, especially the *Just So Stories* he first told to tiny Effie. There, Kipling's joyous, even raucous, participation in children's games remains inseparable from a parental/authorial stance that gently affirms its superior knowledge. As the creator of stories that use repetition to satisfy the child's hunger to have them "told just so," Kipling resembles the mother who fulfills Punch's boastful "'Told you so" to Judy. The preamble to his first trio of "Just So Stories" in 1897 suggests that Kipling had come to treat the child's participation in bedtime stories with the same mixture of respect and authority as the ayah who had deferred to Punch's need in his own suspended condition between contrary states: "You could alter and change [afternoon stories] as much as you pleased; but in the evening there were stories meant to put Effie to sleep, and you were not allowed to alter those by one single little word. They had to be told just so; or Effie would wake up and put back the missing sentence. So at last they came to be like charms, all three of them,—the whale tale, the camel tale, and the rhinoceros tale" ("The 'Just-So' Stories" 89).

Just as Meeta's tale about the ranee who became a tiger appeals to a much younger Punch because of its familiarity, so does the mother's last speech in "Baa Baa, Black Sheep" reconfirm and revalidate an older child's memories. Her willing reversion to a word like *pagal* helps, in fact, to reintroduce the lost Indian household world of Meeta and the ayah that the aged Kipling still gratefully remembered in the opening pages of *Something of Myself*. At the same time, however, the mother demands an adaptation to the changed circumstances brought about by the separation her child has undergone. Mere regression is not possible for its own sake. New clothes are required to replace those soiled in the muddy ditch—clothes appropriate for Punch's older self. Limits and regulations must be observed, lest a too anarchic Punch—or a Mowgli or Beetle or defiant Elephant's Child—be seduced into thinking that he can behave like the Bandar-log or a Wild Thing. Despite his suppressed anger at the mother for the damage done by her desertion, Kipling prefers to accentuate the positive. He thus endows her, albeit tentatively, with the restorative powers he will himself adopt as a parent and writer.[3] His art must be placed in service of the Queen.

The insights gained in "Baa Baa, Black Sheep" and *The Light That Failed* were therefore best carried out in works in which child protagonists, whether boys like Mowgli and Kim or girls like Taffy, who is credited with inventing the alphabet in the *Just So Stories*, are simultaneously treated as highly resourceful and yet highly vulnerable. Mowgli can act out a child reader's boldest fantasies of imperial domination; at the same time, however, this confident master planner, who can enlist the might of Hathi and the cool intelligence of Kaa in coordinating strategic maneuvers that would do credit to a Napoleon, must come to accept that a man-cub has no place in the elementary world of the jungle. Conversely, Taffimai or Taffy, the little daughter and "Best Beloved" of a primitive Neolithic man, is at once an abject failure (since her first pictograph communicates a message totally contrary to the one she had wanted to convey) and a budding genius whose "great invention" will someday be perfected as an art called "writing" (*The Jungle Books and Just So Stories* 384).

It seems hardly arbitrary that Mowgli, abandoned by his actual woodcutter parents (as Hansel and Gretel were in the Grimm fairy tale), should be compensated for that severance by a proliferation of parental surrogates and by two adopted mothers, Raksha (the Demon) and the wealthy Messua, all of whom jealously vie over the boy. Nor is it arbitrary that Taffy's first letter, though misread by its recipient, should demand that her mother replace the broken weapon that her father is so assiduously trying to repair. From Kipling's first published children's story, "The Potted Princess," which appeared in *St. Nicholas* magazine in January 1893, less than a month after the birth of his own Best Beloved, Josephine, to *Rewards and Fairies* (1910), the writer who never forgot his boyhood deprivations also made sure to remember—and inscribe—the continuing feminine attachments on which his creativity depended.

It seems significant that only a few weeks after the birth of his "first child and daughter," Kipling should have published in *St. Nicholas* magazine an Indian children's story which is immediately presented as "the true tale that was told to Punch and Judy, his sister, by their nurse, in the city of Bombay," as they wait "for their mother to come back from her evening drive" ("The Potted Princess" 164). The mother's absence of six painful years in "Baa Baa,

Black Sheep" has been compressed into a short evening drive. And yet Kipling's first story *for* children is in many ways a sequel to the earlier story *about* the child he had once been. When, at the end of "The Potted Princess," Mamma returns, the children try to repeat the ayah's story for her benefit, while she is hurriedly changing her clothes to dress for dinner.

But Punch and Judy are not as skilled storytellers as the ayah. Even without a knowledge of the plot of "Baa Baa, Black Sheep," an adult reader of "The Potted Princess" can detect meanings that neither the child auditors in the tale nor the child readers of *St. Nicholas* magazine could fathom. The ayah's story is clearly intended as a compensatory fiction. It is designed to offset Punch's exaggerated sense both of his vulnerability and of his importance. When the ayah tries to soothe an angry pink crane by chanting a Hindustani song about another, thorn-pricked crane whose "life went away *tullaka-katullaka*—drop by drop," Punch chases the bird, pricks himself, and promptly acquires "two tiny pink scratches" he grandiosely identifies with his own waning life blood: " 'Ohoo!' said Punch, looking at both his fat little legs together, 'Perhaps I shall die!' " (164, 165). The boy's intimations of mortality are short-lived, but his pain has caused Judy to cry. To soothe her and to give the boy a stricter sense of limitations, the ayah immediately plunges into a tale never before heard by the children: "And the Rajah had a daughter . . ." (165).

The writer who had so recently acquired a daughter has the ayah tell a story that is deliberately antifantastic. Although the tale is set in a magical era when sorcerers could turn "men into tigers and elephants" (165), the princess whom a prince must release turns out to have been shut up in a "grain-jar" that proves to be utterly ordinary. As the narrative unfolds, Punch becomes its sole auditor, since Judy, waiting for her mother, has lost interest in the story. Just as the ayah tricks Punch into assuming that the jar will have "to be opened by magic," so do the rajah's sorcerers in the story trick all the princess's suitors but one into believing that, to offset some powerful spell, they will have to consult "the magicians in their fathers' courts, and holy men in caves" (166). By engaging in "magic charm-work which cannot last," these suitors become "all wearied out"; but the one prince of "low birth" whose father "married the daughter of a potter" and who has always remained "the son of his mother" requires no such elaborate schooling (167, 166).

Instructed by "his mother, the Ranee," this commonsensical young
man succeeds where all others have failed:

> "At the very last, . . . the Potter-Prince came into the plain
> alone, without even one little talking beast or wise bird, and all
> the people made jokes at him. But he walked to the grain-jar
> and cried, 'A pot is a pot, and I am the son of a potter!' and
> he put his two hands upon the grain-jar's cover and he lifted
> it up, and the Princess came out! Then the people said, 'This
> is very great magic indeed'; and they began to chase the holy
> men and the talking beasts up and down, meaning to kill them.
> But the Rajah's magicians said: 'This is no magic at all, for we
> did not put any charm upon the jar. It *was* a common grain-
> jar; and it *is* a common grain-jar such as they buy in the bazar;
> and a child might have lifted the cover one year ago, or on any
> day since that day. . . .'" [168]

When the ayah ends her tale as abruptly as she had plunged into
it, Punch seems taken aback by the anticlimactic rebuff of his ex-
pectations. He wants to cling to the magical thinking of the child.
The potter-prince who lifted the jar's lid is insufficiently heroic to
suit the boy:

> There was a long silence at the end of the tale.
> "But the charms were very strong," said Punch, doubtfully.
> "They were only words, and how could they touch the pot?
> Could words turn you into a tiger, Punch baba?"
> "No. I am Punch."
> "Even so," said the ayah. "If the pot had been charmed, a
> charm would have opened it. But it was a common, bazar pot.
> What did it know of charms? It opened to a hand on the cover."
> "Oh!" said Punch; and then he began to laugh, and Judy fol-
> lowed his example. "Now I quite understand. I will tell it to
> mamma." [169]

Yet Punch's incomplete mastery of the ayah's cautionary tale becomes evident when he tries to relay her narrative to his mother.
As Punch, with Judy's assistance, tries to re-create the tale, the children only succeed in befuddling their listener: "as they began in
the middle and put the beginning first, and then began at the end
and put the middle last, she became a little confused" (169). Eager
to dramatize what he has been unable to present verbally, Punch

reaches for an "eau-de-cologne bottle that he was strictly forbidden to touch," and, in his excitement, spills its contents "down the front of his dress, shouting, 'A pot is a pot, and I am the son of a potter!'" (169). Once again, it would seem, the boy who tries to impress his mother will be forced to change his clothes.

The Punch of "The Potted Princess" is the same naive pagal of the opening of "Baa Baa, Black Sheep." But Kipling has by now changed his own clothes. By having the ayah show Punch that a story about female imprisonment has a considerable bearing on the identity of a boy still wearing a "dress" like his sister Judy, Kipling can bypass his earlier emphasis on "manlydom" and recover a femininity he now sees as crucial to his creativity. The potter-prince's mother, the low-born ranee who is nothing but the ayah's self-personation, has prepared her boy for a task that hardly proves to be epic. There is no need for male acts of prowess or male incantations or charms; instead, what is called for is the kind of realism that had become the mark of the literature for girls which Kipling found in the much-prized "bound copy of *Aunt Judy's Magazine*" he saved until the end of his life and in the women writers he evokes so fondly in *Something About Myself* as having had such an impact on his young mind: Mrs. Ewing's "history of real people and real things" that he knew "almost by heart," "Mrs. Gatty's *Parables of Nature* which I imitated," as well as "those good spirits" whose works he avidly devoured but whom he never was "lucky enough" to meet personally, Jean Ingelow and Christina Rossetti (7, 33, 22).

In the ayah's story, a mother's son releases and gains for himself the femininity his stereotypical male rivals were unable to free. And Punch, who comes to recognize, however vaguely, that pleasure and value may reside in stories that limit attainment to "common" skills, has himself been released from an excessive self-projection as an all-powerful male. Just as the son of John Lockwood Kipling, the designer who worked in a Staffordshire pottery when he first met Alice Lockwood in the hamlet of Rudyard, may well have aggrandized himself as a boy by fantasizing that he was the child of more exalted parents, so would the fictional Punch clearly have preferred to be the recipient of a "strong magic" that might have encouraged him "to go out and kill giants and dragons, and cut off their heads" ("The Potted Princess" 166). Yet he is willing to see himself as an ordinary potter-prince in a story which shows him that the ordinary can, under proper circumstances, prove extraordinary in its own right. The ayah has, after all, made sure not to injure Punch's sense of self-importance.[4] She spares him the embarrassment of correcting some of his misconceptions.[5] Nonetheless, it seems significant that this masculine little boy should find himself relaying the story told by one adult woman to another adult woman; moreover, as intermediary between ayah and mother, he also accepts his younger sister as conarrator, though Judy has grasped far less of the story's import than he did and even lacks his own minimal skills as a storyteller.

Words, Punch admits at this stage of his early life, cannot convert him—or a ranee—into a tiger. Words even fail him when he tries to transform the ayah's story into a narrative of his own. Still, he has enjoyed his nurse's liberating joke so exceedingly that, in his excitement, the boy still in pinafores spills his mother's perfume not on her but on himself. "The Potted Princess" depicts a baptism of sorts. The feminine "essence," for which Beerbohm so cruelly mocked Kipling, now bathes a very different writer. Kipling was ready to go beyond his misogynist and antimatriarchal fictions for adults in the restorative children's stories that tumbled from his brain after the composition of "The Potted Princess."

In the first of the stories that "had to be told just so" for Effie, the "single, solitary shipwrecked mariner," who proves as practical as the potter-prince, is afloat on the wide sea because he "had his mother's leave to paddle or else he would never have done it, because he was a man of infinite-resource-and-sagacity" ("The 'Just-So' Stories" 91). As Kipling playfully suggests here, the sailor who prances and dances and bangs and clangs is not really a man at all but rather a resourceful little boy who can act as the grown-up author's link to his child auditor. His prowess is celebrated. It results, after all, in an evolutionary change by which whales "nowadays" are prevented from eating "men or boys or girls" (93). Still, this hero's mastery of the aggressive whale merely culminates with his return "home to his mother, who had given him leave to trail his toes in the water" (93).

Even after the death of his "American" daughter removed for Kipling the kind of creative interaction he dramatized in "How the Alphabet Was Made," he was able to tap the creative power shared by Taffy and her "Daddy." (When Taffy notes that "*Mum* shuts one's mouth up," her father draws the carp mouth open: "That makes *Ma-ma-ma!*" [*The Jungle Books and Just So Stories* 392].)

Whether Kipling's boy heroes are called Mowgli or Kim or Rikki-Tikki-Tavi, or even given the seeming adult stature of King Solomon (or, Suleiman-bin-Daoud, as Kipling prefers to call that wise and all-powerful magician), their resourcefulness inevitably is linked to female power. In this sense, the title of the story Kipling placed last in his first *Jungle Book* seems apt: humans and animals remain coequal "Servants of the Queen." Mowgli must obtain Messua's approval before he can approach "the girl in a white cloth" and say his last farewell to his jungle companions. Similarly, the fairies who want to leave England in " 'Dymchurch Flit' " must rely on the permission of the Widow Whitgift to depart: "She was all their dependence.'Thout her Leave an' Good-will they could not pass; for she was the Mother" (*Puck of Pook's Hill* 191).

Kipling, too, depended on maternal goodwill to sanction the exile he came to accept. In "The Enemies to Each Other," the retelling of *Paradise Lost* that he placed at the beginning of his 1924 volume of *Debits and Credits*, Lady Eve compounds the mistakes that led to the expulsion from Eden. Asked by the peacock "which is greater, the mother or the child," she replies, "Of a surety, the mother" (19), and, emboldened, tears down the mirror-altar in which Adam had sought to worship himself. When Adam asks "my Co-equal" why she has stripped him of his self-respect, Eve replies: "Because it has been revealed that in Me is all excellence and increase, splendour, terror and power. Bow down and worship" (20). Only laughter and the acceptance of gender strife finally can cause both partners to face the limitations of their existence. Still, Eve is reluctant to give up a sense of her innate superiority to Adam. Although she allows that she is "no goddess in any sort, but the mate of this mere Man whom, in spite of all, I love," she cannot forbear to regale the peacock "with tales of the stupidity and childishness of our pure Forefather" (22). Eve's, however, is a story for grown-ups. And even *we* can only tell one tale at a time.

Notes

1. In his recent biography of Kipling, Martin Seymour-Smith wonders: "How are we to explain the antipathy of Max Beerbohm?" Yet in confronting his own question (strangely situated in a discussion of *Stalky*, which he, but not Beerbohm, excoriates as "one of the bad books" [273]), Seymour-Smith comes up with no answers. Instead, he prefers to attack the "Kiplingites" for ignoring Beerbohm's persistent criticism of Kipling in no less than nine caricatures, "P.C., X, 36," and two essays. Seymour-Smith, who maintains that Kipling suppressed not only all "homosexual tendencies

in himself" but also "any tenderness or 'femininity'" (103), seems uninterested in all of the children's books except for *Stalky* and, to a lesser extent, *Kim*, which he reads as a "safe" indulgence on Kipling's part "of paedophilic emotions" (303). His inattention to the *Just So Stories* or even *The Jungle Books* is deplorable, since a closer look at them would have greatly complicated his stance toward Kipling's suppressed femininity. Given his own thesis, Seymour-Smith might have easily answered his question about Beerbohm by analyzing the caption of Beerbohm's cartoon, "De Arte Poetica. J.B. to R.K.," in which John Bull, who misreads Shakespeare and Tennyson as masculine writers, praises Kipling for being more "wholesome" than Byron or Shelley. As McElderry implies, Beerbohm could not forgive Kipling for supplying "manly vigor" as the "proper antidote" to a Wildean aestheticism to which both men had been temperamentally attracted but which Kipling, unlike Beerbohm, felt compelled to deny (134).

2. "Toomai of the Elephants," which appeared in the December 1893 issue of *St. Nicholas*, preceded the publication, also in *St. Nicholas*, of "Tiger-Tiger!" and "Mowgli and His Brothers."

3. Randall Jarrell's remarks about Kipling's inability to include his parents in his revenge fantasies are extremely astute: "From the father's bas-reliefs for *Kim* to the mother's 'There's no Mother in Poetry, my dear,' when the son got angry at her criticism of his poems—from beginning to end they are bewitching; you cannot read about them without wanting to live with them; they were the best of parents. It is *this* that made Kipling what he was: if they had been the worst of parents, even fairly bad parents, even ordinary parents, it would all have made sense, Kipling himself could have made sense out of it. As it was, his world had been torn in two and he himself torn in two; for under the part of him that extenuated everything, blamed for nothing, there was certainly a part that extenuated nothing, blamed for everything—a part whose existence he never admitted, most especially not to himself" (341).

4. The ayah informs Punch that there "was a new star" on the night of his birth. But her confirmation of the boy's sense of being special also carries an ominous counterweight: "I saw it. A great star with a fiery tail all across the sky. Punch will travel far" (165). Does Kipling mean to set this story around the same time in which the opening of "Baa Baa, Black Sheep" takes place? The allusion to a comet, the traditional harbinger of disaster, would suggest that once again the ayah knows about the changes that will come about after Punch's travel "far" beyond India.

5. When she tells Punch that the "prince of low birth was so lowly that the little boys of the city driving the cattle to pasture threw mud at him," her listener fails to grasp the degradation: "'Ah!' said Punch, 'mud is nice. Did they hit him?'" (166). The ayah avoids an answer by introducing the prince's mother, the ranee, in the unqueenly activity of "gathering sticks to cook bread" (167). The cross-reference to "Baa Baa, Black Sheep," where Punch mires himself in mud to forget his own degradation, seems intentional.

Works Cited

Beerbohm, Max. *A Christmas Garland*. London: William Heinemann, 1922.

———. "Kipling's Entire." In *Around Theatres*. London: Rupert Hart-Davis, 1953.

Carrington, C. E. *The Life of Rudyard Kipling*. Garden City, N.Y.: Doubleday and Co., 1955.

Caserio, Robert L. "Kipling in the Light of Failure." *Grand Street* 5 (1986): 179–212.

Cruikshank, George. *Punch and Judy, with Twenty-Four Illustrations*. London: George Bell and Sons, 1881.

Jarrell, Randall. "On Preparing to Read Kipling." In *Kipling, Auden and Co.: Essays and Reviews (1935–1964)*. New York: Farrar, Straus, and Giroux, 1980.

Kipling, Rudyard. "Baa Baa, Black Sheep." Vol. 6 of *The Writings in Prose and Verse of Rudyard Kipling*. New York: Charles Scribner's Sons, 1913.

———. "The Enemies to Each Other." Vol. 31 of *The Writings*. New York: Charles Scribner's Sons, 1926.

———. "In the Rukh." In *All the Mowgli Stories*. London: Macmillan, 1964.

———. *The Jungle Books and Just So Stories*. New York: Bantam Books, 1986.

———. "The 'Just-So' Stories." *St. Nicholas* 25 (December 1897): 89–93.

———. *The Light That Failed*. Vol. 9 of *The Writings*. New York: Charles Scribner's Sons, 1913.

———. "The Man Who Would Be King." In *The Phantom 'Rickshaw and Other Stories*. Vol. 5 of *The Writings*. New York: Charles Scribner's Sons, 1913.

———. "The Potted Princess." *St. Nicholas* 20 (January 1893): 164–69.

———. *Puck of Pook's Hill*, ed. Sarah Wintle. Harmondsworth: Penguin Books, 1987.

———. *Something of Myself: For My Friends Known and Unknown*. London: Macmillan, 1937.

———. *The Story of the Gadsbys*. Vol. 6 of *The Writings*. New York: Charles Scribner's Sons, 1913.

Kristeva, Julia. *Revolution in Poetic Language*. Intro. Leon S. Roudiez; trans. Margaret Waller. New York: Columbia University Press, 1984.

McElderry, Jr., Bruce R. *Max Beerbohm*. New York: Twayne Publishers, 1972.

Seymour-Smith, Martin. *Rudyard Kipling*. New York: St. Martin's Press, 1990.

Wilson, Angus. *The Strange Ride of Rudyard Kipling: His Life and Works*. New York: Viking Press, 1978.

Stalky *and the Language of Education*

D. H. Stewart

When he wrote *Stalky & Co.* (1899),[1] Rudyard Kipling had become a master stylist. The book retains its appeal nearly a century later but no longer as a manual for training administrators of the British Empire, which is how many early critics interpreted it. Rather, it can be read as a celebration of language, boys' language—how they sift and assimilate both their cultural heritage and their immediate experiences through it, and how this prepares them to confront the challenges of adulthood. The book is about education, and a reader's experience with its language constitutes the very process of education as Kipling envisions it.

Stalky & Co. tells the story of three English schoolboys in about 1880. The school, the United Services College at Westward Ho! was a corporation established in 1874 by military officers who could not afford distinguished schools but who wanted their sons well enough educated to pass entrance exams into military academies. Operated "on the cheap" (Smith 8), the school occupied a row of connected buildings facing the Atlantic in North Devon. Kipling immortalized those "twelve bleak houses by the shore" where the boys endured plenty of raw weather and never much food (*Something* 46).

Because the three boys (Stalky, M'Turk, and Beetle) and all other characters are modeled on real people, the book is often treated solely as a roman à clef. Indeed, the three (L. C. Dunsterville, G. C. Beresford, and Kipling himself) later wrote autobiographical accounts augmenting or revising their fictional selves. But exclusively biographical readings seem inadequate. Kipling's imagination ran with a free rein once he escaped the bonds of journalism during his "seven years' hard" in India (*Something* 56). Moreover, he developed a "poetic" process of composition that emphasized the sound and rhythm of language. This polyglossic (and polysonic) style coupled with his high-speed imagination radically transformed events and people, blurring fact and fantasy. The distance between fictive language and "reality" became Shakespearean, which explains why a

Children's Literature 20, ed. Francelia Butler, Barbara Rosen, and Judith A. Plotz (Yale University Press, © 1992 by The Children's Literature Foundation, Inc.).

gap opens between form and content and tempts critics to treat him sometimes as a photographic realist and sometimes as a verbal magician.

Few critics undervalue Kipling's skill with language.[2] It is his morality or ideology that antagonizes. But if one approaches his style first in terms of recent "orality-literacy" theory, then a special claim can be made for *Stalky & Co.*'s value to teachers and students. Walter J. Ong, one of the best known advocates of this theory, calls attention to the primacy of orality ("written words are residue," *Orality* 11), dramatizes its evolving relationship with the "technologies" of writing, printing, and electronic texts, and warns against the "impoverishment" resulting from our "addiction" to unreflective visualization in literary criticism (*Interfaces* 103). The theory is especially applicable to *Stalky & Co.*, which re-creates the old oral-rhetorical tradition that survived in English schools. It illustrates the study of Latin as a "puberty initiation rite" reserved for boys (Ong, *Presence* 251, *Rhetoric* 120–24). The book is a virtual case study of oral and literate "language acquisition," exhibiting the full range of competencies that empower skillful users. In "The Last Term," Beetle's "shouting and declaiming against the long-ridged seas" like Demosthenes concentrates in a momentary image the book's "acoustic" appeal.

Further, a second claim for the book's value can be made based on the relationship between language and morality or ideology that Kipling may have discovered in Friedrich Froebel's theory that genuine knowledge derives from "mind-world-language," which is threefold, yet in itself one.

In "The Propagation of Knowledge," Beetle was reading about mad Elizabethan beggars in Isaac D'Israeli's *Curiosities of Literature* (1791–1823):

> Then, at the foot of a left-hand page, leaped out on him a verse—of incommunicable splendour, opening doors into inexplicable worlds—from a song which Tom-a-Bedlams were supposed to sing. It ran:
>
> > With a heart of furious fancies
> >   Whereof I am commander,
> > With a burning spear and a horse of air,
> >   To the wilderness I wander.

> With a knight of ghosts and shadows
> I summoned am to tourney,
> Ten leagues beyond the wide world's end—
> Methinks it is no journey.

He sat, mouthing and staring before him. . . . [225–226]

Our term for this experience is "the shock of recognition," but we understand "shock" as an internalized, cerebral experience because our reading is almost exclusively visual and passive. Kipling adds a physical, oral dimension. The song "leaped out on him," and he "mouthed" it.

Throughout his work, Kipling foregrounds the oral-aural power of language as if to demonstrate the thesis from orality-literacy theory that ears are more sensitive than eyes.[3] In "Slaves of the Lamp, Part I," the boys sing a music-hall song, "Arrah, Patsy, mind the baby!" In "Slaves of the Lamp, Part II," Stalky, now an officer fighting in northwest India, plays the song on a bugle to guide a fellow officer's attack. The sound of word games in school echoes in deadlier imperial games, where words are used mainly to give orders.

Kipling saturates *Stalky & Co.* with sound. The boys convert most texts they read into living language. In "The United Idolaters," *Uncle Remus* sets the boys shouting and dancing:

> Ti-yi! Tungalee!
> I eat um pea! I pick um pea!
> Ingle-go-jang, my joy, my joy!

The chants seemed to answer the ends of their being. . . . They all sang them the whole way up the corridor. . . . The book was amazing, and full of quotations that one could hurl like javelins. [144]

The war games in "The Satisfactions of a Gentleman" occur amid a mad jumble of phrases from the Bible, Horace, and Captain Marryat's *Peter Simple.* The boys mangle French by compounding it with English: "Tweakons" means "let us tweak." "*Je cat, tu cat, il cat. Nous cattons!*" ("Cat" means vomit in boys' argot.) In "In Ambush," the boys, dancing like dervishes, intone "the primitive man's song of triumph, '*Ti-ra-la-la-i-tu!* I gloat! Hear me!'" In "An Unsavoury Interlude," this becomes "*Je vais gloater tout le* blessed afternoon."

"In Ambush," the lead story in the 1899 edition of *Stalky*, contains almost audibly explosive language. The three boys trespass on Colonel Dabney's land when his gamekeeper fires a shotgun at a fox, narrowly missing the boys. Instead of slinking back to the college, M'Turk marches up to Colonel Dabney to report the keeper's outrage. (Shooting a fox is a cardinal sin among gentry.) Querulous old Dabney at first belabors the boy for trespassing and asks, "Do you know who I am?" Righteously indignant, M'Turk relapses into Irish dialect: "No, sorr, nor do I care if ye belonged to the Castle [Dublin Castle] itself. Answer me now as one gentleman to another. Do ye shoot foxes or do ye not?"

Kipling underlines the sound of this by noting that M'Turk had been "kicked out of his Irish dialect" at school. Then he elaborates:

> Forgotten—forgotten was the College and the decency due to elders! M'Turk was treading again the barren purple mountains of the rainy West coast, where in his holidays he was viceroy of four thousand acres, only son of a three-hundred-year-old house. . . . It was the landed man speaking to his equal—deep calling to deep—and the old gentleman acknowledged the cry. [35]

The passage is remarkable for several reasons. Language here has the force of gesture. It is reminiscent of Odysseus' meeting with Nausicaä and her people. Naked and alone, Odysseus has only his language for protection against capture and enslavement, his upper-class Greek that validates his identity and position. Here a boy speaking the right dialect (it is gentry Irish, not shanty Irish) breaks across the barriers of age and locale (Dabney speaks gentry Devon, not the "potwalloper Devon" that Kipling records affectionately elsewhere). But Kipling carries us beyond class-specific language with the biblical allusion—"deep calling to deep" (Psalms 42:7). This is David in prayer, a glancing allusion too portentous for the context if we take it literally, but deftly resonant for dramatizing orality's impact.

Kipling deploys language harmonically, so that informed hearers pick up counterpoints behind the surface melody. For example, "The Propagation of Knowledge" recounts students' cramming for a literature exam. It is so densely packed with allusions to major and minor writers that only literary specialists can now hear the harmonies that Kipling devises.[4] At the same time, it demonstrates the vitality of the literary heritage as students reconstitute it in living language. For example, when Stalky reads the steward's speech from *King Lear* (II,ii), he drops "d" from "and" and all his terminal g's. One must read aloud to savor the passage.

Most readers of Kipling register the high volume of his prose. He is "noisy." In a letter to his aunt (Mrs. Alfred Baldwin—September 13, 1909), he wrote, "In your own drawing room your own piano is all right—for an audience in a larger room it must be a concert grand, tuned to concert pitch. And yet the notes you play are the same."[5] The public performer dominates, but Kipling's versatility opens a wide array of moods and melodies, from strident to tender.

Stridency is the most obvious in *Stalky*. The distinctive "key" of Mr. King (the boys' Latin teacher) is sarcasm and invective. As the boys construe Horace, King interrupts: "Idiot! . . . May I ask if [the passage] conveys any meaning whatever to your so-called mind?" Today we frown on sarcasm from teachers, but in his autobiography Kipling claimed that

> one learns more from a good scholar in a rage than from a score of lucid and laborious drudges. . . . I think this "approach" [sarcasm] is now discouraged for fear of hurting the souls of youth, but in essence it is no more than rattling tins or firing squibs under a colt's nose. I remember nothing save satisfaction or envy when C—— [William Crofts, the model for King] broke his precious ointments over my head. [*Something* 51]

Beetle mimics King perfectly in "An Unsavory Interlude."

Less prominent, but nonetheless present, are the modulated notes to communicate gentler moods. In "A Little Prep.," the headmaster reads to the boys an account of an alumnus' gallant rescue in battle of a schoolmate who dies, and one boy says in a hushed voice, "That's nine of us, isn't it, in the last three years?" Later the hero recounts his exploits to the awestruck boys, and Stalky questions him in a "voice tuned to a wholly foreign reverence." The muted sentences derive their power by contrast with the customary racket of boy talk.

In addition to "voicing" texts and making language audibly active, Kipling introduces a kind of theory about the importance of orality in education. In "Regulus," Mr. King recites Virgil: "For . . . forty minutes, with never a glance at the book, King paid out the glorious hexameters (and King could read Latin as though it were alive)."[6] His purpose is to instill "balance, proportion, perspective—life." "Character—proportion—background," he says, "that is the essence of the Humanities." He tries to counteract the science teacher's "modern system of inculcating unrelated facts about chlorine, for instance, all of which may be proved fallacies by the time the boys grow up." The science teacher answers with a question: "Is it any worse than your Chinese reiteration of uncomprehended syllables in a dead tongue?"

In the end King wins the argument when a particularly studious boy, a goody-goody, goes berserk in a fight and earns high marks for courage. He gains the sobriquet "Regulus," a valorous Roman martyred for republican virtue. King insists that Latin has given the boy backbone. At least a little of King's message "sticks among the barbarians" to influence their actions.

We know that Kipling approved of King's use of Latin "for a discourse on manners, morals, and respect for authority" because he repeated King's ideas in 1912 when he spoke at Wellington College. Granting that boys remember only a few old Latin tags and quotations after seven years of study, he insists that they

> give one the very essence of what a man ought to try to do. Others . . . let you understand, once and for all, the things that a man should not do—under any circumstances. There are others—bits of odes from Horace, they happen to be in my case—that make one realize in later life as no other words in any other tongue can, the brotherhood of mankind in time of sorrow or affliction.[7]

Latin tags fixed themselves in memory because teachers "performed" them aloud and boys repeated them aloud. By contrast, boys learned chemistry by making "stinks" in the laboratory. The Latin classroom remained the same in Kipling's school as it was a thousand years earlier, a place of oral recitation. As a result, not only "exalted sentiments" but some of the language itself "stuck" among the barbarous boys. In "The Satisfaction of a Gentleman," Kipling records a hilariously garbled Latin telegram that a former student manages to construe correctly.

Kipling's passion for language in *Stalky* seems to have begun with his discovery that words were like javelins in the hands of skillful users. However daunting the boyish jargon, the dialects, and allusions may be for today's readers, we may still share the joy of language unleashed. We may "mouth" some lines, amazed at "opening doors into inexplicable worlds." We may conclude that Kipling enhances reading ability and language facility by challenging readers with lexical, grammatical, and rhetorical surprises and by quickening the aural response to texts as a supplement to chronic visualization, so that (as he said), words somehow become "alive and walk up and down in the hearts of all hearers."[8]

Three of Kipling's remarks about *Stalky* may help remove obstacles that critics hostile to his ethos have created. At the end of his career he wrote that the book "is still read and I maintain it is a truly valuable collection of tracts" (*Something* 113). In the face of countless denunciations of the book (Quigly catalogs them in her edition, xiii), Kipling's insistence on its value prompts one to reexamine it carefully. Responding to early protests against *Stalky*, Kipling made several surprising, perhaps playful, claims. In 1899, he wrote Cormell Price, headmaster at USC, that *Stalky* "will cover (incidentally) the whole question of modern education" (*Letters* 2. 359). To another person, he wrote: "It's in the nature of a moral tract—only a perverse generation insists on calling it comic, and a boy's book, and a lot of other things which it isn't. It's all cribbed from Froebel, with a few slight alterations to disperse plagiarism. . . ."[9]

If we can take the reference to Froebel seriously, it places *Stalky & Co.* in a new light. Friedrich Froebel (1782–1852) was the champion of the kindergarten movement in Germany, and Elizabeth Peabody (Nathaniel Hawthorne's sister-in-law) popularized it in America. The first sentence of Froebel's *The Education of Man* is "In all things there lives and reigns an eternal law," and the book is full of ideas that might have attracted Kipling. Many self-willed, "bad" children turn out to have "the liveliest, most eager, strongest desire for spontaneous goodness" (6–7). Often educators themselves ("men of mischief") make boys bad by misinterpreting high-spirited behavior as malicious (124). The ideal school serves as an "intelligent consciousness" that "hovers over and between the outer world and the young scholar." It "mediates" between the two, "imparting to them language and mutual understanding" (138–39).

Most importantly for this essay, Froebel claims that

the *mind* and the *outer world* (first as *nature*), and *language* which unites the two, are the poles of boy-life, as they also were the poles of mankind as a whole in the first stage of approaching maturity (as the sacred books show). Mind-world-language [are] three fold, yet in itself one, knowledge. [129]

According to Juliet Dusinberre (15–19), Froebel reinstated the body as the center of experience and linked it organically with mental development; hence his insistence on manual training. Babies are animals en route to full humanity. Important corollaries derive from this: First, the child must evolve "naturally," without undue adult constraint, to avoid the perversions detailed by Rousseau, Wordsworth, and other Romantics; hence disobedience to parents is at times permissible. Second, the child prodigy, the genius, is linked both to childishness and insanity, that is, the retention of vital spontaneity within the usual automatism of adults. Third, the mother's role is exalted because moral ideals are born from maternal affection, not self-interest. (Kipling dramatizes this corollary in "The Brushwood Boy" (1895), which precedes *Stalky*.) Thus Froebel is a touchstone for the "cult of childhood" that blossomed in the 1890s and culminated in Barrie's *Peter Pan*.

No doubt Kipling sympathized with many of Froebel's notions. After all, he was a boyish prodigy familiar with unstable mental states.[10] His letters to his children evidence concern for their physical and mental development equally (*O Beloved Kids*). In his tales for little children, it is language that links the child and the world, and language is the basis and medium of education.

Finally, he may have found a literary application of Froebel's bracketing of the physical and mental. Froebel's *Mother-Play and Nursery Songs* contained fifty engravings illustrating all trades and professions. Each picture includes symbolic hand gestures and a song. By touch, by sight, and by hearing, the child absorbs lessons. This ingenious array of sensory appeals reminds one of Kipling's *Just So Stories* that he recited to his children and also illustrated. But *Stalky & Co.*'s appeal is exclusively oral-aural, like a mother's songs. Here Kipling devised a "phonotext" that frequently cancels print's visuality, invites the reader back to "voicing," and thus restores the power inherent in sounded words (Ong, *Presence* 111–13). He does this by saturating his text with aphorisms, clichés, and formulaic expressions, the hallmarks of orality, borrowed directly or imitated from biblical, classical, or folk repositories, even from "the great holiday world" of music-hall gags: for example, "Satan rebuking sin with a vengeance"; "a Daniel come to judgement"; "the bleatin' of the kid excites the tiger"; "I can connive at immorality, but I cannot stand impudence"; "he came, he sniffed, he said things."

The link between harsh school life and the oral, parodic-literary nature of school language, used in tandem with, or as an alternate to, physical aggression, lies in the purpose for which the boys are being educated—a purpose with which Kipling aligns himself at the end of the book.

Now, if we combine the "Froebel clue" with Kipling's unusually hyperbolic and polemical style in *Stalky & Co.*, we may reach conclusions at variance from much critical opinion. Let us consider three "objectionable" passages.

(1) All editions of *Stalky* end with "Slaves of the Lamp, Part II." Ex-students reunite ten years after graduation. Coarsened by their experience as imperial governors (one shivers with ague, another's "face was like white glass"), they behave like boys and tell the story of an absent comrade (Stalky) who won a skirmish in northwest India by duplicating a trick played on a schoolmaster ("Slaves of the Lamp, Part I"). The story ends with Kipling's boast: "Just imagine Stalky let loose on the south side of Europe with a sufficiency of Sikhs and a reasonable prospect of loot." When he claims responsibility for creating Stalky by contriving the school trick years before, an old schoolmate asks, "What's that got to do with it?"

> "Everything," said I.
> "Prove it," said the Infant.
> And I have. [297]

Kipling credits his own stories for creating a generation of imperial buccaneers.

Stalky's model did indeed render distinguished military service and deserves praise. We, however, read Kipling *after* the Boer War, the battles of Loos, the Somme, and Gallipoli, and the Amritsar Massacre, when other Stalkies behaved with disastrous stupidity. We suspect that time trapped Kipling. Having mocked Dear Ferrar's Eric and other "pure-minded boys" for their priggishness, he substituted Stalky and other clever-minded boys whom we mock. The Erics of the world may be nuisances, but the Stalkies risk people's lives. We may wish to believe that Stalky's prank in "Slaves of the

Lamp, Part I," vandalizing a schoolmaster's quarters, anticipates Graham Greene's "The Destructors" or William Golding's *Lord of the Flies*. Indeed, the blatant "I" in the last sentence of "Slaves, Part II" is so obtrusive that it seems to nullify the book's pretentions to fiction and reduce it to propaganda.

(2) The titular hero of "Regulus" is a teacher's pet named Winton. He is a good student, a polite boy who apologizes at once for any infraction. Teachers like him because he is unlike the "Army brats," the bullies, who populate the USC. But his nickname is Pater, and other boys tease him about his "caree-ah." He is earnest. But when boys press him too far, language fails him. He explodes, goes "berserk," physically attacking a schoolmate and the boys who try to stop him. To mitigate punishment, a teacher pleads his case with the headmaster: it was the lad's first offense. The headmaster counters with, "Could you have damned him more completely? . . . Winton's only fault is a certain costive and unaccommodating virtue." Later the chaplain observes that he will "never be anything more than a Colonel of Engineers" rather than a gallant leader.

The story cuts two ways, exposing both goody-goody students and goody-goody teachers. Like Mr. Brownell in "The United Idolaters," academicians take pride in themselves as social and moral activists—for which Kipling makes them uncomfortable. They dislike reminders of their pomposity, low social station, and venality. Reverend John says, "Ours is a dwarfing life—a belittling life, my brethren. God help all schoolmasters!" Both he and the headmaster admit that "we must all bow down, more or less, in the House of Rimmon." But before we object too strenuously, we should remember Kipling's tribute to teachers in the book's prefatory poem, "Let us now praise famous men."

(3) In "The Moral Reformers," the Reverend John Gillet, calling Number Five study his "Tenth Legion" (Caesar's favorite), encourages the boys to punish two senior students who habitually bully a youngster named Clewer. Number Five subjects the miscreants to the entire repertoire of schoolboy "tortures" (*Letters* 2. 352–53). They inflict pain, not injury (except to senior pride). They exact contrition as well as confession because their message is, Repent and sin no more. Punishment matches crime.

Kipling's description of the punishment provokes indignation because the boys relish the process of reducing bullies to abjection. Executioners are not supposed to enjoy their work; but the boys,

especially Beetle, become intoxicated by the retribution they inflict
and the pain they cause. "The bleatin' of the kid excites the tiger."
Certainly there is nothing pleasant about torturing two louts until
they weep and plead for mercy. The hurt and humiliation are too
painful to be funny.

"The Moral Reformers" may have offended more readers than
any story in the book. It "proves" that the three boys are "little
beasts," "small fiends in human likeness," "mucky little sadists, as
critics have called them." It infuriated Edmund Wilson so that he
called the book Kipling's worst, "crude in writing, trashy in feeling,
implausible in a series of contrivances that resemble moving picture
'gags'" (23). Andrew Rutherford, a sympathetic critic, concluded
that "a sophisticated Philistinism, a deliberate brutality of speech,
is one of the most unpleasant features of Stalky & Co." (183). The
story so upset H. G. Wells that he denounced Stalky as "the key to
the ugliest, most retrogressive, and finally fatal idea of modern imperialism; the idea of a *tacit conspiracy between law and illegal violence*"
(307; Wells's italics).

If we cannot stomach a nonjudgmental account of education for
empire, we must always remind ourselves that Kipling's tales are
also sheer adventures in language. The exuberance of child talk
bubbles over, so that our initial pleasure in reading comes from recalling our own thrill at language acquisition, verbal play. Almost
nothing in the Stalky tales actually happened or could have happened in reality. Kipling exaggerated his three heroes' adventures
beyond what memory and reason dictate. Poetical and rhetorical license supplement each other and yield an experience that is
almost autonomous. Our delight is similar to that provided by Lewis
Carroll. The boys' and the narrator's verbal audacity starts and
holds the reader's imagination, carrying him through a series of
incredible pranks. The language is so convincing that the events it
narrates seem credible, "realistic," which of course they are not.

But Kipling writes prose, not jabberwocky; his language is referential as well as autonomous. It provides vicarious experience
and instills moral values. Here something peculiar happens. By his
own embodiment of Froebel's theory, and by ignoring or nullify-
ing Victorian ideals that animated children's stories, Kipling sets
the reader adrift. If we try to locate ourselves in the fictive world
of Stalky & Co. by using Victorian standards (or modern "progres-
sive" standards, for that matter), we remain lost--titillated perhaps

by Kipling's stylistic virtuosity but suspicious that our experience is somehow spurious, even immoral.[11]

One way to chart our whereabouts is to stay attuned to the tone of Kipling's volatile prose. He revised texts by performing them aloud, a practice that exaggerates tone. But tone is hard to communicate to readers unaccustomed to *hearing* texts or to readers belonging to "response communities" different from those that the author presupposes. Both Kipling's narrator and his characters can move with little warning from, for example, neutral description to braggadocio to sarcasm. Mr. King is a master at sarcasm and irony, but when the boys mimic his ironies ("the crass and materialised ignorance of the unscholarly middle classes"), a doubling occurs that forces the reader to listen carefully for the object of Kipling's satire.

Once he passed beyond his early infatuation with postromantic writers, Kipling seems to have been equally at home among preromantics. He called John Donne "Browning's great-great grandfather" and described himself as Robert Ferguson preceding some yet-to-be-discovered Burns (*Letters* 2. 115, 279). His mature style (or styles) always skips back beyond the lush sonority and "fragrance" of the nineteenth century to sparer models of the eighteenth that were still heavily influenced by school Latin. No doubt the telegraphic language of high-speed presses, of machinery generally, magnifies his stylistic novelty and enables him to respond enthusiastically when "all unseen, Romance brought up the nine-fifteen" ("The King"). But there is an older tradition at work in Kipling's style descending from Cicero, Horace, and Juvenal, reinforced by the scientific and Protestant plain style.

In *Stalky*, another way to chart our whereabouts is to follow Kipling's pointers to imperial, pagan Rome. Number Five study is the Tenth Legion. Winton becomes Regulus. Beetle defaces a complete set of Gibbon's *Decline and Fall*. Old Latin tags turn up continually; but even without them, the oral process of transmitting the Latin heritage echoes in the masculine, polemical harshness of boy talk. "A little of it stuck among the barbarians" who, with the aid of it, become responsible procurators. Kipling, in his own style and that of the boys, blended common speech with classical rhetoric, a striking combination.

If we come to terms with Kipling's rough-and-tumble language, we may suspect that its alleged brutality misses the point. In "The Moral Reformers," Reverend John claims that "most bullying is mere thoughtlessness." M'Turk corrects him: "Bullies like bullyin'. They mean it. They think it up in lesson and practise it in the quarters." The older boys who have tormented little Clewer are "flunk-outs" whose parents sent them to the USC in desperation to get them into an academy. They have "hammered [Clewer] till he's nearly an idiot."

Bullying is reprehensible, and Kipling shows, quite plainly, the pleasure produced when it combines with self-righteousness. For all the rhetorical extravagance in the "torture" scene, the aim is not to encourage bullying but to stop it. This is Kipling's message to imperial governors.

Kipling's ideal school is one that leaves boys to themselves as they grope through frantic deliquencies toward adulthood. But his school presupposes an "intelligent consciousness," embodied in the best teachers, that "hovers over" and "unites" the outer world with students' inner worlds. Language bridges and links them. It is a fierce language, capacious, contentious, but generous. It neutralizes hypocrisy without neutralizing values authenticated by two thousand years of Western history. One is not surprised that Kipling praised Horace and Juvenal for upholding republican virtues in decadent Rome. In them he may have heard Froebel's "eternal law." [12]

In his introduction to an edition of *Stalky & Co.*, Steven Marcus accepts the charge that Kipling's school prepared boys to become part of the governing caste of the British Empire, which included brutalizing them and girding them for "domination of the weak by the strong." [13] Conceding that this is "calculated to outrage the values that most educated persons today affirm," he then notes that the book contains values "described by old, obsolete words like honor, truthfulness, loyalty, manliness, pride, straightforwardness, courage, self-sacrifice, and heroism" (7).

If they appear at all, such words are as embarrassing among the boys at Westward Ho! as they are among children today. However, in *Stalky*, according to Marcus, they signal virtues that exist as active and credible possibilities; whereas in our world, they are absent or corrupted. In Kipling, these unspoken virtues propel the boys (and the reader) into the *agonia* that occurs when young minds collide with the adult world. As Isabel Quigly notes, "*Stalky & Co.* is the only school story which shows school as a *direct* preparation for life" (xv).

Kipling achieved this by assigning vital roles to adults in every story and also by revitalizing language—from old Latin tags to earthy dialect and music-hall tunes. Hyperliterate that he was, he reactivated the "oral encyclopedia," the storehouse of values that outlast ephemeral political and economic systems. Perhaps this explains how, in addition to imperial bluster, he reaffirmed "the brotherhood of mankind in time of sorrow or affliction."

Defunct British imperialism seems to have transmitted through Kipling the legacy of values bequeathed by ruined Rome. Late-twentieth-century readers will determine whether these values outweigh imperialism's vices, whether traditional values of any kind can survive in a depleted, overcrowded world. Kipling had his doubts when he conceded that the generation for which he wrote "conked out" in the First World War. And yet the tough boy talk of *Stalky & Co.* goes on calling to us, like the songs of mad Elizabethan beggars, inviting us to recall times when grander and less sentimental aims than ours governed behavior. Perhaps the offending "I" in the book's last sentence, with its candid affirmation of a traditional rhetorical ethos, vindicates Kipling's implied claim: I tried to create a conscience for my race. At the very least, the "I" is both stalky and self-transcending.

Notes

1. One should be aware that many editions of the book are unsatisfactory. The Stalky tales appeared initially in magazines between 1897 and 1929. Only nine of them were included in the first edition with the title *Stalky & Co.* (1899). The remaining five tales were added to *The Complete Stalky & Co.* in 1929. The best edition currently available is edited by Isabel Quigly. It is annotated and contains a valuable introduction.

2. The most notable exception is Vernon Lee (Violet Paget), who analyzed three paragraphs of *Kim* and accused Kipling of "bad syntax, bad grammar, bad rhetoric." No one seems to have noticed that her transcription of Kipling's text contains over a dozen misprints. In any case, she failed to realize that Kipling's texts are often visual signals for oral performance, not silent reading. If you "voice" them, flaws that Lee records vanish. (*The Handling of Words and Other Studies in Literary Psychology* [London: John Lane, 1923]). The Kipling essay appeared originally in 1910.

3. "Sound situates man in the middle of actuality and in simultaneity, whereas vision situates man in front of things and in sequentiality" (Ong, *Presence* 128). "Sight isolates, sound incorporates" (*Orality* 72).

4. Today readers will find the notes in the edition mentioned above indispensable. It is ironic that Kipling, often damned as an uneducated hooligan, is now celebrated for his almost Joycean allusiveness. For example, Nora Crook claims boldly that "Kipling wants to make readers of us all and to keep up literature, not to hoard his riches" (xv).

5. Quoted by permission of the National Trust from the Kipling Papers, University of Sussex Library.

6. It is worth reminding ourselves that since the decline of classical rhetoric, teachers of literature have grown increasingly text-bound. We pretend to be champions of culture, repositories of the finest utterances of humanity. But how many of us are trained to recite (from memory, dramatically) a thousand lines? Neither the certified teacher nor the Ph.D. is routinely tested as an oral performer; yet oral performance, as Kipling claimed, is the surest way to impress students with the values and beauty inherent in grand language. He wrote that gramophone records of good teachers "on the brink of profanity, struggling with a Latin form, would be more helpful to education than bushels of printed books" (*Something* 52).

Peter Green testified to the survival of Kipling's ideal up to the Second World War. He began his translation of Juvenal with an acknowledgment: "I first became acquainted with Juvenal through the good offices of Mr. A. L. Irvine, my old sixth-form master, who—with what I took at the time, wrongly, to be pure sadistic relish—set us to translate Satire X aloud, *unseen*, and afterwards made us learn long stretches of it by heart, together with parallel passages from Dr. Johnson's *The Vanity of Human Wishes*. But in fact, of course, this was by far the best introduction to a notoriously difficult poet that one could hope for. . . . This book is, in a sense, the belated fruit of a seed sown some twenty-five years ago, and I am happy to acknowledge my debt to an inspired and inspiring teacher" (7).

7. "The Uses of Reading" (1912), Sussex Edition of *The Complete Works*, xxv, 85.

8. "Literature" (1906), Ibid., xxv, 3.

9. To "Dear Musician" (October 9, 1899), Livingston Collection, Houghton Library, Harvard. I have used A. W. Yeats's transcription. According to Thomas Pinney in a letter to me, the passage was inscribed on a flyleaf of *Stalky & Co.*

10. Anthony Storr includes Kipling in his psychiatric study of nineteenth- and twentieth-century authors who illustrate "separation, isolation and the growth of imagination" (Chap. 8). Kipling deserved space in a recent study of manic-depressive creators: D. Jablow Hershman and Julian Lieb, *The Key to Genius* (Buffalo: Prometheus, 1988), but the seminal study for Kipling's generation was Cesare Lombroso's *The Man of Genius* (1891).

11. Robin Gilmour concludes his sympathetic analysis of *Stalky & Co.* with praise for Kipling's subversion of Victorian sentimentality about children, but also with condemnation. "The optimistic Victorian moralism of 'fair play' expunged in Kipling's revision of the Hughes code is not replaced by anything of comparable largeness or decency, but by something narrower, more efficient, more 'realistic'" (31). Quite the contrary, Kipling reopens the "spaciousness of old rhetoric" (Richard Weaver's phrase) that reanimates voices across two thousand years of Western history.

12. Kipling's interest in education (as distinct from his writing for children) has received little attention, but Richard A. Maidment helps fill the gap. He describes the USC's exemplary curriculum and schedule (37, 191) and portrays Cormell Price as an educator in the spirit of Froebel (124–25).

When it suited him, Kipling praised the USC as a military school. At Price's retirement (July 25, 1894), he claimed that the headmaster produced "men able to make and keep empires" (18). But the four more mature stories, composed years after the first edition of *Stalky & Co.*, emphasize unmilitary values. Little wonder that Price himself labeled the first edition "an amusing travesty" (144).

13. But Kipling explicitly rejected domination of the weak by the strong in the epilogue to *Puck of Pook's Hill* (1906): "Teach us the Strength that cannot seek, / By deed or thought, to hurt the weak." These lines would seem to augment the claim in *Stalky's* poetic prologue, "Save he serve no man may rule."

Works Cited

Crook, Nora. *Kipling's Myths of Love and Death*. New York: St. Martin's Press, 1989.

Dusinberre, Juliet. *Alice to the Lighthouse: Children's Books and Radical Experiment in Art*. New York: St. Martin's Press, 1987.

Froebel, Friedrich. *The Education of Man*. Trans. W. H. Hailman. New York: Appleton, 1887.

———. *Mother-Play and Nursery Songs*. Trans. Fanny E. Dwight and Josephine Jarvis. Boston: Lee and Shepard, 1891.

Gilmour, Robin. "*Stalky & Co.*: Revising the Code." In *Kipling Considered*, ed. Phillip Mallett. New York: St. Martin's Press, 1989.

Green, Peter, ed. *The Sixteen Satires of Juvenal*. Baltimore: Penguin, 1967.

Kipling, Rudyard. *O Beloved Kids: Rudyard Kipling's Letters to His Children*, ed. Elliot L. Gilbert. San Diego: Harcourt, 1983.

———. *Something of Myself*, ed. Robert Hampson. London: Penguin, 1988.

———. *Stalky & Co.*, ed. Isabel Quigly. Oxford: Oxford University Press, 1987.

———. *The Letters of Rudyard Kipling*, ed. Thomas Pinney. Iowa City: University of Iowa Press, 1990.

Maidment, Richard A. "Imagination and Reality in Rudyard Kipling's View of Education: A Literary Study." M.A. thesis. University College at Swansea, Wales, 1981.

Marcus, Steven, ed. *Stalky & Co.* New York: Collier, 1962, Introduction rep. in *Kipling and the Critics*, ed. Elliot L. Gilbert. New York: New York University Press, 1965.

Ong, Walter J. *Interfaces of the Word*. Ithaca: Cornell University Press, 1977.

———. *Orality and Literacy: The Technologizing of the Word*. London: Methuen, 1982.

———. *The Presence of the Word*. New Haven and London: Yale University Press, 1971.

———. *Rhetoric, Romance and Technology: Studies in the Interaction of Expression and Culture*. Ithaca: Cornell University Press, 1971.

Quigly, Isabel, ed. *Stalky & Co.* Oxford: Oxford University Press, 1987.

Rutherford, Andrew. "Officers and Gentlemen." In *Kipling's Mind and Art*, ed. Andrew Rutherford. Stanford: Stanford University Press, 1964.

Smith, Janet A. "Boy of Letters." In *The Age of Kipling: The Man, His Work and His World*, ed. John Gross. New York: Simon and Schuster, 1972.

Storr, Anthony. *Solitude: A Return to Self*. New York: Free Press, 1988.

Weaver, Richard. *The Ethics of Rhetoric*. Chicago: Henry Regnery, 1953.

Wells, H. G. "Kipling." In *Kipling: The Critical Heritage*, ed. R. L. Green. New York: Barnes and Noble, 1971.

Wilson, Edmund. "The Kipling That Nobody Read." In Rutherford 1964.

Kipling's Combat Zones: Training Grounds in the Mowgli Stories, Captains Courageous, and Stalky & Co.

Carole Scott

Kipling's obsession with the mastery of rules, laws, and codes of behavior dominates his work as it did his life. He wrote a charter for his children that identified in detail their "rights" to the Dudwell River near Bateman's; he created a Jungle society with a code "as perfect as time and custom can make it" (*The Second Jungle Book* 125); and he knew how to manipulate the rules to hasten his son's classification into active military service in World War I. Anyone at all familiar with Kipling's childhood will readily understand these concerns. The shock of being moved at the age of five from a pampered life with his family in India to the care of a harsh foster mother in Southsea, England, must have been traumatic enough. To be rescued after five long years from this "House of Desolation" only to be sent away again in less than a year to public school, a place of strict, often physical, discipline and institutionalized bullying, reinforced Kipling's sense that the world was a dangerous and uncertain place. These early experiences shaped his vision of the world and taught him how to survive: one must understand the system of order, master its code of rules, and apply them relentlessly.

Many writers, especially writers for children, have created unforgettable imaginary realms with their own sometimes fantastic rules; the entrances to such "otherworlds" are often surprising—a mirror, a wardrobe, a rabbit hole—dramatizing the borders of these magical realms and emphasizing their distinctness from the "real" world from which the children have come. It is not surprising, considering the drastic and painful changes to which little Rudyard had been subjected, that the grown Kipling would similarly plunge his young fictional protagonists into parallel worlds with new rules and new modes of survival, and that these otherworlds would be decidedly nonutopian. To Kipling, life was brutal, and his books for young

Children's Literature 20, ed. Francelia Butler, Barbara Rosen, and Judith A. Plotz (Yale University Press, © 1992 by The Children's Literature Foundation, Inc.).

people express this clearly, too clearly perhaps for modern tastes. For just as we find it hard to understand why a proud and loving father would push a seventeen-year-old into battle long before it was necessary, we wonder at his fascination with rules and laws, and why they are associated with such a high degree of violence. We are concerned that he expresses not only casual tolerance, but even encouragement, of behavior and attitudes that we consider unnecessarily brutal and cruel, even sadistic, especially in books for young people. Kipling exalts the harshest side of the manly code, especially the enthusiastic approval of physical punishment and violence and the stalwart indifference to pain, while encouraging the suppression of softer "feminine" feelings that he thought made men vulnerable. Published within a span of five years (1894–99), each of the three works I have selected for analysis, the Mowgli stories (which I shall be treating as one work), *Captains Courageous*, and *Stalky & Co.*, features a testing ground for the protagonist, a combat zone with its own set of laws, code of behavior, mode of being, and appropriate style of language.

The sense that Kipling's harsh code goes too far is not just a modern reaction. Despite his many admirers, there has always been an undercurrent of criticism, even revulsion (particularly in the period between the two World Wars) against the sentiments he expresses.[1] When Martin Seymour-Smith in 1989 describes Kipling's publicly expressed philosophy of life as "cheap, shoddy, unworthy and impractical" and his public utterances revealing of a man "grotesque, merciless and insensitive" (8), he follows in the tradition of Richard Buchanan who, in 1900, declared that Kipling was "on the side of all that is ignorant, selfish, base and brutal in the instincts of humanity" (25) and that "the vulgarity, the brutality, the savagery, reeks on every page" (31). Max Beerbohm's well-known caricatures of Kipling, which began in 1901 and continued for almost thirty years, express a similar opinion.

However, in spite of the criticism, there is no doubt that Kipling's exaltation of the ideals of warfare and its opportunities for manly conduct and heroism was widely shared in his time; it is not often that a new writer achieves popularity as fast as he did. Indeed, his successful expression of the exultant warrior mentality in his books for young people makes them of special cultural significance, for they helped to shape the minds of the young men who were later to die in the mud of Flanders fields. The books teach the ways to achieve success and self-esteem in later life, creating a picture of manliness, courage, and obedience to a clearly enunciated code of behavior from which one may not deviate for any reason. It is not surprising that the young men encouraged to display these traits would advance cheerfully to be mown down by the relentless German machine guns, and would even show their gallant sportsmanship by kicking footballs before them as they went, steadfastly "playing the game." John Kipling naturally falls into this metaphor when he writes his father from the war zone, "Remember our C.O. was 7 months on a "Brigade" staff & what he doesn't know about the game isn't worth knowing" (Gilbert 213).

The rules of war are very different from the rules of games, but Kipling and his contemporaries were not at all clear on this issue; tragically, it took the Great War and its spokesmen, Wilfred Owen, Siegfried Sassoon, and Rupert Brooke, to change the popular vision of the time. For the metaphor of war as game, which Kipling endorsed but by no means invented, had been nurtured by such poets as John Masefield and Sir Henry John Newbolt, whose "Vitaï Lampada" (1898) became a public school favorite. Beginning with the image of a school cricket match, Newbolt's poem ends with the later depiction of the boys at war. I reproduce the first and last verses:

> There's a breathless hush in the Close tonight—
> Ten to make and the match to win—
> A bumping pitch and a blinding light,
> An hour to play and the last man in.
> And it's not for the sake of a ribboned coat,
> Or the selfish hope of a season's fame,
> But his Captain's hand on his shoulder smote—
> Play up! play up! and play the game!
>
> . . . .
>
> The sand of the desert is sodden red—
> Red with the wreck of a square that broke;
> The Gatling's jammed and the Colonel dead,
> And the regiment blind with dust and smoke;
> The river of death has brimmed its banks,
> And England's far, and Honor a name;
> But the voice of a schoolboy rallies the ranks:
> Play up! play up! and play the game!

While it is true that moving onto the playing field or the battlefield involves entering into a distinct arena, where there are opposing teams and winners and losers, carrying the metaphor further is frightening. It is noteworthy that Newbolt's lifelong friend Douglas Haig was the general most responsible for the squandering of life, because he stubbornly persisted in relying on the soldiers' courage and fortitude instead of realizing that these qualities were meaningless in the face of the "stuttering rifles' rapid rattle."

In *The Great War and Modern Memory*, Paul Fussell discusses in detail the common attitude to war in the decades prior to 1914. He particularly notes the sense that when ordinary men moved into battle they took on the dimension of heroes, and points out how the elevated diction of warfare, very different from the language of everyday life, contributed to this perception. Thus the enemy is "the foe," the dead on the battlefield are "the fallen," to die is to "perish," warfare is "strife," and a soldier is a "warrior." The vision that war is glorious and transforms its participants into figures of mythical proportion is aptly illustrated in the mid-century incident that led to Tennyson's "Charge of the Light Brigade." "Someone had blundered," the poem tells us; but the stupidity and bungling that sent close to six hundred men to their deaths for absolutely no purpose is passed over lightly. Instead, the poem focuses upon the glorious bravery of the men of the Light Brigade, and how valiantly and honorably (though futilely) they gave their lives, ennobled by their sacrifice and enshrined in the hearts of posterity for time immemorial. It was not surprising that young men reared on the glowing illusion that "laying down one's life" or "making the supreme sacrifice" for family and country was a beautiful and somehow sanctified act should flock to the recruiting stations at the declaration of war. Thomas Babington Macaulay's "Horatius," written a few years before Tennyson's poem, put it well:

> . . . how could man die better
> than facing fearful odds
> For the ashes of his fathers
> And the temples of his Gods.

No wars are pretty, but the gulf that lay between rhetoric and reality in the Great War was especially striking.

In this context, Kipling's fictional realms, the "otherworlds" he created as arenas of conflict or combat zones, are more understandable. They are definitely men's worlds; most of the players are male, and the few women we encounter are, like Harvey's mother or the fishermen's womenfolk in *Captains Courageous*, safe on land outside the field of combat. At home the women are soft, nurturing, and emotional. They fear, they weep, they suffer vicariously for their menfolk. Harvey's mother breaks down completely, incapable of any kind of action, when she thinks he is drowned; the passion with which Kipling describes how the entire railroad system conspires to speed her to her recovered son is sentimental to the point of excess. Messua, too, is pictured as vulnerable, suffering for her maternal love and kindness to Mowgli when the villagers stone her; incapable of self-preservation, she must depend on her adopted son for protection. The only self-sufficient female is Raksha, but of course she is a wolf! The men, on the other hand, display no such soft emotions; they are fierce, courageous, hard, even cruel; they exult in pain and they exult in winning. But to escape from the female world and female feelings, they must move over the boundary into another world.

In both the Mowgli stories and *Captains Courageous* we find the main character clearly crossing over from his ordinary world into a completely different one. Mowgli has somehow strayed from the sphere of humankind, and when he walks into Raksha's lair he has entered the Jungle world where animals talk and have created a social structure and history, and where he must learn to survive on their terms. Harvey tumbles from his old life in the luxury liner headlong into another realm. Saved from drowning in the ocean, he is literally reborn into the microcosm of the fishing boat named the *We're Here*, where he takes the place of a young man lost at sea just a few days before. He has shed his old identity as he has his wad of money, and must take on new habits, new behavior, and a new perspective on his place in society, playing the part of a man in a man's world, subject to the common code that ensures the survival of the floating community. In *Stalky & Co.*, although we receive some description, especially regarding M'Turk, about the homes from which they have come, there is no account of the boys' arrival at the school. The boundary over which they have stepped is not dramatized, although it is clear that it exists, for their excursions into the surrounding countryside are carefully prescribed, and being out of bounds is punishable. The incident where the Head banishes himself from this sequestered world to preserve it from the danger of diphtheria outside emphasizes its separateness.

The Law of the Jungle in the Mowgli stories is described by Kipling as preeminent and "as old and as true as the sky" with a code that is absolute, seemingly immutable, and unquestionable. The reader is never told how or by whom it was established, or how it might be changed. Driven by a supposedly ageless and eternal vision imbued with a rational wisdom that accepts and incorporates the apparent vagaries of animal behavior and provides a clear pattern fair to each, the law defines each creature's hierarchy, its rights and obligations, and the rules of interaction with its own kind and with other species. Thus the tiger can claim one night of the year when he is entitled to kill Man; a mother wolf has the right to a portion of any wolf's kill for her litter; the jackal may run with the tiger and take what he leaves; and the elephant who lives a hundred years and more has the responsibility to proclaim the Water Truce. Only the Bandar-log, the Yahoos of the Jungle, are outside the law and are consequently viewed with contempt by all of the other animals. While time moves on and the players change, the principles and rules remain; the law has "arranged for almost every kind of accident that may befall the Jungle People, till now its code is as perfect as time and custom can make it" (125). Because it is clearly understandable and dependable, it governs even out-of-the-ordinary situations, like the time of drought, or Mowgli's kidnapping by the Bandar-log and his incarceration among the snakes of the ruined city, when the Master-words of the Jungle ensure safe passage.

The notion of the supremacy of the law, driven by a Darwinian belief in the perfectibility that "time and custom" will unquestionably bring about, suggests a supreme power whose vision is realized in this exact code. Whether this supreme power is divine, or a reflection of the Victorian imperialistic sense of responsibility for bringing light and civilization to benighted areas of the world, is not important here; in fact, the sense of mission characteristic of both is clearly expressed in Mowgli's need to "let in the Jungle" in an attempt to cleanse the nearby village where superstition and greed has led to behavior that violates the morals of the Jungle Law. Because he is so clever and learns the Jungle Law better than the animals, Mowgli becomes invincible. He achieves individual power by following the law and interpreting it with human intelligence, illustrating that the individual is the expression of this deeper power rather than a free agent who can operate outside it.

Those of us who were introduced to the Mowgli stories in childhood probably accept without question that the Jungle in this context is an appropriate source of values. We still delight in Mother Wolf's claiming of the naked man cub, protecting him against the villainous Shere Khan, and watching benignly as he suckles with her own brood. Like Mowgli we feel the joys of companionship with the other wolves and his sense of belonging as he learns to claim, "We be of one blood, ye and I"; and we know his loneliness when he is thrust out of this idyllic existence because of his growing manhood. We share his sense of increasing competence as he learns the rules and becomes Master of the Jungle, and his distaste for the moral turpitude of the village.

When we think a little more objectively, however, the notion of finding codes of behavior in the Jungle, a place usually used as a metaphor for savagery and lawlessness, seems contradictory and strange. And when we analyze these codes more carefully, we find that a great many of them regulate the ordered hierarchy of power, particularly power over killing and ownership of the kill. When you wish someone well you wish him "good hunting," and Chil the Kite's function as the scavenger of the dead is cheerfully acknowledged: "almost everybody in the Jungle comes to [Chil] in the end" (238). Moments of great accomplishment are similarly violent: Mowgli laughs when he sets fire to Shere Khan's coat, and later, having killed him, dances in triumph upon his skin pegged out on the Council Rock. "Letting in the Jungle" features Mowgli's relentless revenge against humankind, and the story is followed by "Mowgli's Song Against People," which celebrates the obliteration of a village. The nature of the language as well as the splendid rhythms of the death chants and songs gives a legendary quality to this long tale of hunting, killing, and revenge. The violence is continuous, but the everyday tone encourages us to accept it as the way things are, where winning means survival. "'When tomorrow comes we will kill for tomorrow,' said Mowgli, quoting a Jungle saying; and again 'When I am dead it is time to sing the Death Song. Good Hunting Kaa!'" (229). There are really only two occasions where death seems frightening. The first is in "Kaa's Hunting," where Kaa tells Mowgli "what follows is not well that thou shouldst see" (47) and we are left with the image of the mesmeric Dance of the Hunger of Kaa that will lead to the death of many of the Bandar-log, unable to resist in their hypnotized state; the second is in "The King's Ankus" where men kill not for food, but for greed. Somehow the killing on these two occasions seems unsporting and not played by the appropriate rules.

Like the Mowgli stories, *Captains Courageous* presents an autonomous world whose code of behavior is absolute, and where the stakes once again are life and death. Here it is not other people, or humanized animals, but the sea that is the threat. The neverending fatal power of the ocean is poignantly acknowledged at the ship's homecoming and at the service where wives, sweethearts, and mothers suffer from the news of the latest losses at sea, and grieve for those who have died before.

Kipling has sought to create not a fantasy world, but one characterized by verisimilitude, having spent hours of careful research and interviews to represent an accurate picture of the fisherman's life. The strong sense of a natural law whose incontrovertible power and strength must be understood and whose rules followed faithfully and with insight is expressed just as strongly in *Captains Courageous* as it is in the Mowgli stories. As Mowgli seeks to emulate the superior senses of the animals, so Disko Troop, the "master artist who knew the Banks blindfold" (50), is recognized by the entire fleet for his amazing knowledge of the contours of the sea beneath him and for his almost uncanny gift for sensing "the roving cod in his own sea" (36); he steers his craft even in fog and darkness, "always with the fish, as a blindfolded chess-player moves on the unseen board" (77).

This oneness with his natural environment, together with his thoughtful control of his crew, gives Troop unchallenged power over both nature and human nature. But he has achieved this stature through mastery of the rules of the sea and the lore of those who sail upon it; he has learned not only the maritime geography, but the way of the currents, the wind, and weather; not only how to catch and preserve the fish, but the reasons why they will congregate in certain places; not only the rules that make a ship's crew work together—who is assigned which task, who takes precedence at mealtime, who stands which watch—but also the more delicate codes of behavior and of ethics that cause him to take on the tragic amnesiac Pratt and his guardian Salters, even though they are not outstanding fishermen. His boat is a minicosmos that includes representatives of various nationalities and religious beliefs, including the cook's unearthly magical rituals and second sight. The deep natural morality that inspires Troop's way of life and work is highlighted by the contrast of Uncle Abishai's boat: "foul, draggled and unkempt, . . . a blowzy, frowzy, bad old woman" (68) manned by a drunken crew who all go down with the boat in clear sight of the

We're Here. In their drunkenness, their violations of the code of sea-manlike behavior, and their prideful and foolish underestimation of the power of the sea, they have broken all the rules and they must pay with their lives.

Of the three books I am considering, *Captains Courageous* involves the least violence and cruelty. It is also, interestingly enough, the work in which the lawmaker, Disko Troop, is the most human. His rules are less ideal codes than practical behavior, and he is allowed to make mistakes; one of Dan's continuing sources of merriment is that his father is "mistook in his jedgment" regarding Harvey's true account of his father's wealth and position in society. Nonetheless Kipling seems to take a good deal of pleasure in detailing Harvey's physical trials: being worked to exhaustion, suffering painful "gurry sores" (the mark of a real fisherman); being knocked around gener-ally if he doesn't move or learn fast enough. The seaman teaching Harvey "emphasized the difference between fore and aft by rub-bing Harvey's nose along a few feet of the boom, and the lead of each rope was fixed in Harvey's mind by the end of the rope itself" (47). And the incident where Harvey and Dan accidentally catch the corpse of the dead sailor with "the head that had no face under its streaming hair" (121) does seem gratuitous. Kipling convinces us that Harvey ultimately enjoys what could be considered abusive treatment of a minor, and that the end result is a matured and enriched youth well on the way to the assumption of his manly responsibilities.

The approach is reminiscent of Lord Northcliffe's propaganda piece to families of men at the front entitled "What to Send 'Your Soldier.'" A very acceptable gift, he says, is peppermint bulls' eyes:

> The bulls' eyes ought to have plenty of peppermint in them, for it is the peppermint which keeps those who suck them warm on a cold night. It also has a digestive effect, though that is of small account at the front, where health is so good and indigestion hardly ever heard of. The open-air life, the regular and plenteous feeding, the exercise, and the freedom from care and responsibility, keep the soldiers extraordinarily fit and contented. [Fussell 87]

The cold, wet, exhausted soldier eating his unheated canned ra-tions, crouching at the bottom of a rat-infested trench with shells screaming overhead, the decaying dismembered bodies of his comrades around him, would have some difficulty recognizing North-cliffe's absurd description. Yet it is clear from the soldiers' letters home that a cheerful and willing response and sturdy inattention to physical comfort was the attitude that was expected of them. John Kipling, in his last letter home, writes, "We have to push through at all costs so we won't have much time in the trenches, which is great luck. Funny to think one will be in the thick of it tomorrow" [Gilbert 222].

In *Stalky & Co.* the codes are much more complex, and the kinds of behavior described present a challenging dynamic that mediates between a number of conflicting possibilities. In the world outside the school we have the accepted codes of the village, the farmers and shopkeepers who inhabit it, and representatives of the gentry. The boys bring some of these codes from home with them, as we see for example in the event where M'Turk and Colonel Dabney share outrage at the shooting of a fox. Within the school we find the rules of the masters such as King and Prout, with their sometimes narrow perspectives of what is acceptable; the ordinary boys with ordinary rules, limited and rudimentary in daring, imagination, and intel-ligence; and at another level the startling trio of Stalky, M'Turk, and Beetle, who play out with the Head a symbolic stichomythia of creative behavior, each interweaving with the others to form new variations on the accepted patterns.

Nonetheless, it is clear that the Head is the source of absolute order; for even the Three, though they can manipulate everyone else, bow to his authority. In fact, one of the especially significant events of the later part of the book is the discovery of the reason for the Head's punishing them in a manner and for an offense that they did not understand at the time. To maintain the fiction that he is infallible is so important that Abanazar covers up the true reason (the Head had to impress one of the trustees) and reinterprets the offense to the other two (the Head knew they had been dueling). It is apparently necessary that the boys' vision of the Head as a god-like figure be protected, for he is the only visible source of authority and of ultimate values in the book; human failings are not per-mitted him as they are to Disko Troop. As he tells Beetle, "There is a limit . . . beyond which it is never safe to pursue private ven-dettas, because . . . sooner or later one comes into collision with the higher authority" (141). When the Head ironically points out that the enforcing of limits involves some "flagrant injustice," M'Turk refers to him as a "dearr man," and Stalky laughs heartily at the thought. The boys must preserve the system of authority that they need, helping to construct and maintain it through their willing collusion.

The Jungle and the *We're Here* present worlds where the laws are clear, and the sense of order dependable. The characters know the rules and the dangers of flouting them, and though Mowgli must use his intelligence to interpret the Jungle Law as it should apply to the world of people, within the discrete boundaries in which the rules apply there is little need for any individual to redefine the codes of ethics and behavior.

In sharp contrast to the serenity born of the clear order in the Jungle and the *We're Here*, *Stalky & Co.* is permeated with a sense of uneasy rambunctiousness where the expected structural order is consistently sabotaged, and various codes of behavior vie with each other for supremacy. While it is true that the Head reigns supreme, like Disko Troop a natural leader and arbiter setting the ethical standards of which codes and rules are the ultimate expression, the other masters' authority is constantly challenged by Stalky, Beetle, and M'Turk, who usually emerge victorious. In addition, the hierarchical structure that the boys in general set up and defer to, the system of prefects whose seniority is usually respected, is also overturned by the three protagonists, who consider their judgments and intelligence vastly superior. The tension that Philip Mason notes between Kipling's love of rules and his respect for human potential is very evident here. Mason believes that in "all his life [Kipling] was to be divided between his instinct as an artist and his understanding of the administrator; between an emotional sympathy for the waif and the outlaw but a firm belief that, if chaos is to be kept at bay, men must be ruled by laws and the individual may have to suffer. He is usually on the side of the system but often against its manifestations; always on the side of the Head but often against the housemaster" (47).

In *Stalky & Co.* it is important to remember that the setting is the United Services College, which is preparing boys for a career in the military, as Stalky's ditty makes clear:

> It's a way we have in the Army,
> It's a way we have in the Navy,
> It's a way we have in the Public Schools
> Which nobody can deny!   [250]

The later part of the book does tell us about the boys' actions in battle, not at all like the Great War to come, but part of the preservation of the Empire against the tribesmen who stir up unrest. This war and the characters' actions are as outrageous as the school environment illustrated, and Kipling goes to some extremes to suggest the continuity between the two, for example the two chapters entitled "Slaves of the Lamp," where the closing song of the boys' pantomime reappears in a military telegram, and Stalky is recognized in action by his singing "Arrah, Patsy, mind the baby." Though this connection is common to all the books considered here (Mowgli takes his sense of values into the human world with him; Harvey's experience of men and boats serves him well in his father's shipping empire), the war stories told by Dick Four and Tertius fifteen years later reveal a Stalky little different from the schoolboy. War is almost as much of a game as the battles at school, replete with glee at outwitting the enemy, bravado which now shows as bravery, and cheek to higher authority.

There is no doubt at all that Kipling intends us to admire the boys-become-men, and especially Stalky, for their derring-do, their sense of adventure, their intelligence, their humor, their camaraderie, and their flouting of authority. He suggests that these qualities are what makes the Empire great and lauds their expression in military life. The fact that USC prepares boys for the military makes the school's sense of disorder and violence justifiable, and the friction a way to define a deeper kernel of truth. The code is based not on superficial rules but on a deeper understanding of manliness, which finds its ultimate expression in the final chapters where the boys' early training prepares them not only for honorable behavior, but for survival. Stalky can thus use a comrade's dead body to cover and keep hidden a passageway he does not want others to use, and he can carve a symbol on the chest of a man he has just killed to confound his enemies and put them at war with each other. The callousness at school toward physical punishment becomes, in this context, simply preparation for a life whose high point is the glorification of war and the fighting man. Once again, conquest is survival.

The contrast in the degree of physical punishment in the three books is of particular interest. Mowgli is treated with kindness and chastised only once, after he consorts with and is kidnapped by the Bandar-log; Bagheera provides "half-a-dozen love taps" which wouldn't have wakened a panther cub but which "for a seven-year-old boy amounted to as severe a beating as you could wish to avoid" (48). Similarly, in *Captains Courageous* Disko Troop strikes Harvey just one time, causing him to fall down onto the deck with a bloody nose. In both of these cases Kipling expects the reader to accept that the punishment is correct, deserved, and very efficacious. But in *Stalky & Co.* there is an endless ritual of beatings, lauded as a much better punishment than lines or other tiresome impositions. These are administered by the Head, and the boys are always both impressed by his actions and grateful for their punishment. In fact, in the most extreme case, after the Head is cheered by the entire school for his bravery in dealing with a diptheria case, his decision to beat every boy in the school for unruly behavior is met with "wonder and admiration. . . . Here was a man to be reverenced" (248). And partway through the beatings he is cheered again. A scene which is particularly revealing is the one in which the Head discusses limits while beating the boys. Kipling's representation of the process of punishment is quite evocative; afterward the boys run down to the lavatory and, while admitting they had suffered severe pain, laughingly compare welts with the aid of a mirror. One is reminded that flagellation is considered "le vice Anglais" and is apparently a standard feature of most British pornography.

> It was a fair, sustained, equable stroke, with a little draw to it, but what they felt most was his unfairness in stopping to talk between executions. Thus:— "Among the—lower classes this would lay me open to a charge of—assault. You should be more grateful for your—privileges than you are. There is a limit—one finds it by experience, Beetle—beyond which it is never safe to pursue private vendettas, because—don't move— sooner or later one comes—into collision with the—higher authority, who has studied the animal. Et ego—M'Turk please— in Arcadia vixi." [141]

In addition to these beatings exerted by the Head, we find in "The Moral Reformers" (a rather distasteful chapter, at least to sensitive eyes), the Padre turning over a discipline problem to the Three, who subject two bullies to a well-documented and carefully detailed succession of painful bullying techniques—techniques that the bullies themselves had used on a young victim. This rough justice, though probably deserved and certainly effective, seems motivated by revenge as well as justice (Beetle had been bullied when young) and leaves rather a sour taste. It really isn't fun, though the Three seem to enjoy it. It seems that though Kipling apparently found Stalky exceedingly funny, the challenge to order required him to reinstate it in the book through constant violence; it appears that the threat to order provoked a deep anxiety that both humor and violence relieved.

It is very possible that the sharp and not altogether pleasant memories that inspired Kipling to write *Stalky & Co.* are expressed not only in the noticeable degree of hysteria that permeates the book, but also in the absence of a clear dividing line between the "Coll." and the "real world," and in the disordered hierarchy and unstable rules that operate in the school. It has become commonplace to look back upon Kipling's childhood experiences through the eyes of the boy in "Baa Baa, Black Sheep" and perceive the agony of a child deserted by his parents and abused by his foster family. But anecdotes from the biographies also suggest that Rudyard was a pampered little boy, spoiled by the family's Indian servants and sorely in need of some discipline. Furthermore, two images of the child reveal a boy who, when he could not see well, took a stick and slashed what he thought was his grandmother to determine if the blurry image was indeed her, and who would come to lunch with his boots red with blood from the pig slaughtering that so fascinated him. There are also mixed messages about his time at school. Was he mistreated at United Services College, or did he simply object to the usual restraints and rough-and-tumble normal in a group of adolescent boys? Certainly he was perceived as being very physically mature for his age, and his demeanor at school was described as challenging and arrogant. In fact, he had discovered, shortly before writing *Stalky & Co.*, that his schoolmasters had suspected him of homosexual behavior, a suspicion that made him extremely angry, for he considered such acts "beastliness." The violence in the book may be expressing some of this anger.

Such anecdotes provide no firm base for an interpretation, but they do provide some additional perspective to the disconcerting violence that simmers so close to the surface of *Stalky & Co.*, erupting not only in the canings, but in the killing and persecuting of animals, the smashing of furniture and windows, the shooting at other boys, and the near-burning of the dormitory. Revenge frequently inspires the violence, for example, the Three's killing a cat and placing it under the floorboards of King's house to decompose in retaliation for his suggestion that they smelled bad, or their smashing up King's study when they are evicted from their own. "Didn't I say I'd get even with him?" says Stalky (250); "Ti-ra-la-la-i-tu, I gloat! Hear me!" (54) cry the boys as they celebrate their revenge. The sense of sweet satisfac·ion celebrated in these and other incidents is more frighteningly evident in a later story, "Mary Postgate," where the pleasure of the revenge Mary feels at the death of a German soldier is expressed as sensual ecstasy.

Where rules are broken, they must be mended, and this, it appears, can only be accomplished with violent action. The more uncertain the rules, the harsher the violence that is needed to reestablish the necessary order. While Kipling portrays the duel between order and disorder in social terms, clearly this must also be a metaphor for the surge of personal desires and inappropriate motivation, and the necessity to restrain or redirect them into acceptable channels. Kipling's writings suggest that he held within him serious unresolved conflicts that find expression in the obsession with rules and with the violence necessary to keep order dominant. With equal violence, he disciplines and divides emotions and feelings appropriate for men from those fit only for women. This macho vision of masculinity is hard to sustain for someone like Kipling, whose ambivalence toward the first important woman in his life, who petted and then abandoned him, is depicted so well in "Baa Baa, Black Sheep," where the young boy throws up his arm to defend himself against his mother's caress. By attempting to deny that part of his personality he identifies as "feminine," Kipling is forced to exaggerate the "masculine" characteristics that become, as one would expect in this dichotomy, stereotypically expressed in the bravado, indifference to pain, and brutality of the manly code he proposed.

Kipling was clearly a sensitive man camouflaged by brave words and an assertive, even brash personality. His ongoing attempt to master and to hide his vulnerability, to guard the tender self within, reveals itself in the need to dedicate himself to something greater, a more powerful authority structure whose preservation, whatever the cost, must be ensured. Mowgli's commitment to the Law of the Jungle, Harvey's involvement in the survival of the *We're Here*, and Stalky and his friends' collusion in maintaining the authority of USC's headmaster all illustrate Kipling's belief in an ordered, all-male structure whose shaping power turns boys into men.

Many cultures celebrate rites of passage to dramatize that boys are now grown and ready to take their place in adult society. Frequently the rituals involve isolating the young men from the community and subjecting them to tests by which they must prove their worth, tests which in many cases challenge the youths' ability to endure pain, humiliation, and even physical mutilation in their quest for a new adult wisdom.[2] By plunging his young protagonists into "otherworlds" with clearly delineated codes, rules, and powerful authority structures that hone the boys' potential into strength and self-reliance, Kipling creates his own ritualized arenas in which the boys can prove themselves. The willing, even joyful submission to pain is associated with the need to suppress aspects of the feminine, which Kipling depicts as soft, fragile, incompetent, and rendering the individual too vulnerable to survive in a demanding world. As the need to reject the female self becomes increasingly insistent, the ideal of self-sacrifice grows stronger, so that the giving and acceptance of pain becomes an exercise in power, acknowledging both the strength of the authority figure and the strength of the individual who, by enduring pain, shows himself worthy.

In real life, the self thus divided is in danger. Kipling's public self, the brash jingoist who continued to laud the increasingly anachronistic ideals of manhood and empire, appears to have flourished at the expense of a vulnerable private self that suffered not only from the early loss of his "best beloved" daughter, but from the death of his son in combat, sacrificed to the ideals and code that Kipling espoused. He spent his later years immured in the gloomy Bateman's, protected by his wife from the demands of a too-insistent world; access to his works after death was similarly controlled by his wife and later his daughter, who appear to have decided which of his unpublished writings were appropriate for release to the public.

In his fictional realms, however, Kipling's boys relish their tough, strict training in the combat zones he has created for them, and cheerfully endure and enjoy their preparation for a challenging world where their success seems assured. In each case the "otherworld" Kipling has delineated seems tailor-made as a training ground for the "real" world to which the boys must return; their mastery of the rules and codes, whether they be Jungle Law, sea lore, or military school regulations, promises them mastery not only of the self, achieved by a code-based self-discipline, but of the world in which they will take their rightful place.

Notes

1. See, for example, Philip Mason's chapter "Admiration and Dislike" or Harold Orel's "Rudyard Kipling and the Establishment: A Humanistic Dilemma."

2. A contemporary example of such a rite is depicted in a September 1990 *Los Angeles Times* series featuring "Hell Week," which young men in the Navy must endure if they are to become SEALs, members of the elite sea-air-land commando force that is sent on dangerous clandestine missions. "Why do they endure 'Sucking Up Pain' and Mind Games?" the subheading asks, as it describes a week which includes only three hours of sleep and constant physical abuse.

Works Cited

Buchanan, Robert. "The Voice of the Hooligan: A Discussion of Kiplingism." In *Kipling and the Critics*, ed. Elliot L. Gilbert. New York: New York University Press, 1965. 20–32.

Fussell, Paul. *The Great War and Modern Memory.* New York and London: Oxford University Press, 1975.

Gilbert, Elliot L., ed. *O Beloved Kids.* Orlando, Fla.: Harcourt Brace Jovanovitch, 1984.

Kipling, Rudyard. *Captains Courageous.* Vol. 16 of *The Collected Works of Rudyard Kipling.* 1941. New York: AMS Press, 1970.

———. *The Jungle Book* and *The Second Jungle Book.* London: Octopus Books, 1984.

———. *Stalky & Co.* Vol. 14 of *The Collected Works of Rudyard Kipling.* 1941. New York: AMS Press, 1970.

Mason, Philip. *Kipling: The Glass, the Shadow and the Fire.* New York: Harper and Row, 1975.

Orel, Harold. *Critical Essays on Rudyard Kipling.* Boston: G. K. Hall and Co., 1989.

Seymour-Smith, Martin. *Rudyard Kipling.* London: Macdonald and Co., 1989.

Puck & Co.: Reading Puck of Pook's Hill *and* Rewards and Fairies *as a Romance*

Corinne McCutchan

The Puck books, *Puck of Pook's Hill* (1906) and *Rewards and Fairies* (1910), are unlike anything else that Rudyard Kipling wrote for children. The Jungle books, *Just So Stories*, and *Stalky & Co.* are collections of stories and occasional poems that may have a common style or motifs or themes or characters, but none of their elements depends for its reading on a reading of all the others in the same book. Any one story may be extracted and read in isolation without a significant loss of appreciation. The stories about Mowgli in the Jungle books come closest to interdependence and are best read in chronological order, but it would be wrong to say that a reader could not fully understand "The King's Ankus" without reading "The Spring Running" or vice versa. But the elements of the Puck books, I will argue, are far less self-contained and far more interdependent because the Puck books are a single, intricately integrated work rather than simply the two collections of stories and poems they appear at first to be.

At first glance the Puck books present a formidable array of story and verse. Their frame narrative establishes the premise that two children, Dan and Una, conjure up Puck himself by acting out parts of *A Midsummer Night's Dream* in a fairy ring on midsummer eve in the shadow of Pook's Hill—that is, Puck's Hill. Puck gives them "seizin"—formal possession—of Old England, which means that from time to time he introduces them to men and women from England's past who tell the children stories about their lives. The supernatural narrators include (in order of appearance) a Norman knight who tells of the Conquest, a British-Roman soldier who describes the decay of the Roman Empire, a Tudor artist, a medieval Jewish physician who gives the secret history of the Magna Carta, Elizabeth I, a dying Regency beauty, an Iron Age tribesman, an Anglo-French gypsy with tales of Washington, Napoleon, and Talleyrand, and a seventh-century archbishop. Between each tale is

Children's Literature 20, ed. Francelia Butler, Barbara Rosen, and Judith A. Plotz (Yale University Press, © 1992 by The Children's Literature Foundation, Inc.).

at least one poem, often two, which elaborates or comments upon
some aspect of the adjacent narratives. All told, *Puck of Pook's Hill*
and *Rewards and Fairies* comprise twenty-one tales and thirty-eight
poems, and it is my argument that between them they compose a
single unified work, specifically, a romance.

The unity of *Puck of Pook's Hill* and *Rewards and Fairies* is not a
new idea, though it is often ignored, but rather an idea that has
never been satisfactorily worked out. Peter Hinchcliffe, making the
best attempt to date, writes that "despite their apparently random
chronological arrangement the stories in these two books are a coherent unity, much more than Kipling's other collections of stories"
(156). He even believes that "one ought to consider both books as
forming one interconnective narrative" (157). But the Puck books
provide an obstacle to searching out their own interconnections. In
his autobiography, Kipling wrote of the books: "I worked the material in three or four overlaid tints and textures, which might or
might not reveal themselves according to the shifting light of sex,
youth, and experience. It was like working lacquer and mother-o'-
pearl, a natural combination, into the same scheme as niello and
grisaille, and trying not to let the joins show" (205). And, as Hinchcliffe points out, "They are slick in a good and almost literal sense,
presenting the smoothest of surfaces to the reader, as Kipling's own
description of them implies. They are also intentionally complex,
and a full reading of the Puck stories ought to do what Kipling
suggests and look for the shapes that lie beneath the 'lacquered'
surface" (157).

When he looks beneath the surface, Hinchcliffe finds that "arranging the tables of contents of the two books in parallel columns
reveals a nicely symmetrical pattern of complementary stories"
(158). The symmetry leads him to believe that the stories told by
the Roman soldier and the gypsy "are the core of each book, and
their subject is the dynamics of leadership and the proper relations
between leaders and followers" (158). He is further convinced of
their centrality because they "form the only continuous narratives
in the two volumes, for the other stories told by the same narrators,
Puck and Sir Richard [the Norman knight] and Harry Dawe [the
artist], are all separate episodes" (163). But after a neat description
of the parallel arrangements, he himself must say, "Yes, but—the
symmetry is not perfect after all" because to make his scheme fit
he has omitted a story whose presence "requires the construction

of a whole new scheme. . . . The structure that seemed so obvious disappears and is replaced by another, equally coherent, as soon as we shift our point of view" (159). His symmetry only works so long as he assumes that a single theme, the dynamics of leadership, holds the assortment of poems and stories together. Leadership is an important theme in the Puck books, but as soon as Hinchcliffe begins to look at the equally important theme of healing, his scheme collapses, as he himself points out. His focus on the leadership theme is natural, since his article compares the Puck books to *Heartbreak House* and *Howards End* as three treatments of the related but broader theme of the destiny of England—from the conservative, socialist, and liberal points of view. But the cause of sorting out lacquer, mother-o'-pearl, niello, and grisaille so that the joins *do* show is better served by looking at the Puck books from a structural or generic point of view that comprehends and makes coherent all the formal and thematic elements of the books, but is not disrupted by a shift from one theme to another.

That Kipling intended the Puck books to be some kind of unified text is evident in their structure: a frame narrative used in combination with the books' basic formal unit, the poem-story-poem triad. Kipling had frequently used frame narratives within short stories, but never before and never again for a collection. And never before had he used his invention of the poem-story-poem triad: a short story flanked by two thematically related poems. Although Kipling used the triad again in later collections, the poems tend to frame and contain the narrative rather than create transitions from one story to the next as they do in the Puck books.

For example, the darkly ironic "Marklake Witches" is told by a narrator who, alone among the Puck books' ghosts, does not seem to realize that she has died, that tuberculosis has killed her, and that the doctors she trusted kept the truth of her condition from her. Each of her three doctors "protects" her in this way because each is in love with her, although all of them know that she is "not for any living man" (119). This phrase is echoed and amplified in "Brookland Road," a ballad about a mortal's love for a fairy maid, which gives a displaced lyrical expression to the grief of the men in the story at the death of the heroine. Its refrain is "Oh! maids, I've done with 'ee all but one, / And she can never be mine!" The connection with "Marklake Witches" is clear, but the refrain applies just as well to the iron-age hero in the next story, "The Knife and the Naked

Chalk," whose maid can never be his because *he* "dies." With their stone weapons, Tyr's flint-working tribe cannot fend off the wolves that stalk and kill them, so Tyr goes alone to an iron-working tribe to barter for iron knives. The ironworkers' god requires that his right eye be put out as a pledge of good faith, and he agrees. On his return, maimed and bearing "the Magic Knife," his tribe makes him a god by according him the status of the hallowed dead. Even though he is still clearly alive in fact, his lover, like the rest of his tribe, regards him as a dead man in principle and consequently marries another man.

Such subtle connections might be merely the effect of Kipling's well-known care in arranging the stories in his collections. And, certainly, there are obstacles to seeing any stronger formal and thematic unity among the tales and poems of the Puck books. Most striking is that the stories do not occur in chronological order, moving from the beginning of the Iron Age through the Roman Empire to the Middle Ages and on to the eighteenth century and the Napoleonic era. Even if arranged in a neat linear order, the stories in the Puck books would not form a continuous history of England—centuries, including most of the nineteenth, are omitted. Moreover, as Hinchcliffe found, no single theme can adequately embrace the whole collection, unless it is a theme so broad as to be virtually meaningless. And by its very polygeneric nature as an amalgam of frame narrative, verses, and stories, it has no unifying plot and no unifying hero of the kind we would expect in an epic or a novel. But polyphonic plots, polythematic narrative, and plural heroes turn out to be definitive or at least typical of medieval and Renaissance romance, such as the great cycles about Arthur and Spenser's Faerie Queene. And it is this generic tradition in which Kipling places *Puck of Pook's Hill* and *Rewards and Fairies*.

References to romance and elements taken from the tradition appear throughout the Puck books, beginning with the first book's title. Puck is, of course, the Puck of *A Midsummer Night's Dream*, but Kipling connects Shakespeare's romance to other romances. In the course of the books, Puck tells us that Oberon and Titania were succeeded by Huon of Bordeaux and the Lady Esclairmonde, characters from a thirteenth-century French romance. Kipling's Puck has also known Merlin and the world of Arthur. That Kipling knits together different romances of different periods and cultures suggests that the books in which he does so are a romance as well. He seems to be particularly aware of the example of Spenser, titling his story about Elizabeth I "Gloriana." More significantly, Kipling gives the children names strongly suggestive of *The Faerie Queene*: Una, the name of the first book's heroine, and Dan, which by association with Daniel of the Bible recalls the lion that befriends and defends Una in the forest. But the eponymous hero of Kipling's romance is not a queen or a king, but Puck, who like his royal counterparts is not a hero in the novelistic or epic manner, but one character among many, albeit with a special role.

It might be objected at once that Arthur is the hero of Arthurian romance just as Gloriana is the heroine of Spenser's great poem. But they are not hero and heroine in the way that Odysseus is the hero of the *Odyssey* or Jane Eyre of *Jane Eyre*. There are many heroes in the great Arthurian romances who are not Arthur—Yvain, Gawain, Lancelot, Tristram, Galahad—and many Spenserian heroes who are not the Faerie Queene—Redcrosse, Britomart, and Artegall, to name a few. In the cases of Arthur and Gloriana, the role of the titular hero or heroine is largely the role of a focal point, the role of a quasi-mystical repository of the whole range of virtues and abilities represented by the knights of Logres or Faerie. One of the clearest signs that Kipling was consciously working in the romance tradition and yet modifying it according to his own vision is that he fills this traditional role, but with a nontraditional figure, his own version of Puck.

In their creation of Arthur, writers of Arthurian romances from Chrétien de Troyes to Alfred Tennyson have put their distinctive mark on the king of the Britons, and yet remained true to the tradition in which they worked. In the creation of Puck, Kipling follows folklore, Shakespeare, and other traditional romance sources like *Huon of Bordeaux* and Celtic mythology, yet invents an original character of his own. Still a trickster, but now a pedagogue, Kipling's Puck is a beneficent otherworldly figure giving instruction to Dan and Una as the Lady of the Lake instructed Lancelot. The traditional Puck the Shape Shifter has become a Puck who remains (with one exception) recognizably himself and who yet, like a good actor or a good writer, takes on the characteristics of speech, demeanor, and even the languages and moods of the ghosts he produces. He is courteous with Richard, merry and teasing with Parnesius, calm and mysterious with Kadmiel.[1] As their link with the living world of Dan and Una, Puck has become the Gate Keeper of Old England

and, since he acts the part of a liege lord in giving the children seizin of it, its fairy king. Given the ennoblement of his position, he quite logically objects to the "butterfly wings and gauze petticoats" school of fairy iconography (*Puck of Pook's Hill* 49) and even the word *fairy*, which connotes such fluffy preciousness. "People of the Hills" and the Sussex dialect "Pharisees" are his terms of choice. He goes out of his way to emphasize the courage and prowess of the People of the Hills:

> "I've seen Sir Huon and a troop of his people setting off from Tintagel Castle for Hy-Brasil in the teeth of a sou'-westerly gale, with the spray flying all over the Castle, and the Horses of the Hill wild with fright. Out they'd go in a lull, screaming like gulls, and back they'd be driven five good miles inland before they could come head to wind again. Butterfly wings! It was Magic—Magic as black as Merlin could make it, and the whole sea was green fire and white foam with singing mermaids in it. And the Horses of the Hill picked their way from one wave to another by the lightning flashes! *That* was how it was in the old days!" [49]

In this one passage, Kipling connects his Puck with specific characters from romances other than Shakespeare's *A Midsummer Night's Dream*. The places he mentions are taken from pre-Shakespearean sources, Hy-Brasil from Celtic mythology and Tintagel from Arthurian romance. This allows the reader to retain Shakespeare's Puck, but to cease to see that Puck as definitive: in the world of the Puck books, Shakespeare's Puck is *one* Puck of many, a fictionalization of a "real" being whom Dan and Una meet face-to-face. When he appears and delivers some of Puck's lines from Shakespeare's play, he remarks, "I'm rather out of practice . . . but that's the way my part ought to be played" (44). He does not say, "That's the way I said it" or "That is how it was."

Part of the purpose behind freeing his Puck from the Shakespearean model would be the obvious ones suggested above: if Puck is to be the producer of history for the children rather than the player of practical jokes on them, if he is to be the spirit of Old England, its genius loci, stage manager, and psychopomp of its heroic dead, then his character must undergo some revision. But besides this practical consideration, Kipling needs Puck to fill the niche in romance for the king or queen who figures the unity of the realm and the text. In Kipling's romance, Puck holds the same position as the sovereign in one of the great romance cycles, but with the difference that his fellowship is not exclusively royal and knightly, but a fellowship of all the classes, sexes, and races that have gone to make up England. As he harmonizes himself with each narrator in turn, he creates an impression of plenitude, of possessing rather than merely mirroring the best and most essentially English qualities of each and uniting them within himself as a composite personification of all.

"A Charm," the opening poem of *Rewards and Fairies*, implies that he is exactly that. Throughout the two books Puck is characterized as a very earthy fairy—one of the narrators calls him "Spirit of Earth." In "A Charm" earth is explicitly identified with England's humble and forgotten dead whom history has overlooked:

> Take of English earth as much
> As either hand may rightly clutch.
> In the taking of it breathe
> Prayer for all who lie beneath—
> Not the great nor well-bespoke—
> But the mere uncounted folk
> Of whose life and death is none
> Report or lamentation.

As John E. Stevens writes, "The whole tendency of social thinking . . . in medieval romance from Chrétien to *Gawain* is towards a philosophy of an elite" (58). But the kind of social and historical thinking Kipling sets forth in his romance is intensely egalitarian, meant to cut across lines of class and race. In the Puck books we find, instead of a royal court, the fairy ring in the meadow, with Puck for sovereign and the children and their visitors for the court. Just as the children's "father had made them a small play out of the big Shakespeare one" (*Puck of Pook's Hill* 43), Kipling makes a small romance out of the big romance tradition. Kipling's small romance is romance from below, from the perspective of children, from the experience of long-dead actors most of whose names are forgotten or obscurely remembered, from the magic of a supernatural being who traffics with "hempen homespuns" (44) and harmless fun rather than royalty and holy grails. As "A Charm" announces, his first concern is not with the great names of history—though they appear from time to time—but with the ordinary people who

shared the English earth with them in life and share it with them
now in death. The magic effect of "A Charm" and of the Puck books
as a whole is to awaken the reader to the value of the ordinary
people of the present day as well as the past:

> These shall show thee treasure hid,
> Thy familiar fields amid,
> At thy threshold, on thy hearth,
> Or about thy daily path;
> And reveal (which is thy need)
> Every man a King indeed!

With "every man" as his hero, Kipling can scarcely afford the epic
treatment for any. That is, he cannot afford to let any one hero,
however superb, dominate the books as a whole. Instead he limits
each hero or heroine to as little as one tale and no more than five
and lets the arrangement of the tales and poetry impress the reader
with the admirableness of English virtues rather than the admirableness of one or two Englishmen.

Romance, then, permitted Kipling to create a socially varied cast
of heroes and heroines. But he does not vary in his idealistic attitude toward them and their tales. In this idealism lies another reason that in composing a work of long fiction, Kipling would be
drawn toward romance. Stevens writes that "the central experiences
of romance are idealistic" and that medieval romance "grew into
being to express 'the claim of the ideal' in an age which needed to
formulate a secular idealism" (227). In the Renaissance, Spenser too
embraced idealism, allegorizing a cardinal virtue in each book of his
romance. In his turn, Kipling brought to his romance an idealism
that embraces themes as varied as his narrators and their tales.

Again and again Kipling asks us to share the feelings of good
men and women who do what is right. Occasionally he asks us to
condemn the vices that mar the almost good or motivate the wicked,
but he gives the good characters the most attention and sympathy.
This sympathy is saved from devolving into sentimentality because
the heroes tend to take their goodness as a given, as something
inevitable rather than something to their credit. Of the attitude
toward virtue in romance, Rosamund Tuve writes:

> This emphasis upon allegiance to virtue as a thing not admit-
> ting of choice or deserving of compliment is much stressed,

and Spenser or romance-writers often find very similar words for it: "I have nothying done but that me ought for to do" says Lancelot (Vinaver, I, 274), and Red Crosse, "all I did, I did but as I ought" (II.i.33), or "Suffise, that I have done my dew in place" (II.viii.56) which is Arthur. [348n]

This is precisely the attitude taken and very nearly the precise words spoken by heroes and heroines in the Puck books. There is a striking similarity between the phrases of duty performed and the ubiquitous refrain of narrators in *Rewards and Fairies* ("What else could I do?" "What else could I have done?") and Kadmiel's "Why not?" at the end of *Puck of Pook's Hill*.

Just as no one character (other than Puck) can claim to be the hero of the books, no one virtue and no one theme can claim to be central. The principal themes that Kipling treats idealistically are the themes that occupied him throughout his career: the responsibilities of leaders and followers, justice and law, religious tolerance, vocation (the talent or destiny innate in a character), craft (the art or skill that furthers the vocation), and healing. Each verse, each framing introduction, each story, and each poem works some variation or some new combination upon one or more of these themes, so that over the course of the two books each theme is seen in relation to the others and in the light of varying circumstances, personalities, and ethical choices. They are intertwined, inseparable from each other and from the complete text of the Puck books as arranged by Kipling.

In fact, the strongest evidence that Kipling consciously designed the Puck books as a romance is that their organizing principle turns out to be the one most characteristic of romance: *entrelacement*. As Tuve explains, entrelacement is not the same as mere juxtaposition of different narratives or themes; nor is it the same as breaking off one narrative line and taking up another to create the impression of simultaneity while moving along a plot and subplots chronologically. The polyphonic narratives of medieval and Renaissance romance are organized so that each element, however divorced in time or place or characters from other elements, reflects backward upon all that precedes it and forward upon all that follows. The interrelatedness of all the elements was not simply the result of cause and effect, but expressive of qualifications and refinements of a theme or mood or meaning:

[T]hough the intervening episode will look like a digression from the line previously followed, it will transpire that the line could not go on without something furnished in the seemingly unrelated second line of narrative, the "digression." Or, if the digression has rather the character of a flashback or an elaboration or a supplying of background, it will turn out to carry onward some second "new" theme as well as the first one which needed the background; and from that in turn we digress, or seem to, and then come back, not to precisely what we left but to something we understand differently because of what we have since seen. (Tuve 362–63)

In the Puck books all the stories and series of stories seem to be digressions from each other. The chronological discontinuity is perhaps more "digressive" than in earlier romances, but the interlacing of the themes is all the more powerful. Kipling builds up overlapping "digressions" that continue or transform or elaborate a set of themes and motifs so intricate and so intertwined that they cannot be separated from each other without a great loss of intellectual and emotional response.

To trace the interlacing of the entire text of the Puck books is beyond the scope of this essay. Yet two of the more emphatic strains running through the books, leadership and healing, can be outlined here.

Puck of Pook's Hill begins with two groups of stories, the first concerning the aftermath of the Norman Conquest and the second the waning of Roman control of Britain. Both De Aquila in the former and Maximus in the latter are charismatic and brilliant leaders, but De Aquila is clearly the superior because he seeks the prosperity of the conquered Saxons and looks forward to erasing the distinction between Normans and Saxons, going so far as to make the Saxon Hugh one of his chief retainers and encouraging Norman-Saxon intermarriage. Maximus, on the other hand, belongs to an empire that has driven the conquered Picts to desperation and poverty north of Hadrian's Wall, and Maximus himself abandons a Britain threatened by Viking invaders to two young officers, Parnesius and Pertinax, in an attempt to make himself emperor. The distinctions Kipling draws between good and bad leaders here are fairly clearcut, especially since the good leader prospers while the bad leader loses his head. But in *Rewards and Fairies*, good leaders suffer more and more despite their goodness and new relationships between leader and follower begin to appear. In the poem "Cold Iron," a Christ-figure king waits at table on a captive rebel baron and forgives his treason. In "Gloriana," Elizabeth I cannot quite forgive herself for practicing Maximus's brand of realpolitik even though her goals—prosperity, defense of the realm–are those of De Aquila. She seeks reassurance from Dan and Una that she did the right thing in letting *her* pair of young followers sacrifice themselves in a naval diversion, but only Dan agrees that she was right.

While Gloriana is maimed in conscience, Tyr in "The Knife and the Naked Chalk" is maimed physically and cut off from a normal life by the excessive adulation of his people. "Brother Square Toes" and "A Priest in Spite of Himself" place George Washington in the opposite predicament: cut off from his people by their excessive anger at him for refusing to start a war with England. His only peers, his only true followers, are the Senecas Red Jacket and Cornplanter, whom he can call "my brothers" and "my children" (161). But while human fellowship and goodwill are valued by Tyr and Washington, they mean little to Washington's opposite number in the same tales, Talleyrand. The Frenchman reprises Maximus's self-serving ambition, but, unlike Maximus, cannot inspire love in his followers, only fear and grudging respect. This failing, and even more his lack of concern about it, show him, despite his success, the inferior of nearly every other leader in the books, including Harold of England in "The Tree of Justice." Although, as De Aquila affirms, he was a good leader, Harold lost the battle of Hastings and, in the forty years by which Kipling has him survive it, suffers more than any other leader in the Puck books, stoned by his own people for trying to tell them who he is. He is brought before Henry I and his court decrepit, starved, and only intermittently lucid. And yet the point of the tale is that the Normans ultimately refuse to mock him, and his former retainer, Hugh, weeps openly for his degradation. Kipling's final word on leadership, then, seems to be that good leaders have no guarantee of success or of love or even of keeping their identity intact, and yet what else could they do?

Kipling interlaces leaders through his romance, puckishly complicating the evidence as he invites the reader to pass judgment upon them. At the same time, he uses the recurrent appearances of physicians and healers to pass judgment upon the "diseased" moral and political climates they inhabit. Parnesius's brother practices medicine in the waning of the Roman Empire, the Widow Whitgift during Tudor religious persecutions, Kadmiel in the reign of King John, Nick Culpeper at the time of the English Civil War, Simon's Aunt during the Spanish persecution of Dutch Protestants. The era of the Napoleonic wars (when Kipling's favorite world powers, England, France, and America, were enemies) generates five healers: René Laennec, Doctor Break, Jerry Gamm, Pierre Tiphaigne, and Toby Hirte. Though their methods and efficiency vary, all of the healers in the Puck books are sincere and dedicated. If in this Kipling idealizes the medical profession, it is because he uses it to set a standard for disinterested human decency. Roundhead Culpeper saves a Royalist village from bubonic plague. Kadmiel, a Spanish Jew, saves anti-Semitic England from its lawlessness and injustice. René Laennec treats an English girl while he is a prisoner of war in England. Even French Royalist Tiphaigne, who makes a brief appearance in "Brother Square Toes," cares for a man whom he supposes to be a French Republican sailor. If there were only a single occurrence of such dedication, it might seem to be a matter of idiosyncratic decency or Hippocratic duty. But found again and again throughout the Puck books in men and women whose personalities vary widely, such occurrences allow Kipling to present disinterested compassion as an essential virtue incumbent upon all people, not healers alone.

Two healers appear in what I call the smuggler group in *Puck of Pook's Hill*, and I would like to look at these last three stories (and their poems) for a more detailed example of entrelacement. The other two groups in the book—the Conquest group and the Roman group—comprise tales told by the same narrator about the same characters and general time period. Yet the last three tales in the book are also properly regarded as a group, as closely related as those of Conquest and Roman groups, and equally important in the book as a whole.

As my name for them suggests, these tales are held together by the motif of smuggling. "Hal o' the Draft" is about smuggling guns, "'Dymchurch Flit'" about smuggling the People of the Hills, "The Treasure and the Law" about smuggling gold and, metaphorically, justice. The Norman-Saxon story, "The Knights of the Joyous Venture," of course concerns smuggling African gold *into* England, but the smuggler group is all about sending something out of England—purgative where the Conquest group is acquisitive and the Roman group defensive. They are also concerned with the theme announced in "Prophets have honour all over the Earth," which introduces "Hal o' the Draft":

> Prophets have honour all over the Earth,
> > Except in the village where they were born;
> Where such as knew them boys from birth,
> > Nature-ally hold 'em in scorn.

Each of the heroes of the smuggling stories is scorned (in some sense) by those who are closest to him. Hal and his precious craft are less important to the Sussex people than their booming trade in smuggling guns. The Widow Whitgift and her two sons—one blind, one mute—live alone and apart from the rest of the Marsh men and work their good deed unremarked and unthanked by any but the fairies. Kadmiel secretly improves the Magna Carta, but only Bishop Langton knows the alterations are his. The common English people of the day—not to mention their descendants—know nothing of their benefactor. And Kadmiel's uncle regards him as a traitor for sinking the treasure that would have financed King John in a war to revoke the Charter.

The smuggling stories also differ from the other two sets because they take a different view of the rewards of virtue. Although we are still in the realm of successful skill and virtue with the heroes of the Conquest and the defenders of Hadrian's Wall, the smuggler heroes are not rewarded with magic swords, rich manors, hoards of gold, promotions, praise, or an official triumph. Hal's reward is a lesson in humility. The reward given the Widow Whitgift—that there will always be one of her descendants "that could see further into a millstone than most" (192)—is not a reward that many would want; the present-day beneficiary is the Bee Boy, who is "not quite right in the head." Kadmiel is given no material reward at all, simply returning to business in Bury at the end of his adventure. His satisfaction comes from knowing that he has brought about a just law. There is an aptness, then, about the smuggling theme—it is a metaphor for good deeds done in secret and at the risk of the actors' lives. Hal and his friend Sebastian are, as the local magistrate points out, compounding a felony by not turning in the smugglers. The Widow risks the lives of her sons to ferry the People of the Hills out of England across a stormy Channel. Kadmiel risks his life over and over again to carry out his plan.

But to get the full effect of Kipling's patterning of his major themes, we should begin at the beginning of the group. Or, rather, at the end of the previous group. In "A Pict Song" the Picts vent their hatred of Rome who "never looks where she treads, / Always her heavy hooves fall, / On our stomachs, our hearts or our heads." Their refrain is "We are the Little Folk—we! / Too little to love or to hate. / Leave us alone and you'll see / How we can drag down the Great!" In the poem that opens the smuggler group, "Prophets have honour all over the Earth," Kipling takes up the idea of enemies dragging down the great and softens it to "a man's folk" puncturing the pride of the Great who grew up with those

> That don't care nothing what he has been.
> He might ha' been that, or he might ha' been this,
> But they love and they hate him for what he is.

At the same time that it establishes a connection with the previous group, "Prophets" points forward into the next. The importance of religion is foreshadowed by the poem's New Testament title (an allusion to Matthew 13:57) and by its allusions to the prophet Jonah. Prophecy and second sight will figure in the group, but Jonah is particularly appropriate because much of his book is about his vocation from God and his resistance to it. The allusion to the prophet's story also introduces the idea of justice tempered with mercy: Jonah is sent to prophesy destruction to Nineveh, but when the Ninevites repent, God relents and spares those whom He wryly refers to as "sixscore thousand persons that cannot discern between their right hand and their left hand" (4:11).

The humorous tone of the Almighty's last words in Jonah is matched by the comic tone of "Hal o' the Draft," in which the themes announced in "Prophets" appear in one of Kipling's practical-joke tales. The frame narrative takes up the vocation theme, Hal telling the children how "he was born at Little Lindens Farm, and his father used to beat him for drawing things instead of doing things, till an old priest . . . coaxed the parents to let him take the boy as a sort of painter's apprentice" (168). Hal so excels at painting and other arts that he becomes vain. To humble his pride the old priest sends him back to his village to repair its ruined church. As in the preceding poem's promise, the little folk drag down the great: the villagers, who are using the church to warehouse the guns they smuggle, sabotage Hal's attempts at repair and put off the legal but less profitable delivery of guns to Hal's friend,

Sebastian Cabot. One of them even dresses as the Devil and capers about in the church in the moonlight to discourage interference. The comic tone of the story almost prevents a dark interpretation of this situation; nevertheless the physical decay of the church and the venal purpose to which it is put form an image of religious and spiritual decadence that implicates both the gun-running villagers and the self-satisfied Hal. But as with Nineveh, justice is tempered with mercy. When Hal discovers the village conspiracy, he reports it to the local magistrate, who seizes the guns but spares the villagers.

So by the end of "Hal o' the Draft," the entire social structure—magistrate, artist, sea captain, villagers—is complicit in the crime, but relieved of its painful consequences. Even Dan and Una, living in the same village four hundred years later, identify with the smugglers: "And what did we—I mean, what did our village do?" says Dan (177). "A Smugglers' Song," which closes the triad, further links smuggling to all strata of society, especially children, to whom it provides some crucial instructions:

> If you wake at midnight, and hear a horse's feet,
> Don't go drawing back the blind, or looking in the street,
> Them that asks no questions isn't told a lie.
> Watch the wall, my darling, while the Gentlemen go by!
>> Five and twenty ponies,
>> Trotting through the dark—
>> Brandy for the Parson,
>> Baccy for the Clerk;
>> Laces for a lady; letters for a spy,
> And watch the wall, my darling, while the Gentlemen go by!

This may seem an overly cheerful treatment of a treasonous business, but it matches the tone of "Hal o' the Draft," with which it functions as comic relief between two exceptionally dark tales: "The Winged Hats," which forebodes the rape of Britain by the Vikings, and " 'Dymchurch Flit.' "

In moving from "A Smugglers' Song" to "The Bee Boy's Song" Kipling moves from a song of secrecy and evasion to a song of telling and knowing:

> *Bees! Bees! Hark to your bees!*
> *'Hide from your neighbours as much as you please,*
> *But all that has happened, to us you must tell.*
> *Or else we will give you no honey to sell!'*

It is also a poem that warns against human hatred:

> Don't you wait where trees are,
>   When the lightnings play;
> Nor don't you hate where Bees are,
>   Or else they'll pine away—
>   Pine away—dwine away—
>   Anything to leave you!
> But if you never grieve your Bees,
>   Your Bees'll never grieve you.

This song of folk apiology seems to promise another light tale to follow. But "'Dymchurch Flit'" concerns hate, abandonment, and failure of communication. The connection between "The Bee Boy's Song" and the story turns out to be that the fairies, like the bees, cannot live where there is hate: "for Good-will among Flesh an' Blood is meat an' drink to 'em, an' ill-will is poison," says the narrator (188). And the problem of the story is the fairies' great difficulty in telling human beings that they are being poisoned by ill-will and that they want to "flit" out of England.

As we move from poem to frame narrative, straightforward telling as advised in the poem becomes complicated by confusion and misunderstanding, symbolized by the deceptive landscape of Romney Marsh, the scene of the coming tale. Puck describes it:

> "You've seen how flat she is—the Marsh? You'd think nothin' easier than to walk eend-on acrost her? Ah, but the diks and the water-lets, they twists the roads about as ravelly as witch-yarn on the spindles. So ye get all turned round in broad daylight."
> [186–87]

Just as the appearance of the landscape is confusing, there is confusion about the appearance of the People of the Hills. When Puck first meets the children he repudiates the notion that fairies are "little buzzflies with butterfly wings and gauze petticoats" (*Puck of Pook's Hill* 49). But such clear vision is strikingly absent in "'Dymchurch Flit.'" It is the only story in which Puck appears disguised so that the children do not recognize him immediately. And along with the appearance of a countryman, he seems to have taken on a countryman's ideas about the "Pharisees" and their powers: "Their liddle wings could no more cross Channel than so many tired butterflies. . . . Nor yet they couldn't get their boat an' crew to flit by without Leave and Good-will from Flesh an' Blood" (188).

The changed image of the fairies suggests the extent to which human knowledge and perception of the fairies has become "as ravelly as witch-yarn on the spindles" by the time of the story. What seems to be the fairies' smallness is a sign of the humans' smallness, their ignorance and insensitivity, which is leading them to religious intolerance and the horrors of persecution. As the fairies crowd into the coastal marsh, looking for passage across the Channel, the humans see the effects of their presence—"They saw their cattle scatterin' and no man scarin'; their sheep flockin' and no man drivin'; their horses latherin' an' no man leadin'; they saw liddle low green lights more than ever in the dik-sides"—but they misinterpret the meaning of the signs:

> "They reckoned the signs sinnified trouble for the Marsh. Or that the sea 'ud rear up against Dymchurch Wall and they'd be drownded like old Winchelsea; or that the Plague was comin'. So they looked for the meanin' in the sea or in the clouds—far an' high up. They never thought to look near an' knee-high, where they could see naught." [189]

Still less do Flesh and Blood think to look into their own hearts. The confusion in "Hal o' the Draft" is comic and reparable—the Devil in the church is a kind of a practical joke. But in "'Dymchurch Flit'" the Devil has got into the Church in earnest: the Marsh folk can hear "cruel Canterbury Bells ringin' to Bulverhithe for more pore men an' women to be burnded" (188). And the results are tragic and irreparable, almost a national Fall in which the good folk, rather than the wicked, are driven into exile.

Against this depravity is set the Widow Whitgift, whose vocation, as her name suggests, is a gift: second sight. She answers questions "like where lost things might be found" and she practices folk medicine, knowing, for instance, "what to put about a crooked baby's neck" (190). In her person, then, the themes of prophecy, vocation, and healing are combined. In her story, her second sight enables her to heal the entire Marsh of the disturbing effects of the fairies' swarming into it. She alone hears and heeds the fairies and acts with compassion, sending her sons to take the fairies on the dangerous crossing to France.

When the tale is done, Kipling closes the triad with "A Three-Part Song," a simple hymn to love of the land:

> I'm just in love with all these three,
> The Weald and the Marsh and the Down countrie;

> Nor I don't know which I love the most,
> The Weald or the Marsh or the white chalk coast!

These could be the words of anyone fond of Sussex, including
Kipling himself, but they recall Puck in particular as the only fairy
who does not abandon England in the Dymchurch flit. He is a lonely
and isolated figure, the last of the People of the Hills, but at least
he is not a landless exile like those who have left. He is bound to
the land, and the hero of the next tale, himself a solitary exile, calls
him "Spirit of Earth."

That hero, Kadmiel, has no land of his own because he is a Jew.
Landlessness is, according to "The Song of the Fifth River," the
condition of Israel: "In every land a guest, / Of many lands a lord, /
In no land King is he" (196). But by way of compensation "He that
is Wholly Just" has ordained that the Secret River of Gold "keeps
the secret of Her deeps / For Israel alone, / As it was ordered to
be." By treating the financial vocation of Israel as a gift from a just
God, Kipling makes the unpalatable stereotype as palatable as he
can. More to his credit, he points out the historical cause-and-effect
connection between the Jews' inability to possess land and their re-
sorting to money-lending. This connection is made explicit in "The
Treasure and the Law," along with the fact that the "compensation" of the Jews' second sight regarding gold is no substitute for a
homeland and the protection of the law.

Vocation and prophecy figure together at the beginning of Kadmiel's narrative. At his birth it is foretold that he will be "a Lawgiver
to a People of a strange speech and a hard language" (200). Nevertheless, his craft, his profession, is to be a physician, and his study
of medicine in the schools of the Near East allows Kipling to draw
a contrast between the enlightened, tolerant, and scientifically advanced East and the lawless, anti-Semitic, backward West where the
savagery of the people toward the Jews is matched only by the savagery of the nobility toward the people. As in "'Dymchurch Flit'"
hatred is the root of ignorance: "So I sailed," says Kadmiel, "with
Elias to Bury in England, where there are no learned men. How
can a man be wise if he hate? At Bury I kept accounts for Elias, and
I saw men kill Jews by the tower" (202).

He also sees the war of the barons of England against King John,
sees the barons borrow money from his uncle to pay for their war,
sees the Magna Carta, and sees his chance to fulfill the prophecy.

When Bishop Langton comes to borrow more money, Kadmiel makes terms so that the fortieth law of the Magna Carta reads not "To no *free man* will we sell, refuse, or deny right or justice" but "To *none*." The change includes the Jews along with the Christians in the Charter's protection—at least theoretically. But it is still up to Kadmiel to save the whole Charter: his uncle intends to lend a secret hoard of gold to King John. Now Kadmiel's medical craft and legal vocation merge. He uses his medical knowledge to gain access to the gold and speaks of his actions in medical terms, as if the prescription for England's deadly lawlessness is a purgative or surgery: "I saw well that if the evil thing [the gold] remained, or if even the hope of finding it remained, the King would not sign the New Laws, and the land would perish" (206).

Kadmiel's patient, ailing England, survives, but not, as "'Dymchurch Flit'" and other stories in the Puck books illustrate, without relapses into cruelty and ignorance. This chronic danger of backsliding seems to motivate the prayer of petition that makes up most of the closing poem in the group, "The Children's Song." The children concerned represent the future of England, and the rather preachy verses have them ask for such things as will be useful to their motherland. Requests for purity and honesty and self-control are what might be expected from Kipling the conservative imperialist, but Kipling the creator of Sir John Pelham, the Widow Whitgift, and Kadmiel emphasizes humanitarian, even liberal, virtues. Among other things, the children ask for strength "that cannot seek, / By deed or thought, to hurt the weak" but will rather "comfort man's distress," and for "forgiveness free of evil done, / And Love to all men 'neath the sun!"

In this examination of the smuggler group, I have tried to show something of the manner in which themes and motifs are interlaced in the Puck books and to demonstrate that the whole of Kipling's thinking in respect to even one theme can be grasped only by reading all the poems and stories as an interlaced whole. Outside the context of its framing poems and its group, "Hal o' the Draft" seems to be on the side of scofflaws and opportunists. Outside its context, "'Dymchurch Flit'" makes a connection between hatred and sickness, but without Hal's comedy for a preface, the cruelty in it does not appear so emphatically as the product of a devil-ridden Church. Without the retrospective view possible from Kadmiel's tale, the religious intolerance of the Reformation might seem to be an isolated episode, not a recrudescence of a besetting national sin and a violation of the Magna Carta's justice. By the same token, reading "The Treasure and the Law" without first reading " 'Dymchurch Flit' " could create the impression that Kipling had an overly optimistic view of the power of law to restrain oppression and violence. But as Kipling has arranged it, the smuggler group presents a complex vision of the relations among law, mercy, racial and religious hatred, the talents and skills of individuals, and the constant need in England's history for healing of sickness—spiritual, physical, and political—a vision that must be taken into account each time these themes occur in *Puck of Pook's Hill* or *Rewards and Fairies*.

Unfortunately, it is not possible to cover all the connections among the tales and poems in the Puck books here. Even in discussing a single group, I have left out many details that belong in an exhaustive reading. My limited purpose has been to suggest a new way of reading the Puck books—as a romance—and a new way of regarding Kipling—as akin to the romance writers of the Middle Ages and the Renaissance and to those of his contemporaries, like William Morris, who also turned away from the traditional novel and toward romance as a vehicle for their idealism. Reading *Puck of Pook's Hill* and *Rewards and Fairies* in the way romance should be read demonstrates that Kipling's idealism went far beyond mere imperialism and sentimentality. Moreover, such a reading of these rich and engaging books will also show Kipling to be an unrecognized master of a major fictional form, as well as the master of tale and rhyme he has always been known to be.

Notes

1. Indeed, in this chameleon response to different persons and their characteristics, Puck on the whole most closely resembles Kipling himself. In his short stories and poems Kipling frequently adopted personae and idioms either borrowed from those he met and drew out in conversation or painstakingly devised for those he could only imagine. Even in playing with his children—and Dan and Una are his own son and daughter, disguised only in name—Kipling reveled in historical roles (Oliver Cromwell, for instance) and addressed the children in "period" language. Moreover, Puck resembles Kipling physically, being stocky and blue-eyed, and is, as Kipling was, happy and at ease in the company of children and an eager collector of varied acquaintances. For the appearance of a self-portrait in a romance, Kipling might have once again found his precedent in Spenser, whose authorial figure, Colin Clout, appears in *The Faerie Queene*, 6.10, playing his shepherd's pipes to "Nymphes and Faeries" who are "all raunged in a ring."

Works Cited

Hinchcliffe, Peter. "Coming to Terms with Kipling: *Puck of Pook's Hill, Rewards and Fairies*, and the Shape of Kipling's Imagination." *University of Toronto Quarterly* 45: 1 (1975): 75–90. Reprinted in *Critical Essays on Rudyard Kipling*, ed. Harold Orel. Boston: G. K. Hall, 1989. 153–68.

Kipling, Rudyard. *Puck of Pook's Hill*, ed. Sarah Wintle. London: Penguin, 1987.

———. *Rewards and Fairies*, ed. Roger Lewis. London: Penguin, 1987.

———. *Something of Myself for My Friends Known and Unknown*. New York: Doubleday, Doran, 1937.

Stevens, John E. *Medieval Romance: Themes and Approaches*. London: Hutchinson University Library, 1973.

Tuve, Rosamund. *Allegorical Imagery: Some Medieval Books and Their Posterity*. Princeton: Princeton University Press, 1966.

The Trinity Archetype in The Jungle Books and The Wizard of Oz

Juliet McMaster

The magical and mystical significance of the number three is common to myth, religion, and children's literature. But though the cluster of three is important, it is also expected that the units within the cluster be subtly differentiated, and in some sense opposed and complementary. The most familiar constellation of this grouping and opposition is of course the Christian doctrine of the Trinity, the three in one. But the Trinity of Western culture is only one example of many such groupings in which the three elements are joined and opposed in a structure that is psychologically, morally, and artistically satisfying. Not surprisingly, the pattern occurs, with a parallel assignment of qualities to the three units, in a number of books written for children. My own concern is with the pattern as it is adapted in two works not far separated in time, but in space and culture further apart than two continents: Rudyard Kipling's two *Jungle Books* and L. Frank Baum's *The Wonderful Wizard of Oz*. In each we find a trinity of companions for the protagonist, and in each the companions are differentiated and specialized in recognizably parallel ways.

The three persons of the Trinity, God the Father, God the Son, and God the Holy Spirit, though indivisibly one, each specialize. God the Father, the Yahweh of the Old Testament, is creator and lawgiver, strong in justice and discipline. God the Son, the Christ of the New Testament, is the redeemer, saving man out of love and through sacrifice. God the Holy Spirit, always a more mysterious entity, seldom appears as a character, but is familiar in iconography as the bird that mediates between God and the Virgin in depictions of the Annunciation, and is invoked by Milton as the being who "Dove-like satst brooding on the vast Abyss" (I. 21). The particular qualities assigned to these familiar dramatis personae are, respectively, omnipotence, benevolence, and omniscience; or, to use less Latinately theological terms: for God the Father, power; for God the Son, love; and for God the Holy Spirit, knowledge.

Children's Literature 20, ed. Francelia Butler, Barbara Rosen, and Judith A. Plotz (Yale University Press, © 1992 by The Children's Literature Foundation, Inc.).

This alignment of the persons of the Trinity with power, love, and knowledge (though each may partake of the characteristics of the others) has been a well-established tradition in Christian theology since the time of Augustine (Whitla 46–51).[1] And in the Renaissance these perfect attributes of the divinity were assigned (in an imperfect, human form) to man, made in God's image. In his devotional poem "The Litanie," Donne addresses a stanza each to the Father, the Son, and the Holy Spirit, and then follows with a prayer to the Trinity:

> As you distinguish'd undistinct
> By power, love, knowledge bee,
> Give mee a such selfe different instinct
> Of these; let all mee elemented bee,
> Of power, to love, to know, you unnumbred three.   [309]

Man's best self, like God's, comprises the elements of power, love, and knowledge.

In nineteenth-century England, these attributes of the deity and of man were given a more popular currency by the so-called Bridgewater Treatises. The Earl of Bridgewater, when he died in 1829, left a large bequest to the Royal Society for the publication of a series of works "On the Power, Wisdom and Goodness of God, as manifested in the Creation." These works were duly commissioned and published in the two decades following. The wide publicity of the Bridgewater Treatises is testified by the choice of Bridgewater's name by the phony "Duke" in *Huckleberry Finn*—where the "Bridgewater" of his claim swiftly degenerates into "Bilgewater" (Twain 100–01).

But the constellation of Power, Love (or Benevolence, or Goodness, as it is moralized), and Knowledge (or Wisdom) is of course not peculiar to Christianity. Its most familiar appearance in classical mythology is in the often-depicted episode of the Judgment of Paris, in which the young Paris has to judge between Hera the queen of heaven, Aphrodite the goddess of love and beauty, and Athena the goddess of wisdom. Each offers Paris the bribe that is hers to give: again, Power, Love, and Knowledge. While "love" in the Christian tradition is *caritas,* love of humankind, in the classical tradition it is more apt to modulate toward sexual passion, and is often attached closely to beauty and the aesthetic sense. Paris's choice of Aphrodite, because of her offer of the most beautiful woman, leads to the Trojan War: the three attributes, when opposed to one another instead of balanced in a harmonious unity, may be dangerous. The archetype appears in the Hindu world picture too, in which Siva as Power, Vishnu as Love, and Brahma as Knowledge provide a parallel with the Christian Trinity and the classical myth of the Judgment of Paris.[2] These three, then, Power, Love, and Knowledge, are apt to appear in relation to one another in Christian, classical, and even Eastern works.

They also are found in literature for children. And here the interplay of the three complementary qualities, achieved in the godhead and striven for by the human being, can provide a pattern that is both satisfyingly familiar and inventively varied.

In his sequence of stories about Mowgli in *The Jungle Book* (1894) and *The Second Jungle Book* (1895), Kipling makes creative use of this archetype. The narrative about the boy brought up by wolves in the jungle, torn between his inheritance as man and his nurture as wolf, makes its impact as a story about education and the growth of the self. It has strong mythological elements, as many commentators have noticed.[3] Its powerful appeal for the adolescent arises from its vivid projection of a protagonist poised between two states: Mowgli is "two Mowglis" (I, *TT*, 121),[4] partaking of both animal and human identity, child and adult, outcast and leader; belonging in the jungle paradise, but irresistibly drawn to the dubious haunts of human civilization. The pathos of his condition, also powerfully attractive to the adolescent, is that he doesn't know what is happening to him. He finds himself weeping, and needs to be told what tears are (I, *MB*, 40); smitten by a crisis of loneliness and sexual longing, "he looked himself over to be sure that he had not trod on a thorn" (II, *SR*, 270).

In this complex "amphibian" existence (Knoepflmacher 521), Mowgli as infant, boy, and man struggles toward consciousness and understanding as toward physical maturity. He is provided with mentors, beings beyond himself who embody the qualities of knowledge, power, and love that he must acquire. It has been noticed, in fact, that "Mowgli is over-lavishly provided with tutors" (Stewart 117). But some, such as Father Wolf, simply teach him the skills of survival as a wolf (I, *MB*, 25), while Messua's instructions pertain to language skills among human beings. More essential to the growth of Mowgli's identity is what he learns from creatures who are neither wolf nor human: first his two sponsors at the looking-over at the Council Rock, Baloo the bear and Bagheera the panther;

and to these is added Kaa the python. It is these three mentors who are constructed as the power, love, and knowledge that must become Mowgli's if he is to mature and discover his self. The trio, like the Trinity, are separate and discrete, but also united and complementary. And these mythic roles, whether the reader recognizes them or not, have much to do with the trio's particular appeal as characters and their effectiveness in Mowgli's development.

In the first story, "Mowgli's Brothers," while Kipling is still getting into his stride, he presents the young human child as eminently educable. He has intelligence, but little experience, and no motive for reflection. He has "nothing in the world to think of except things to eat" (I, 26). He is a tabula rasa, innocent and impressionable, and living safely in the protection of the wolf pack that has accepted him. "I have the Pack and I have thee," he tells Bagheera, ". . . and Baloo . . . Why should I be afraid?" (I, 27). It is Bagheera who awakens him to knowledge of evil as well as good, and alerts him to his precarious status as a man among wolves.

> "They hate thee because their eyes cannot meet thine—because thou art wise—because thou hast pulled out thorns from their feet—because thou art a man."
> "I did not know these things," said Mowgli sullenly. [I, 30]

But with the astute guidance of Bagheera he is able to hold his own at the Council Rock when the hostile wolves plan to hand him over to his enemy Shere Khan (the Satan of Mowgli's paradise).

It is in the next story, "Kaa's Hunting," that Kipling presents the trio of mentors in their developed roles of Power, Love, and Knowledge. In fictional time this story is set between the beginning and the end of "Mowgli's Brothers," when Mowgli is a young boy of seven (the age of rationality), on the threshold of self-awareness. He is also receiving his formal education in the Law of the Jungle. Mowgli is still conceited and unreflecting, but he is about to undergo a lesson and a test. The introductory poem stresses the education theme:

> "There is none like to me!" says the Cub in the pride of his earliest kill;
> But the Jungle is large and the Cub he is small. Let him think and be still.   [I, 45]

And as we encounter Mowgli in the classroom scene that opens the story, he is showing off his newly acquired knowledge. Mowgli as human must learn more than any one species, for man's status in the evolutionary scheme does not allow him to specialize:

> The big, serious, old brown bear was delighted to have so quick a pupil, for the young wolves will learn only as much of the Law of the Jungle as applies to their own pack and tribe, and run away as soon as they can repeat the Hunting Verse. . . . But Mowgli, as a man-cub, had to learn a great deal more than this. [I, 46]

"A Man-cub is a Man-cub, and he must learn *all* the Law of the Jungle," Baloo explains (47). This is Kipling's version of T. H. White's fable of the embryos in *The Sword in the Stone* (1938), in which man achieves his special status in the universe by choosing not to have specialized equipment, such as horns or a thick hide (265–67). He is to dominate by virtue of his adaptability. This is one reason that Mowgli's most significant mentors are neither man nor wolf, but beasts of other species altogether. Mowgli's status in his world is to come from exceeding the limitations both of man and of wolf.

"Kaa's Hunting" is a satisfactory fable of education. The scene opens in a classroom, where Baloo the pedagogue has been teaching Mowgli the Law of the Jungle. Baloo in his partiality claims that Mowgli is "best and wisest and boldest of Man-cubs" (63) (the familiar configuration is already present), but the claim is premature. Mowgli resists the discipline of learning, and so he is appropriately kidnapped by the Bandar-log, the monkey people, who are parodies of the worst of the tribe of men. They claim to be "wise and strong and gentle" (70)—that is, to have knowledge, power, and love—but their claim is spurious; in fact they are ineducable, for "they have no Law. . . . They have no remembrance" (51–52). Mowgli, who has learned his lessons, is able to use what he has learned to bring his friends Baloo, Bagheera, and Kaa (the power, love, and knowledge that the monkeys will always lack) to his rescue. Once rescued, he again uses what he has learned to thank his rescuers and become reconciled with them. Mowgli's education in this early stage of his career will stand him in good stead in his future adventures and his future development. And his three protectors, with their quasi-allegorized roles, will continue to enable him to grow and learn.

Baloo's role in the trinity is like God's on Mount Sinai. One delivers the Ten Commandments on the tablets of stone, and the other delivers the Law of the Jungle. In his role as teacher Baloo is comic, a "fubsy old pedagogue," a "housemaster," as he has been called (Mason 168; Wilson 127). But he is effective, and in "Kaa's Hunting" Mowgli's life depends on the effectiveness of his teaching. In the battle against the monkey horde Baloo relies on brute strength and power: "He threw himself squarely on his haunches . . . and then began to hit with a regular *bat-bat-bat*" (74). This suggests the physical aspect of his power. And it is notable that Baloo, like Yahweh, is strong on punishment. He physically disciplines Mowgli both before and after his abduction by the monkeys, and this corporal punishment is seen as just and necessary. But his power is more than strength, and at its best it has almost the force of creation. Like God separating the light from the dark and the waters from the land, Baloo with his law and his discipline imposes order on chaos. The Bandar-log are not only parodies of men: they are a force of chaos and disruption. They lack all distinction, discrimination, memory, and rules. One could as soon build a statue out of dry grains of sand as discern a meaningful social or moral structure to their existence. That is why they are seen as dangerous and despicable in the ordered world of Kipling's jungle. For Mowgli to revert to being one of the monkey-people would be to "reel back into the beast" indeed. (Other writers might present such a race as charming and engaging; and indeed, Disney did so in his animated version of *The Jungle Book*.)

Baloo as teacher deals in knowledge as well as power. In fact, his knowledge effectively *is* his power, the power to create and sustain a significant pattern for Mowgli's life in the jungle. He enables Mowgli to find a place among the other species, and to deserve it.

In the later tales, as Mowgli himself becomes strong and informed, Baloo is less prominent. But he is notably present in "How Fear Came," the tale that presents the Genesis of the jungle. And though on this occasion Hathi the elephant rather than Baloo transmits the myth, Baloo knows it as he knows all the others. And he is present again at the final meeting at the Council Rock to complete the series symmetrically.

The complementary roles of Baloo and Bagheera in Mowgli's education are made clear by a representative exchange between them in "Kaa's Hunting":

"A man-cub is a Man-cub, [says Baloo] and he must learn *all* the Law of the Jungle."

"But think how small he is," said the Black Panther, who would have spoiled Mowgli if he had had his own way. "How can his little head carry all thy long talk?"

"Is there anything in the Jungle too little to be killed? No. That is why I teach him these things, and that is why I hit him, very softly, when he forgets."

"Softly! What dost thou know of softness, old Iron-feet?" Bagheera grunted. "His face is all bruised to-day by thy—softness. Ugh!"

"Better he should be bruised from head to foot by me who love him than that he should come to harm through ignorance," Baloo answered very earnestly. [I, 47–48]

It sounds like a dialogue of Justice and Mercy. The passage has some theological overtones, and not only in the formal and biblical rhetoric. Baloo's stern though loving ruling that the being who has transgressed must be punished, and Bagheera's eager defense, sound a little like the exchange between God and the Son over the fate of man in book 3 of *Paradise Lost*. And Baloo's austere "Is there anything in the Jungle too little to be killed?" is a nineteenth-century echo of the Puritan James Janeway's attitude to children: "They are not too little to die, they are not too little to go to Hell" (Darton 56). Bagheera's role here is as appeaser and apologist, tenderly making allowances for man's proneness to fall.

Bagheera performs a Christ-like role in more ways than one. Kipling's clearest signal of his function is in making him a panther, for the panther has been the symbol of Christ since medieval times. In the twelfth-century bestiary translated by T. H. White, the panther is described as "most beautiful and excessively kind. . . . The true Panther, Our Lord Jesus Christ, snatched us from the power of the dragon-devil" (White 14–15). Bagheera is the one who redeems Mowgli at the outset, who "buys" him into the pack at the price of a newly killed bull, when the naked child would otherwise have been handed over to Shere Khan, the satanic tiger. Bagheera doesn't himself turn scapegoat, but he provides one, so that Mowgli may be saved. And when Mowgli leaves the pack to return to humankind at the end, Bagheera buys him out again with another bull. He performs the due ritual at the Council Rock, the spiritual and administrative center of the wolves' society. Kipling's jungle, like Milton's heaven, observes the rigid economics of sacrifice, a life for a life.[5]

If Bagheera is a symbolic embodiment of Christian love, he is also, of course, much more. As Keats recalled in associating "Bacchus and his pards," the leopard or panther is sacred to Dionysus. In keeping with the classical formulation of the parallel attributes, Bagheera has the beauty and the passion that are associated with Aphrodite's sphere. Except for his two mother surrogates, Raksha the wolf and Messua the woman, Mowgli's associates are all notably masculine.[6] But Bagheera, with his sinuous movements and exotic beauty, provides a strong and almost feminine contrast to Baloo's straightforward, bachelorish masculinity. If in the Christian tradition the panther is a symbol of Christ, in the classical tradition following Aristotle, the panther is the type of the feminine (Aristotle 801a). Bagheera is expert at persuasion and accommodation. He is also beautiful. Though black, he has "the panther markings showing up in certain lights like the pattern of watered silk. . . . He had a voice as soft as wild honey dripping from a tree, and a skin softer than down" (I, *MB*, 20). He stands for the passional life, including not only sexual passion (in "The Spring Running" he goes courting) but a range of intense emotions that in the Christian scheme would be called sinful: anger, pride, and a fierce sense of honor. These, too, Mowgli learns and makes his own.

The triple association of power, love, and knowledge is completed by Kaa the python, whom Baloo and Bagheera recruit as the indispensable ally in their rescue of Mowgli. Though Baloo, as we have seen, supplies Mowgli with knowledge of the law, Kaa's brand of knowledge might more fitly be called wisdom. It exceeds the mental accumulation of data and laws and the intelligent application of them, and comprehends contradictions and ironies. (Baloo is never any good at irony, and characteristically speaks "earnestly.") To the monkeys, Kaa is Fear (as Man is Fear in the animals' genesis myth in "How Fear Came"). Kaa opposes the monkeys, the forces of ignorance, not by strength, like Baloo, nor by passionate, ineffective devotion, like Bagheera, but by a hypnotic dance that establishes mastery over the minds of his victims. Like the Holy Spirit to humanity, Kaa moves in mysterious ways. Being footless and cold-blooded, he is alien and undefined to the quadruped mammals, who construct him as Other and find him threatening. " 'He

knows more than we,' said Bagheera, trembling," when he sees Kaa
execute his hypnotic dance (I, *KH*, 81).

Wisdom for Mowgli necessarily comprehends the knowledge of
good and evil; and it is appropriate that Kaa the serpent should
help to induct him into that knowledge (Wilson 126–27). In "The
King's Ankus," a story as mythically suggestive as Chaucer's "Par-
doner's Tale" (on which it is based), Mowgli is clearly located in
his jungle paradise when Kaa begins the process of initiating him
into man's characteristic sin of avarice. In a glow of physical well-
being, Mowgli is basking in the sense that all his essential desires
are fulfilled: "What more can I wish? I have the Jungle, and the
favour of the Jungle! Is there more anywhere between sunrise and
sunset?" (II, 151–52).[7] To test whether Mowgli indeed has no more
to wish for, Kaa leads him to the treasure in the deserted city of
Cold Lairs, which is guarded by another serpent (and one more
learned in human cupidity). Mowgli is tempted by the beauty of
the jeweled ankus that he takes from the hoard, but he himself
does not fall. He only witnesses the deadly avarice of the men who
find the bauble and kill each other for it. The fall of man on this
occasion does not include the fall of Mowgli, whose nurture with
animals has made him immune from this particular sin. (He is indifferent to money, and calls it "the stuff that passes from hand to
hand and never grows warmer" [II, *LJ*, 81].) But his education has
progressed in that he has learned more of the evil of his own kind.
Bagheera drives the lesson home. When Mowgli tells him to bury
the ankus, which as an elephant goad represents human cruelty as
well as human avarice, Bagheera points out, "I tell thee it is not
the fault of the blood-drinker [the ankus]. The trouble is with the
men" (II, *KA*, 174). Mowgli has had an effective lesson in the knowledge of good and evil. The serpent's role in Genesis is here split
into two: the white cobra performs Satan's role in tempting man to
fall, while Kaa as a version of the Holy Spirit has advanced man's
consciousness of good and evil, a consummation theologically accepted as the Fortunate Fall. Man's (and Mowgli's) consciousness of
good and evil leads to wisdom, and is a necessary condition of his
redemption.

Kaa's role as Knowledge becomes clearest of all in "Red Dog." If
"How Fear Came" and "The King's Ankus" are genesis myths, "Red
Dog" is closer to being classical epic. Like the *Iliad* and the *Aeneid*,
it shows the clash of two races, with heroic battles and fierce indi-

vidual encounters; its rhetoric is formal and poetic, the dialogue decorative and ceremonious; and Kaa the python provides the epic "machinery." Mowgli plays the role of the crafty Odysseus who defeats the enemy by employing a stratagem; and Kaa instructs him on the means to destroy the Red Dog as Athena prompted Odysseus's scheme of the Trojan horse.[8] Mowgli, who has developed in humility since the days of "Kaa's Hunting," comes explicitly to seek Kaa's advice. "I am not wise nor strong. Hast thou a better plan, Kaa?" (II, *RD*, 233). (In the same way the epic poet of *Paradise Lost* addresses his muse, the Holy Spirit: "Instruct me, for Thou know'st" [I, 19].) Kaa, thus consulted, settles down to remembrance of things past, recalling all that has happened in the two hundred years since he hatched from the egg; and comes up with a plan that will be a deliberate reenactment of an accidental occurrence of the past: "What will be is no more than a forgotten year striking backward," he says (233). When Kaa has unfolded his plan, Mowgli makes his tribute: "Kaa, thou art, indeed, the wisest of all the Jungle" (238).

As Mowgli goes about enacting the scheme, we see him at the height of his development, and bringing to bear a lifetime of training among the animals and observation among men. The stratagem of luring the Red Dog among the bees and himself escaping to fight the survivors downriver calls on all his varied powers:

> "Mowgli the Frog I have been," said he to himself; "Mowgli the Wolf have I said that I am. Now Mowgli the Ape must I be before I am Mowgli the Buck. At the end I shall be Mowgli the Man." [241–42]

As he has learned to add Kaa's wisdom to Baloo's power and Bagheera's passion, so he has confirmed his mastery as man, the animal who is fully adaptable.

At the end of "The Spring Running," the last of the Mowgli stories, Mowgli takes leave of his three mentors at the Council Rock. Kipling is winding up the different thematic and symbolic strands. Mowgli is still "two Mowglis," wolf and human, and drawn in two directions:

> "By night and by day I hear a double step upon my trail. When I turn my head it is as though one had hidden himself from me that instant. I go to look behind the trees and he is not there.

I call and none cry again; but it is as though one listened and
kept back the answer." [II,291–92]

It has come to pass "that Mowgli should drive Mowgli back to the
Man-Pack" (292). At the ritual leave-taking, Baloo, now very old,
first takes the floor, reminding us of his role: "I taught thee the
Law. It is for me to speak" (293). Mowgli's "wisdom and strength,"
he says, have saved the wolf pack. Love he does not mention for
the moment, for at this point only Kaa and Baloo, of the three, are
present. Kaa too is there with his wisdom to impart: "'Having cast
the skin,' said Kaa, 'we may not creep into it afresh. It is the Law'"
(293). It is the wisdom for all seasons, from Milton's "To morrow to
fresh Woods, and Pastures new" to Tennyson's

> The old order changeth, yielding place to new, . . .
> Lest one good custom should corrupt the world.

And at last Bagheera joins the scene, having been delayed by bringing the sacrificial bull that is to buy Mowgli out of the wolf pack
again so that he may return to his own kind. He too provides a
reminder of his role. His last words to Mowgli are "Remember,
Bagheera loved thee" (294).

The last of the contents of *The Second Jungle Book* is "The Outsong," "the song that Mowgli heard behind him in the Jungle" as he
leaves it. Like Donne's "The Litanie," it is divided into four parts,
one for each person of the trinity, and a final part devoted to "The
Three." Baloo counsels "Keep the law," and envisages the law as the
Trail, a structured path through experience. Kaa presents a series
of wise saws in oracular imagery, and instructs on language and
appropriate silence. Bagheera recalls his own hard-won knowledge
of men, and cautions Mowgli, "Feed them silence when they seek /
Help of thine to hurt the weak." The burden of the combined song
of the three is to enjoin upon Mowgli "Wisdom, Strength and Courtesy." The tripartite structure of "The Outsong" echoes in brief the
developed roles of Mowgli's animal trinity.

The power that Baloo supplies Mowgli is less mere physical
strength than that which derives from discipline and control, and
a full knowledge and observance of appropriate law. The love of
Bagheera bears some relation to the Christian *caritas* (Mowgli refuses to kill his own kind, and spares even the white cobra who had
tried to kill him), but is also recognizable as the emotional inten-

sity that makes him a memorable and sympathetic protagonist. The knowledge of Kaa completes him, and enables him to be the savior of the wolf pack before he leaves them. The interdependence of the three is poignantly demonstrated when Bagheera, usually proudly self-sufficient, first joins forces with Baloo in order to save Mowgli, and then is forced to call for help to Kaa in order to save himself. He uses the snakes' call, "We be of one blood, ye and I" (I.*KH*.74). The three characters and the qualities they represent are not discrete entities, but each partakes partially of the characteristics of the others: Baloo deals in power, law, order, and discipline; but he is also knowledgeable and loving. Bagheera provides a model of sacrifice and devotion; but he is also astute and physically powerful. Kaa is the wisest in the jungle, but he is also beautiful and affectionate like Bagheera, and strong like Baloo: "wise, old, strong, and most beautiful Kaa," Mowgli calls him (II,*RD*,230). Together they form a trio for Mowgli's development of self, as the Trinity acts for the salvation of the Christian, or the three goddesses enlarge the world for Paris.

So far I have developed a set of correspondences that may be rendered diagrammatically thus:

ATTRIBUTES	THE CHRISTIAN TRINITY	JUDGMENT OF PARIS	REWARDS	JUNGLE BOOKS
Power	God the Father	Hera (Juno)	Power	Baloo
Love	Son	Aphrodite (Venus)	Love / Beauty	Bagheera
Knowledge	Holy Spirit	Athena (Minerva)	Wisdom	Kaa

It is possible to find further parallels to the three attributes in various branches of traditional learning also.[9] During the Renaissance the assumption that man was made in God's image was extended to physio gy, and as a complement to the derived classical belief in the four humors there was a theory of three. Man's functions—as described, for instance, by Robert Burton in *The Anatomy of Melancholy* (I,i,2,3)—are the physical or appetitive, the passional, and the rational. Each of these modes of being has its "seat" in the human body. The seat of reason is the brain, the seat of passion is the heart, and the seat of the appetites is the liver.

When one contemplates these familiar organs in the context of children's literature, something chimes with a familiar ring. Who seeks a brain, who seeks a heart, and who seeks . . . ? Why, the Scarecrow, the Tin Woodman, and the Lion, of course, in *The Wizard of Oz*. Well, the Cowardly Lion seeks courage, let it be admitted, rather than a liver per se. But the two have been closely connected in the popular imagination as well as in the Renaissance mind, for a sturdy liver was believed to make for a courageous man, a sickly liver for a pusillanimous one. (The term "lily-livered" is still extant as an epithet for a coward.) To the above diagram on the variations on the Power/Love/Knowledge trinity, then, we may add two further columns:

	LOCATION IN THE BODY	THE WIZARD OF OZ
Power	Liver	Cowardly Lion
Love (passion)	Heart	Tin Woodman
Knowledge (reason)	Brain	Scarecrow

Dorothy's three memorable companions—"her strangely assorted company," as Baum called them (114)—have been a major element in the first success and continued popularity of *The Wizard of Oz*. The *New York Times* review of September 8, 1900, singled out the trio for special comment:

> A Scarecrow stuffed with straw, a tin woodman, and a cowardly lion do not, at first blush, promise well as moving heroes in a tale when merely mentioned, but in actual practice they take on something of the living and breathing quality that is so gloriously exemplified in the "Story of the Three Bears," that has become a classic. [Hearn 35–36]

Their being a trio like the three bears, and not just assorted individuals, clearly has something to do with their particular appeal. It has been pointed out that between them, they represent animal, vegetable, and mineral (Hearn 148). Nearly all critical treatments of the work focus on Dorothy as protagonist and her three companions. As Edward W. Hudlin points out in a recent essay on the mythology of Oz, "The subplots concerning these characters develop the major mythic themes of the work" (453).

Baum himself seems to have been unconscious that the ongoing pattern of ideas that I have been discussing informs his work. He told an interviewer, "The Scarecrow, the Tin Woodman, and the cowardly Lion were real children of my brain, having no existence in fact or fiction until I placed them in the pages of my book" (Hearn 49). He refers to them as Dorothy's "unique companions"— a rather surprising choice of phrase when one considers how many analogues exist for this configuration of the familiar trilogy of Power, Love, and Knowledge. But his unconsciousness of the analogues suggests that we are dealing here not just with an articulated system of ideas, but with an archetype. This configuration of qualities seems to exist in the collective unconscious, and to be thrown up to the conscious level in the minds of various artists from different cultural backgrounds. Baum was far from being an orthodox Christian, but when he spoke of the creation of *The Wizard of Oz* he suggested that he had been moved by something like divine inspiration. According to the Reverend Mr. Ryland,

> I once asked him how he came to write the first Oz book. "It was pure inspiration," he said. "It came to me right out of the blue. I think that sometimes the Great Author has a message to get across and He has to use the instrument at hand. I happened to be that medium, and I believe the magic key was given me to open the doors to sympathy and understanding, joy, peace and happiness." [Hearn, 73]

Making allowances for wide divergence in tone and cultural background, one can still recognize some affinity between Baum, the humble medium through whom the Great Author delivers truths about the Lion, the Woodman, and the Scarecrow, and Milton, the epic poet who calls upon the Heavenly Muse to help him to dramatize the relations of the Father, the Son, and the Holy Spirit, and so justify the ways of God to men.

Baum's use of these traditional and archetypal elements is unique, however. He has inventively varied their presentation, especially in inverting their authority. Kipling gives Baloo, Bagheera, and Kaa to Mowgli as mentors and authority figures, but Dorothy's companions follow her instead of leading her. They are, after all, in the allegorical structure presented, her own attributes. (In the same way Faithful and Hopeful in *The Pilgrim's Progress*, a strong influence in American as well as British literature for children, represent not only the faithful man and the hopeful man, but also Christian's own faith and hope.) Baum's pilgrimage is a democratized configuration, as is appropriate in an American tale. The Scarecrow, Woodman, and Lion, in their quests for brain, heart, and courage, are engagingly humble, for each thinks he most lacks what he most signally possesses. Dorothy uses her companions to achieve her own quest, while simultaneously furthering theirs.[10] For Dorothy, getting home to Kansas is growing up and achieving her identity. She, like Mowgli, is using her knowledge, love, and power to develop her own selfhood.[11]

There are, of course, major differences between the two works, deriving from the differing worldview of their authors. Kipling is a British imperialist, and presents a boy protagonist; Baum is American, and chooses a girl protagonist. But to explore the considerable national and gender differences in the handling of the pattern is beyond the scope of this essay. For the moment my business is with the pattern they share.

The three companions represent not only Dorothy's knowledge, love, and power, but her desire to possess these attributes, and her own healthy self-doubt. A crucial issue is that of self-confidence. The Scarecrow is notably intelligent, but believes he is brainless. He needs the Wizard not to give him a brain, but to give him confidence in the intelligence he has already. The same applies to the Tin Woodman and his heart. "I have no heart, you know, so I am careful to help all those who may need a friend, even if it happens to be only a mouse" (92). *Because* he doubts his own compassion, he is especially tender. Consciousness is a major aspect of the Lion's predicament, too. "As long as I know myself to be a coward I shall be unhappy," he says (67). The Wizard doesn't give him courage, but he supplies him with consciousness of his courage. As Mowgli was shown to be least wise when he showed off about his wisdom, Dorothy's wisdom, like the Scarecrow's, is most evident in her doubt that she has it.

Mowgli's acquaintance with Kaa, Knowledge, came last in the three encounters, when he was already acquainted with Baloo and Bagheera. But for Dorothy the Scarecrow comes first. Knowledge is her priority, as it is his. Like Socrates, Dorothy and the Scarecrow are most wise in believing they lack wisdom, and in seeking it.

> "I don't know anything [says the Scarecrow]. You see, I am stuffed, so I have no brains at all. . . . I don't mind my legs and arms and body being stuffed, because I cannot get hurt.

If anyone treads on my toes or sticks a pin into me, it doesn't matter, for I can't feel it. But I do not want people to call me a fool, and if my head stays stuffed with straw instead of with brains, as yours is, how am I ever to know anything?"

"I understand how you feel," said the little girl. [38–39]

He is the companion with whom Dorothy can identify most fully.

The Scarecrow is constructed as knowledge in various ways. The story he tells of his own creation by the farmer is a fable of representation, where that which is represented becomes immediately real, and consciousness follows. First the farmer makes his head, on which he paints an ear. As soon as the ear is painted, the Scarecrow can hear with it; and as soon as his eye is painted, he can see with it. The body comes last of all. So he witnesses his own creation, and is soon able to articulate it in speech too (43–44). We follow the dawning of his consciousness step by step as his body is created; and the body is subordinate to the consciousness.

The Holy Spirit is the least substantial of the persons of the Trinity; and the Scarecrow's identity is similarly hardly resident in his body. His body can be dismantled and scattered, as it is by the winged monkeys, and yet he doesn't die, and his identity remains intact: once he is reassembled, he is the same Scarecrow again.

The Tin Woodman seeks a heart that will give him the power to love. His role in the trinity is that of the Son. The creation myth that Baum provides for him—his gradual metamorphosis from flesh to tin—is one of suffering through loss. The wicked witch damages him for loving the Munchkin girl. Being made of tin, he loses and laments his love for her, but his loss of sexual love has the effect of increasing his compassion and tenderness for the rest of creation. Later he suffers and perishes for Dorothy's sake, being smashed on the rocks by the winged monkeys. But presently he is resurrected by the Winkie Tinsmiths, and thereafter he is empowered and made royal. He doesn't exactly sit "at the right hand of God, the Father Almighty," but he does become king of the Winkies.[12]

"The Cowardly Lion," says Edward Hudlin, "is the symbol of latent and overt power" (454). While the mythic pattern that he finds in *The Wizard of Oz* is different from the pattern I am exploring, Hudlin's independent identification of the Lion with Power helps to confirm my argument. The Lion is the "King of Beasts" from the outset (65), and he is also physically large and strong. He performs feats of strength and daring—such as leaping the chasm with a passenger on his back, and defeating the Kalidahs—and takes on the role of the strong member of the group. He also reinforces the lesson that power and strength alone are not sufficient for victory: he needs to be rescued from the field of poppies by the courtesy of the mice. Such incidents remind us of other such fables of the association of strength with sensitivity, such as the story of Androcles and the lion, and the lion killed by Samson: "Out of the strong came forth sweetness" (Judges 14:14).

The three companions are made one (with each other as with Dorothy) in the series of episodes in which they have their separate interviews with the Wizard of Oz in his various manifestations. Perhaps by way of avoiding too predictable a scheme, and perhaps in order to show his characters' interdependency, Baum switches around the expected images. Oz appears as "an enormous Head, without body to support it or any arms or legs whatever" (120) not to the Scarecrow as we would expect (since he is in search of a brain), but to Dorothy. He appears as "a most lovely lady" (124) not to the Woodman, as we would expect (since he wants to love his Munchkin girl again), but to the Scarecrow. He appears as "a most terrible Beast" (128) not to the Lion, but to the Woodman. And to the Lion he appears as "a Ball of Fire," although it is the Scarecrow who has identified a lighted match as the one thing he most fears. But perhaps these inept manifestations are simply one more sign that Oz is not a very good wizard.

Dorothy's three companions, then, like Mowgli's, are variations on a recurring archetype of the relation of Power, Love, and Knowledge, and cover, like his, the physical, emotional, and intellectual life. They provide both the satisfaction of a recognizable pattern and the pleasure of a new and original formulation of it. The girl's "strangely assorted company," so strikingly bizarre and original, are yet recognizable as embodying the three attributes, and have kinship with configurations as ancient and respectable as the Christian Trinity and the judgment of Paris.

Archetypes recur. And by way of demonstrating the recurrence of this one it is worth tracing some of the variations on it in familiar works of literature. I present the following examples in no particular hierarchy, for myths are independent of categories of quality. And I apologize in advance for the rather breathless pace of the listing. My purpose here is to accumulate examples in order to demonstrate the universality of the pattern, rather than to compare and analyze.

Dumas's three musketeers provide a familiar and popular version of the Knowledge/Love/Power trio: D'Artagnan, his protagonist, has as his co-mates the intelligent and sensitive Athos, the passionately intriguing Aramis, and the massively powerful Porthos. For the disempowered woman the attributes can be in painful conflict: George Eliot's Maggie Tulliver, in *The Mill on the Floss*, is ultimately destroyed by the conflict between the three men in her life, who are embodiments of the familiar configuration: Philip Wakem lends her books and provides her aesthetic and intellectual awakening; Stephen Guest is the passionate lover; and her disciplinarian brother Tom sternly insists that she follow the rules laid down by her father. A recent version of the trio occurs in William Goldman's *The Princess Bride*, where the princess has three men as allies: Westley provides the intelligence (and at one point his body from the neck down is paralyzed, so that he is virtually a brain without a body); Inigo, a romantic Spaniard motivated by revenge and wielding a sword, is passion; and Fezzik, an amiable giant, all brawn and no brain, is power. The three act as a team, and complement each other's operations.

The pattern may be inverted when the attributes become the hero's antagonists rather than his allies. The most salient example is Milton's dark parody of the Trinity in *Paradise Lost*: Satan the father ("father of all lies" as well as of his daughter Sin and his son Death); Sin, who in keeping with Milton's misogyny is the Daughter rather than the Son, and a lascivious being who enters into incestuous sexual relations with both her father and her son; and Death, "The other shape, / If shape it might be calld that shape had none" (Milton, II. 666–67). (The "holy spirit" of the trinity is frequently ineffable or amorphous.) Dickens provides at least two diabolic trinities in which Power, Love, and Knowledge show their dark sides. The three villains in *Oliver Twist* are the violent Bill Sikes, who as housebreaker and murderer represents the inverse of God the creator and lawgiver; Oliver's half-brother Monks, who professes himself to be motivated by hatred rather than love; and Fagin the corrupter and informer, who knows everybody's secret. Bill Sikes says Fagin looks like "a ugly old ghost just rose from the grave" (136), an appropriate description for the evil shadow of the Holy Spirit (McMaster 263–77). Similarly, in *Barnaby Rudge* Dickens

supplies an appropriate trio to lead the mob: for power the brutish
Hugh, for love the hangman Dennis, and for knowledge the mad-
man Barnaby. In *Victory* Conrad too presents an evil trio as the
antagonists for his protagonist Heyst: Jones, Ricardo, and the Nean-
derthal Pedro represent, says Heyst, "evil intelligence, instinctive
savagery, arm in arm; the brute force is at the back" (329).

One role of the critic is like that of Baloo the lawgiver: to perceive
order and to transmit it, and so to enlarge consciousness. On the
face of it, Kipling's Mowgli tales in the two *Jungle Books*, set in the
Indian jungle and dealing with actual though anthropomorphized
animals, are a world apart from Baum's whimsical fantasy that begins in Kansas but transmigrates to an invented land peopled by
animated androids. But the two narratives have a common integrating principle: they both deal with the maturation of a young
protagonist, and both provide for the protagonist a trio of companions who are there to supply wholeness through difference. By
them the protagonist is empowered and put in contact with his or
her own physical, emotional, and intellectual life. Mowgli learns
from, and then masters, the parts of the integrated system represented by Baloo, Bagheera, and Kaa. Dorothy helps and is helped
by her self-deprecating companions, the Lion, Tin Woodman, and
Scarecrow, who enable her to complete her pilgrim's progress from
Kansas to Oz and back. And both their stories belong in a family
of narratives that are informed by the archetype of the Trinity as a
representation of a harmonious relation between Power, Love, and
Knowledge.

Notes

1. William Whitla, in his study of the incarnation in Browning's poetry, traces
the history of this idea more fully than I can here.
2. For the addition of this Hindu schema (which may have had as much influence on Kipling in his presentation of the Indian jungle as the orthodox Western
Trinity), I am indebted to Cynthia Leenerts of George Washington University.
3. For instance, J. M. S. Tompkins: "The realm of wonder extends beyond the
limits of myth" (69); Philip Mason: "The Mowgli stories . . . succeed because they
give shape and form to archetypal fantasies about the self" (169); Robert F. Moss:
"The Mowgli stories reach well beyond naturalism into fable and myth" (110).
4. Quotations from Kipling are from *The Jungle Book* and *The Second Jungle Book*.
For ease of reference, and so that quotations may be located in any edition, I use
"I" and "II" for the two volumes, and abbreviated titles for the different stories:
"Mowgli's Brothers," *MB*; "Kaa's Hunting," *KH*; "Tiger! Tiger!" *TT*; "How Fear
Came," *HFC*; "Letting in the Jungle," *LJ*; "The King's Ankus," *KA*; "Red Dog," *RD*;
"The Spring Running," *SR*. I include the poems under the titles of the stories with

which they are associated. I do not deal with "In the Rukh," the story sometimes included with the Mowgli stories but written and published separately before them.

5. Philip Mason points out that Kipling "absorbs from the Judaism of the Old Testament a sense of the sacredness of the law, of the necessity for atonement and restoring the balance, of the presence of a righteous anger at the heart of things" (311).

6. Mason notes the almost exclusively masculine personnel in the series, and aligns it with "the world of the Club and the House of Commons" (167). Lionel Trilling has also pointed out the numerous parent surrogates for Mowgli, "the fathers far more numerous than the mothers" (86).

Kipling's stories for children are, of course, not peculiar in containing a high proportion of males. The same can be said, for instance, of Kenneth Grahame's *The Wind in the Willows* (1908) and Tolkien's *The Hobbit*.

7. See Constance Sheerer: "India, for Kipling, represented the Lost Paradise" (27).

8. The memorable passage of decorative prose in "The King's Ankus," describing the wrestling match between Mowgli and Kaa, is probably a reminiscence of the narrative about the Trojan horse in the *Aeneid*. "The beautiful, statue-like group" of boy and serpent (II,150) recalls the Laocoön, one of the most famous of classical sculptures. Laocoön was the Trojan who advised against bringing the wooden horse into Troy, and was destroyed, along with his two sons, by two serpents sent by Minerva/Athena. See book 2 of Virgil's *Aeneid*.

9. See, for instance, Ficino, the Neoplatonist reconciler of pagan philosophy with Christian thought: "No reasonable being doubts . . . that there are three kinds of life: the contemplative, the active, and the pleasurable (*contemplativa, activa, voluptuosa*). And three roads to felicity have been chosen by men: wisdom, power, and pleasure (*sapientia, potentia, voluptas*)" (Wind 82).

10. According to Douglas J. McReynolds and Barbara J. Lips, Dorothy "makes men whole": her three male companions find wholeness only in relation to her. "She makes caricatures into real ones, and does it without losing her own identity in theirs" (90). But these characters are also projections of her own qualities—of her desire for knowledge, wisdom, and power as well as her possession of them.

11. Raylyn Moore also reads *The Wizard of Oz* allegorically: Dorothy's "story is seen to be an allegory of self-reliance, bolstered by the similar experiences of her companions, the Lion, Woodman, and Scarecrow" (135).

12. Edward Hudlin considers the Scarecrow rather than the Woodman to be "the dying and resurrected Corn God . . . the Osiris to [Dorothy's] Isis" (453). Though I differ from him in this identification, we agree in assigning mythic significance to Dorothy's companions.

Works Cited

Aristotle. *Physiognomonica*, trans. T. Loveday and E. S. Forster. Vol. 6 of *The Works of Aristotle*, ed. W. D. Ross. Oxford: Clarendon Press, 1913.

Baum, L. Frank. *The Wizard of Oz*. Chicago: Reilly and Lee, 1956.

Burton, Robert. *The Anatomy of Melancholy*, ed. Floyd Dell and Paul Jordan-Smith. New York: Tudor Publishing, 1951.

Conrad, Joseph. *Victory: An Island Tale*. London: J. M. Dent, 1948.

Darton, F. J. Harvey. *Children's Books in England*. Cambridge: Cambridge University Press, 1960.

Dickens, Charles. *Oliver Twist*. In the Oxford Illustrated Dickens. London: Oxford University Press, 1949.

Donne, John. *The Poems of John Donne*, ed. Herbert Grierson. London: Oxford University Press, 1957.

Hearn, Michael Patrick, ed. *The Annotated Wizard of Oz*. New York: Clarkson N. Potter, 1973.

Hudlin, Edward W. "The Mythology of Oz: An Interpretation." *Papers on Language and Literature* 25 (1989): 443–62.

Kipling, Rudyard. *The Jungle Book*. Library Edition. London: Macmillan, 1950.

———. *The Second Jungle Book*. Library Edition. London: Macmillan, 1950.

Knoepflmacher, U. C. "The Balancing of Child and Adult: An Approach to Victorian Fantasies for Children." *Nineteenth-Century Fiction* 37 (1983): 497–530.

McMaster, Juliet. "Diabolic Trinity in *Oliver Twist*." *Dalhousie Review* 61 (1981): 263–77.

McReynolds, Douglas J., and Barbara J. Lips. "A Girl in the Game: *The Wizard of Oz* as Analogue for the Female Experience in America." *North Dakota Quarterly* 54 (1986): 87–93.

Mason, Philip. *Kipling: The Glass, the Shadow and the Fire*. London: Jonathan Cape, 1975.

Milton, John. *Paradise Lost*. In *The Poetical Works of John Milton*, ed. Helen Darbishire. London: Oxford University Press, 1958.

Moore, Raylyn. *Wonderful Wizard Marvellous Land*. Bowling Green, Ohio: Bowling Green University Popular Press, 1974.

Moss, Robert F. *Rudyard Kipling and the Fiction of Adolescence*. New York: St. Martin's Press, 1982.

Sheerer, Constance. "The Lost Paradise of Rudyard Kipling." *Dalhousie Review* 61 (1981): 27–37.

Stewart, J. I. M. *Rudyard Kipling*. London: Gollancz, 1966.

Tompkins, J. M. S. *The Art of Rudyard Kipling*. London: Methuen, 1959.

Trilling, Lionel. "Kipling." In *Kipling's Mind and Art*, ed. Andrew Rutherford. Edinburgh: Oliver and Boyd, 1964: 85–94.

Twain, Mark. *The Adventures of Huckleberry Finn*, ed. Sculley Bradley. New York: W. W. Norton, 1961.

White, T. H. *The Sword in the Stone*. London: Collins Lions, 1971.

———, trans. and ed. *The Book of Beasts, Being a Translation from a Latin Bestiary of the Twelfth Century*. London: Jonathan Cape, 1954.

Whitla, William. *The Central Truth: The Incarnation in Robert Browning's Poetry*. Toronto: University of Toronto Press, 1963.

Wilson, Angus. *The Strange Ride of Rudyard Kipling: His Life and Works*. London: Secker and Warburg, 1977.

Wind, Edgar. *Pagan Mysteries of the Renaissance*. London: Faber, 1968.

The Empire of Youth:
Crossing and Double-Crossing
Cultural Barriers in Kipling's Kim

Judith A. Plotz

In the opening pages of *A Passage to India*, Forster sets out the question that organizes the book: "they were discussing as to whether or no it is possible to be friends with an Englishman" (4). Can there be candor, devotion, and shared values between those who belong to the rulers and those who belong to the ruled? After scores of missed chances, aborted meetings, and unanswered calls, the issue of friendship among colonizers and colonized recurs in the famous conclusion in which nothing is concluded: "Why can't we be friends now? . . . It's what I want. It's what you want."

> But the horses didn't want it—they swerved apart; the earth didn't want it, sending up rocks through which riders must pass single file; the temples, the tank, the jail, the palace, the birds, the carrion, the Guest House, that came into view as they issued from the gap and saw Mau beneath: "No, not yet," and the sky said, "No, not there." [316]

Forster, writing in 1924, regretfully concludes that the structures of imperial power overshadow the human gestures that ineffectually take place within them. Within those shadows the gap between cultures is too great.

Forster, the eloquent enemy of the Raj, shares with Kipling, its ardent exponent, a concern with *friendship* across the bounds of race, religion, and nationality. As "the Little Friend of all the World," Kipling's greatest hero wins hearts wherever he goes among the Muslims, Hindus, Jains, Buddhists, Christians, Pathans, Bengalis, Punjabis, Irishmen, Englishmen, Tibetans, priests, soldiers, farmers, householders, ethnologists, and spies who are India. And *Kim* too, like its hero, is at once "the Little Friend of all the World" and "the imperial agent" (to use Timeri Murari's term), simul-

Children's Literature 20, ed. Francelia Butler, Barbara Rosen, and Judith A. Plotz (Yale University Press, © 1992 by The Children's Literature Foundation, Inc.).

taneously regarding India with disinterested affection and interested, controlling calculation. On the one hand, Kipling's *Kim* is
unique in colonialist literature as the place where the unimaginable
transpolitical friendship between cultures is richly imagined; on
the other, it is an unapologetically colonialist text in which cross-
cultural love is set forth as the *by-product* of empire, a rare essence
to be extracted *only* from empire. The union of affection and power
Forster perceives as impossible is made credible in *Kim* by the skillful generic engineering that turns this difficult and sophisticated
text into a plausible children's novel.

Kim has long been praised as the most richly and innocently cross-
cultural of Kipling's works. To Kinkead-Weekes, Kim "embodies
the urge to attain a deeper kind of vision, the urge not merely to
see and know from the outside, but to *become* the 'other'" (217). To
McClure, the Kipling of *Kim* "is able to see beyond the horizon of
his times and portray a world of yet to be realized inter-racial harmony" (168) in a story that JanMohamed argues "overcomes the
barriers of racial difference better than any other colonialist novel"
(78). To Tompkins, Kim is doubly a "chain-man," for he is a link,
"a bridge suspended for the passage of understanding between two
territories of Kipling's heart" (24).

Kimball O'Hara, as an adolescent inhabitant of the border territory between childhood and manhood (the book opens when Kim
is thirteen, ends when he is seventeen), is a great criss-crosser of
boundaries. In some ways he is deeply Indian—fluent in Punjabi,
in Urdu ("the vernacular"), even Pushtu; at home in Muslim and in
Hindu dress—but, of course, he is not Indian:

> Kim was English. Though he was burned as black as any native;
> though he spoke the vernacular by preference, and his mother-
> tongue in a clipped, uncertain sing-song; though he consorted
> on terms of perfect equality with the small boys of the bazar;
> Kim was white—a poor white of the very poorest. [3]

Nor is he exactly English either. His facility in the English language
comes from an exiled German (162), a teacher of languages and
a refugee of the barricades of the '48 revolution. Moreover, both
Kim's parents are Irish, a heritage explicitly linked to the boy's
curiosity ("Irish enough by birth to reckon silver the least part of
any game" [61]) and his courage ("The blow had waked every un-

known Irish devil in the boy's blood" [396]). His heritage marks his kinship to the colonized marginal Irish as well as to the English colonizers. Kim's father, that alcoholic sergeant turned opium addict, thrall to drugs Eastern and Western, is also something of a cultural boundary crosser in his simultaneous Roman Catholicism and Freemasonry (4, 183).

Kim is set up as the boy who could be virtually anything. So flexible are the boundaries of Kim's identity—"What am I? Mussalman, Hindu, Jain, or Buddhist?" (234)—that he seems to don a new consciousness with each set of new clothes. Sometimes he appears in "Hindu kit, the costume of a low-caste street boy" (7) or moves invisible among crowds as "a Hindu urchin in a dirty turban and Isabella-colored clothes" (27).[1] Sometimes he is a young sahib in "a white drill suit" (204), sometimes "a Eurasian lad . . . in badly fitting shop clothes" (240). With Mahbub Ali, Kim is from the first "externally at least, a Mohammedan" (214) and is eventually rewarded with a splendid set of Pathan clothes, appropriate border garb with their explicitly Afghan, northern Indian, and even Russian elements. Even the clustering of hyphenated words in the passage describing these glad rags is stylistically characteristic of *Kim*, the great text of hoped-for linkages:

> There was a *gold-embroidered* Peshawur *turban-cap,* rising to a cone, and a big *turban-cloth* ending in a broad fringe of gold. There was a Delhi embroidered waistcoat to slip over a *milky-white* shirt, fastening to the right, ample and flowing; green pyjamas with twisted silk *waist-string;* and that nothing might be lacking, *russia-leather* slippers, smelling divinely, with arrogantly curled tips. [279–80; italics mine]

Though he knows or seeks to know all the castes of India, he is bound to none and drawn to all. Kim is as convincing a disciple of "a certain caste of *faquir* . . . cross-legged, ash-smeared, and wild-eyed" (260–61) as he is a Buddhist lama's faithful *chela*. But even at his most Buddhist, with his "sad-coloured sweeping robes, one hand on his rosary, and the other in the attitude of benediction," Kim reminds the (English) narrator of nothing so much as the very English "young saint in a stained-glass window" (320).

So freely does Kim criss-cross the bounds of British and Indian culture that he is hard to place. The lama is confounded: "A Sahib and the son of a Sahib . . . But no white man knows the land and the customs of the land as thou knowest" (149). The very sweeper grows paradoxical at the appearance of Kim: "There is a white boy by the barracks waiting under a tree who is not a white boy" (165). The intolerant Mahbub Ali is confounded by the protean Kim into tolerance: "Thou art beyond question an unbeliever, and therefore thou wilt be damned. So says my law—or I think it does. But thou art also my Little Friend of all the World, and I love thee. So says my heart" (234). There are attempts by the narrator and occasional characters to place Kim as definingly white and a sahib: "Kim was English" (3); "Kim was white" (3). Kim has "the white man's horror of the Serpent" (72) and the white man's brash valor, "struggling on the brickwork plinth . . . [where] a native would have lain down, Kim's white blood set him upon his feet" (76). "Once a Sahib, always a Sahib," insists Mahbub Ali (175). Yet Kim himself resists such identification. Though he thrice muses on the mystery of his identity, asking "Who is Kim" (193), "Who is Kim—Kim—Kim" (304), and ". . . what is Kim" (462), he won't take simple Englishness as an answer: "I am *not* a Sahib," he tells Mahbub Ali (221); "I am *not* a Sahib," he repeats to the lama (443). By a genial touch "Kim" means *who* in Turkish, so that "who" is "Kim" and "Kim" is "who." (But Kim himself, necessarily self-unknowing, "knows no Turki" [283].)

The orphan child of white parents, Kim is also the adopted son of many substitute parents. As Lionel Trilling notes, *Kim* "is full of wonderful fathers, all dedicated men in their different ways, each representing a different possibility of existence" (123). Kipling's own father (who illustrated the first edition and took a sustained interest in the composition of the book) is the model for the Lahore museum curator. Father Victor of the Mavericks (who knew Kim's real father) paternally entrusts the boy to Colonel Creighton who, along with Lurgan and Hurree Babu, acts as Kim's father in the art and craft of the Great Game. Equipping Kim like a Pathan even to the "mother-of-pearl, nickel-plated, self-extracting .450 revolver," Mahbub Ali calls him "my son" and gives him an affectionate paternal blessing: "please God, thou shalt some day kill a man with it" (280–81). The lama returns from the brink of death and of triumphant merging into the Great Soul in order to rescue Kim as the "Son of my Soul" (473) from bondage to the Wheel. There is a maternal presence as well. The Sahiba nurses Kim with all a mother's affection and Kim gives her a son's gratitude: "'maharanee,' Kim began, but led by the look in her eye, changed

it to the title of plain love—'Mother, I owe my life to thee' " (453).
Indeed, Kim regards all India as his family. When asked, "And who
are thy people," he replies, "This great and beautiful land" (222).

All India, especially that which is out of bounds, is Kim's province. Kim habitually moves in and out of restricted areas, delighting
in "the stealthy prowl through the dark gullies and lanes, the crawl
up a water-pipe, the sights and sounds of the women's world on
the flat roofs, and the headlong flight from housetop to housetop
under cover of the hot dark" (6). His first appearance "in defiance of municipal orders, astride the gun Zam-Zammah" (3) is, as
Kinkead-Weekes has noted, "emblematic" (216): English Kim sits
where his playmates, Hindu Chota Lal and Muslim Abdullah, cannot. While the two other boys fear the new and unfamiliar lama,
Kim delights in novelty and plunges into the museum. Kim is continually moving in and out of secluded precincts, venturing in and
out of restricted areas in defiance of various municipal and cultural
orders. In Lucknow, Kim rides high in the cab as a sahib, but breaks
decorum to leap down into "the road headlong, patting the dusty
feet" of his lama (198). Kim moves in and out of school, now a sahib
in a white drill suit, now a wandering native. He almost moves in
and out of his own skin, sometimes as pale as his Irish genes dictate, sometimes as dark as the fierce sun or the dyes of the bazaar
can make him. He is a border violator who riskily intrudes into the
army camp and later, at much greater risk, into the "mysterious city
of Bikaneer" (276), which he clandestinely maps.

Just as its protagonist is a crosser of borders, so does the novel
Kim incorporate diversity in the interests of unity. The epigraph to
chapter 8 praises "Allah Who gave me two / Separate sides to my
head" (214) and that to chapter 14 pays tribute to the power of the
one universal human meaning in many languages, many creeds:

> My brother kneels (so saith Kabir)
> To stone and brass in heathen-wise,
> But in my brother's voice I hear
> My own unanswered agonies. [410]

The India of *Kim* is not a babel but a harmony of many voices. As
Stewart and Davis have shown, Kipling dramatizes linguistic "code
switching" (Davis 37) back and forth among the four separate language codes Stewart describes in the novel: the narrator's language;
"the voice of the homeland," as expressed in the various dialects

of Irish Father Victor, the Liverpool drummer boy, and "correct" Colonel Creighton; the "native English" ("oah yess") of Kim before his St. Xavier's training, of Hurree Babu, and of the bazaar letter writers; and Urdu itself, amazingly rendered in an English ingeniously made to look and sound un-English (Stewart 29–32). Yet Kipling's single *Kim* idiom contains all the differing codes.

This harmony of multitudes is further promoted by the structure of the work as a road novel. The Grand Trunk Road—in itself a symbol of Kim's journey and of British colonial presence as well—spreads all India before Kim and before the reader:

> And truly the Grand Trunk Road is a wonderful spectacle. It runs straight bearing without crowding India's traffic for fifteen hundred miles—such a river of life as nowhere else exists in the world. . . . There were new people and new sights at every stride—castes he knew and castes that were altogether out of his experience. They met a troop of long-haired, strong-scented Sansis with baskets of lizards and other unclean foods on their backs. . . . Then an Akali, a wild-eyed, wild-haired Sikh devotee in the blue-checked clothes of his faith, with polished steel quoits glistening on the cone of his tall blue turban. . . . Here and there they met or were overtaken by the gaily dressed crowds of whole villages. . . . Kim was in the seventh heaven of joy. The Grand Trunk at this point was built on an embankment . . . so that one walked, as it were, a little above the country, along a stately corridor, seeing all India spread out to left and right. [94, 101–04]

This clear emphasis on the glorious multiplicity of Indian life makes it inviting to read *Kim* as a cross-cultural bildungsroman in which the adolescent's long-sought identity is achieved by a purposeful journey, and by a synthesis of the multitudinous experience of "all India spread out to left and right" and of the many modes of being offered by his Indian and British father substitutes. In such a reading, Kim is the ideal Anglo-Indian, the "idealized embodiment of what Kipling would have liked an inhabitant of British India to be" (Kettle 214), able to be a good British subject as well as a loving son of India because so clearly identified with the wholeness of India in a way no actual individual Indian—bound by caste, bound by religion—could ever be. Indeed, McClure speculates that Kim is not simply the idealized embodiment of the best possible inhabitant of British India, but is in fact a "what if" version of Kipling himself. *Kim* may thus be read as the fantasy of a Kipling who had not been sent to England and the "House of Desolation" but had run away and spent the years from six to sixteen in India, where he prolonged into manhood the freedoms he had enjoyed as a beloved, spoiled, masterful child. Kipling emphasizes in *Kim* the high competence of the "country-born" for ruling India: "These be the sort to oversee justice," says the Sahiba. "They know the land and the customs of the land. The others, all new from Europe, suckled by white women and learning our tongues from books, are worse than the pestilence" (125). As is well known, the brief Indian sections in *Something of Myself* set India up as Kipling's lost childhood paradise, the place where everything was permitted, where all things seemed possible, where he could do no wrong. The vernacular, the Urdu Kipling spoke as a child rather than English, is recalled as a language deeper than language, a language of the self unconsciously in harmony with the world's "sights and smells that made me deliver in the vernacular sentences whose meaning I knew not" (*Something of Myself* 382). As the surrogate self who stayed home in India, in Urdu, who remained forever "below the age of caste" (355) and the division of native and sahib, Kim seems to have offered Kipling a second life.

Of all Kipling's works, *Kim* has found greatest acceptance among Indian readers and writers, largely because of its attempt to make unity out of diversity. Nirad Chaudhuri, indeed, has praised it as "not only the finest novel in English with an Indian theme but also one of the greatest English novels in spite of the theme" (47). Chaudhuri cites the fourfold depiction in *Kim* of "the life of the people and religion in the twin setting of the mountain and the plain" as a remarkable vision of the *wholeness* of India; despite the multiplicity of Indian experience *Kim* succeeds in giving a representation of the fullness. Though Chaudhuri himself is hardly a representative figure (to this day he continues to defend the British Empire while condemning British colonialism), other less nostalgic contemporary Indo-Anglican writers have also found *Kim* an engaging text both for its attempted synthesis and for its vision of individual mobility and freedom. Both G. V. Desani's extraordinary *All About H. Hatterr* (1948) and Salman Rushdie's *Midnight's Children* (1981) send their Kim-like heroes on pan-India quests for totality.[2]

But no matter how buoyantly cross-cultural one's reading of *Kim*, no matter how much *Kim* has been assimilated into Indo-Anglican writing and become a Little Friend of all the Writers, the book is all the same a spy story that hinges on betrayal both of others and of part of the self. Though Kim starts off in Lahore as "Little Friend of all the World," he comes of age as a spy, a secret agent. To be a spy is the antithesis of being a friend; to be a spy is to ape the forms of intimacy for political ends. To be a "perfect spy" like Kim and like Le Carré's charming adult spy Magnus Pym ("Pym the Great"), whose name echoes Kim's, is to deceive even oneself with the sincerity of one's playacting.[3] Thus to Parry the central relationship of *Kim*, that between guru and chela, is spurious despite Kim's real affection for his lama: "the Lama's love for Kim, his reverence for all living things and his innocence are mocked by the stealth and cynicism of the Great Game" (255). The rules of the Great Game force on Kim a role that progressively impedes fully human communion between him and the Indian world.

Kim's temperament, after he is put to use by the British, excludes him from true fellowship with India. Kim has been from the beginning a watcher. He is repeatedly characterized as one who sees unseen. He is a watcher in the shadows, "lithe and inconspicuous" (6), "like a shadow" (22). Repeatedly "Kim watched . . . considering and interested" (23); Kim "kept his watchful eye" (51) or "watched between drooped eyelids" (116). He regularly stations himself out of sight to watch others. At the museum he is the hidden observed: "Kim laid himself down, his ear against a crack in the heat-split cedar door, and, following his instinct, stretched out to listen and watch" (13). In Mahbub Ali's camp, Kim, unseen, spies on the spy searching the tent: "Kim with one eye laid against a knot-hole in the planking . . . had seen the Delhi man's search through the boxes" (42–43). After delivering the message to Creighton, "flat on his belly lay Kim" (62) to watch the British officers. Again lurking in shadow "behind the thick trunks in the cool dark of the mango-tope" (130), then "belly-flat" by the mess-tent door (137), Kim watches the Mavericks.

It is his watchfulness that marks Kim within this text as truly British—one who looks from above, from the cannon, from the raised Trunk Road—and it is this characteristic that his handlers seize upon to make him a spy. In Kipling's world the British are consistently characterized as the masters of clear vision as distinguished from the Indians, who are totally engaged in their small areas of

Indian life. It is the English museum curator who gives the lama a marvelous pair of spectacles: "How scarcely do I feel them! How clearly do I see!" (21). (Despite his English glasses, however, the lama deliberately avoids occasions of sight: "He lowered his head that he might not see" [51]; "The lama never raised his eyes. . . . He looked steadily at the ground" [103]. At the desired moment of vision, indeed, the lama loses all knowledge of his surroundings.) It is the English museum director who sees and comprehends all Asia as he presides over photographs even of the lama's distant Tibetan monastery, even of the "little door through which we bring wood before winter. And thou—the English know of these things?" (14). It is the Englishman who presides over the "mighty map" compiled by Europeans, on which he points out to the learned—but yet ignorant—old Buddhist "the Holy Places of Buddhism" (15). Colonel Creighton and Hurree Chunder Mukherjee watch India overtly through the Ethnological Survey, covertly through the Secret Service. Kim by instinct is also an ethnological surveyor; he leads the lama into the museum with an exhilarated sense that "he is new" (11) and therefore something "to investigate further: precisely as he would have investigated a new building or a strange festival. . . . The lama was his trove" (22). District Superintendent Strickland, also of the Secret Service, is so indefatigable a watcher and so persuasive a tempter that he gets the Sahiba, the embodiment of Mother India, to remove her veil (124). The English in *Kim* see all the world unveiled; they "know of these things" (14). The English are the scientific investigators, the knowers, the masters of ethnography; the Indians are the known, the seen, the collected materials of ethnography, the mere objects of scrutiny. Indeed, Kipling makes some wry comedy out of Hurree Chunder Mukherjee's antithetical roles as scientific investigator with his eye on the Royal Academy and as superstitious Bengali babu. On the one hand the ethnographer-spy is objectively collecting the curiosities of a backward people; on the other hand he is backwardly terrified lest he violate a taboo or incur a curse: " 'How am I to fear the absolutely non-existent?' said Hurree Babu, talking English to reassure himself. It is an awful thing still to dread the magic that you contemptuously investigate— to collect folk-lore for the Royal Society with a lively belief in all Powers of Darkness" (295). Despite his commitment to evolution and Herbert Spencer, Hurree Babu is an Indian and thus never achieves the one-way vision that is represented as the birthright of

sahibs. Kim, however, with his racially and personally innate watchfulness and his double-sided awareness has the gift of surveillance,
which is raised to controlling heights by his training.

In training for the Great Game, Kim learns to cultivate his natural watchfulness so as to see without being *recognized* as an English
boy or as a conscious looker. He must learn to see without provok-
ing response; he must always perceive what he looks at as Other,
never allowing his own humanity—the wrong "side of his head"—
to be engaged in a reciprocal gaze. During the encounter in which
Mahbub Ali first recommends Kim to Creighton as a candidate for
the Game, the three look at each other:

> [Kim] gazed imploringly at the clear-cut face [of Mahbub Ali]
> in which there was no glimmer of recognition; but even at this
> extremity it never occurred to him to throw himself on the
> white man's mercy or to denounce the Afghan. And Mahbub
> stared deliberately at the Englishman, who stared as deliber-
> ately at Kim, quivering and tongue-tied. [178]

Here Kim watches Mahbub who watches Creighton who watches
Kim. None acknowledges the humanity of the other ("no glimmer
of recognition") but each contemplates the other as an object for
possible use and control. Assessing vision such as this is what makes
an agent strong "on the Ethnological side," is what enables a surveyor, a "chain-man" such as Kim becomes, to map and thereby
control new territory: "by merely marching over a country with a
compass and a level and a straight eye," a boy could "carry away a
picture of that country which might be sold for large sums" (267).
The surveying, controlling, acquisitive "straight eye" marks the eth-
nologist and the spy.

Kim's natural aptitude for seeing is matched by his equal resistance to being seen and controlled. The resistance is partly manifested in his talent for disguise: Kim can pass as a low-caste Hindu
street boy, a Muslim ostler, a crazed *faquir,* or the lama's disciple.
More strikingly, however, Kim is designated as an agent of rare
promise when he withstands Lurgan's controlling, hypnotic vision.
As "the only boy I could not make to see things" (283), Kim resists
becoming the object of Lurgan's vision; he will not consent to see
the broken jar as whole:

> "Look! It is coming into shape," said Lurgan Sahib.
> So far Kim had been thinking in Hindi, but a tremor came

on him, and with an effort like that of a swimmer before sharks, who hurls himself half out of the water, his mind leaped up from a darkness that was swallowing it and took refuge in— the multiplication-table in English!

"Look! It is coming into shape," whispered Lurgan Sahib.

The jar had been smashed—yes, smashed—not the native word—he would not think of that—but smashed into fifty pieces, and twice three was six, and thrice three was nine, and four times three was twelve. He clung desperately to the repetition. The shadow-outline of the jar cleared like a mist after rubbing eyes. There were the broken shards; there was the spilt water drying in the sun, and through the cracks of the verandah showed, all ribbed, the white house-wall below—and thrice twelve was thirty-six. [251–52]

Kim's resistance to Lurgan's mastery involves shifting from an intuitive unitary Indian consciousness to his resistant isolated British consciousness, which is associated with the reductiveness and the control of arithmetic. Clear vision in *Kim* belongs to the British, to the realm of rationality, numeration, positivist science (Herbert Spencer), isolation, and control. But this clear vision involves throwing off reciprocity and mutual recognition.

It is notable that Kim's controlling vision, unlike the lama's culminating vision of "all Hind" (471) is a vision of apartness. Kim's arithmetic triumph is to see the jar broken into fragments. It is in this controlling vision that Kim is most strikingly the "imperial agent" Murari has labeled him. Certainly within the text the British operate as over-see-ers of India. Creighton is a figure of watching and control. Controlled vision such as Kim commands here is associated with seeing analytically in apartness from the objects of his vision. Such instrumental seeing, like the curator's spectacles ("How scarcely do I feel them! How clearly do I see!"), constructs the world in dichotomized orientalist terms. As Said and Williams have made clear, Indians in all their diversity are always and forever the passive objects of British action, protection, scrutiny, and control. As "spectacle," as "trove," as something "to admire," both the single unitary "Orient" and the fascinating diversity of Indian civilization are artifacts of empire.

In *The Illusion of Permanence*, Hutchins has emphasized that imperial rhetoric after the Great Revolt of 1857 sets out with full self-consciousness Indian unity and harmony as inventions, as noble

creations of empire. Without the British, there is no such thing as
India; without the British, India is not a real country at all. Its cha-
otic multiplicity is too confusing for its natives to comprehend as
unity. Such comprehension is the task and glory of empire. According to spokesmen of empire such as Seeley and Strachey, it is for-
eigners who gave India herself (as the curator gives the lama spectacles): "The fundamental fact then is that India had no jealousy
of the foreigner because India had no sense whatever of national
unity, because there *was* no India and therefore, properly speaking,
no foreigner" (Seeley [1883] quoted in Hutchins 141).

> What is India? What does the name India really signify? The
> answer that I have sometimes given sounds paradoxical, but it
> is true. There is no such country, and this is the first and most
> essential fact about India that can be learned. . . . India is a
> name which we give to a great region, including a multitude
> of different countries . . . there is not, and never was an India,
> or even a country of India, possessing, according to European
> ideas, any sort of unity, physical, political, social, or religious;
> no Indian nation, no "people of India," of which we hear so
> much. [Strachey (1911) quoted in Hutchins 141–42]

According to one high official of the East India Company in
1853, "there were hundred of European servants of the Company
who knew far more of India and of its inhabitants than any of the
Natives themselves" (Hutchins 155). This British "myth of omniscience" meant that no Indian could ever "be expected to 'know
India'" as well as Englishmen could (Hutchins 156). The lama's assumption that "no white man knows the land and customs of the
land as [Kim] knowest" (142) sees things precisely reversed: *only* a
white man can know India comprehensively.

If a unified India is a self-consciously constructed imperial artifact, so too is a multifarious India. Interpreting the Mutiny as a
protest by traditional archaic communities to disruptive modernization, the British government responded with a policy designed
to maintain, even to exaggerate, traditional divisions of caste, community, and religion. Pre-Mutiny policy had minimized such differences in the interests of national unity. Post-Mutiny policy exaggerated and absolutized such differences. As Wurgraft notes:

> the pre-Mutiny army was largely recruited on the basis of indi-
> vidual qualities without regard to caste; the post-Mutiny Bengal

army was rebuilt with greater attention to regional, caste, and religious differences. Rather than attempting to convert their recruits or at least trying to loosen their caste loyalties, British officers sought to maintain the orthodoxy of their troops by hiring Hindu, Muslim, and Sikh priests and by enacting regulations to enforce orthodox behavior. [6]

The cherishing of Indian diversity may well have been linked to genuine interest and respect, but it was also a calculated policy of exaggerating differences among subject peoples so as to make the mediating British presence essential. Such "ethnographic" acceptance and endorsement of traditional divisions depicts India as a "changeless East" consisting of chaotically diverse and largely antagonistic communities. Such a self-serving analysis dovetailed with an imperial policy of "divide and rule." To perceive India chiefly in terms of eternally antagonistic diversity is to perceive a fertile chaos in need of a guiding creative spirit, a battlefield of warring factions in need of a mediator. In post-Mutiny India, the policy of institutionalizing the "eternal" differences of the Changeless East was a policy to maintain a permanent empire. The British exploited "this divisiveness by playing Indian communities off against one another" under the assumption that "the complex divisions of Indian society made cooperation between them impossible" (Hutchins 174).

In light of these observations, *Kim* seems particularly imperial. Even apart from Kim's service to the Great Game, the novel depends on an imperial framework. Both in the panoramic vision the text valorizes and in the affectionate camaraderie between this Little Friend of All the World and the peoples of India, the book assumes a perpetual Raj. To belong fully to India in *Kim*, to be a genuine Indian among Indians—Hindi-speaking and Hindi-thinking— is to be a swimmer among the sharks in the great chaos of the unregulated sea: "So far Kim had been thinking in Hindi, but a tremor came on him, and with an effort like that of a swimmer before sharks, who hurls himself half out of the water, his mind leaped up from a darkness that was swallowing it and took refuge in—the multiplication-table in English!" Kim's masterful vision of wholes—"all India spread out to left and right"—is a fundamentally *imperial* possession, belonging to the ethnological overseer rather than the swimmer in the sea of life. That Kim's relationships are warmly affectionate, and that his friendships are extensive, are also imperial artifacts. Post-Mutiny imperial policy mediated all

Indian-to-Indian relationships through governing English bodies and rendered obsolete "intricate procedures earlier Indian rulers had devised for eliciting cooperation among communities by honoring their separate distinctness" (Hutchins 175). Kim, indeed, is capable of befriending or at least cajoling Muslims, Hindus, Sikhs, Buddhists, Jains, nautch girls, prostitutes, the aristocratic Hindu dowagers, the powerful polyandrous hillwoman. Yet the multitude of different Indians who count themselves Kim's friends are hardly friends to each other. It is the British *te-rain* that can bring together otherwise separate and hostile groups ("'I say,' began the moneylender, pursing his lips, 'that there is not one rule of right living which these *te-rains* do not cause us to break. We sit, for example, side by side with all castes and peoples'" [47]). So too it is British Kim who mediates between Oriental and Oriental. Though Mahbub Ali holds (in Pushtu) the lama "an unbeliever and an idolater" (465) and the lama holds Mahbub Ali one who "lacks courtesy, and is deceived by the shadow of appearances" (469), they are at one in their love for Kim. As Mahbub Ali remarks sardonically of the Sahiba's affectionate regard for Kim "as her son," "Hmph! Half Hind seems that way disposed" (464).

Just as imperial oversight made possible a unified vision of a multifarious Indian whole and imperial administration made possible a harmony among eternally antagonistic communities, so Kim as the fosterling of "this great and beautiful land" is able to embody a utopian totality and harmony. The exhilarating diversity of Kim's India only becomes available for experience because of empire. With a freedom impossible for any actual Indian, necessarily bound by rules of caste and community, Kim slides in and out of the multiple inhibiting rules of Indian life just as in and out of the rules of different games. What is the realm of necessity and law for Indians is the realm of choice and freedom for Kim. He inhabits an idyll, but it is an idyll of imperialism.

The power of Kipling's novel rests on its character as an imperial idyll—a work which joins conflicting realms, the imperial realm of power and the idyllic realm of love. Empire is far more problematic in *Kim* than in any of Kipling's adult works because power here is imagined to coexist with states contrary to power. Thus politics coexist with love, true discipleship with betrayal, Caesar with God ("the boy, sure of Paradise, can yet enter Government service" [467]), Western action with Eastern contemplation. Only the generic inscription of the work as a children's book allows the coexistence.

Kim is a hard book both to classify and to read. Even those like Seymour-Smith who are most convinced that it is "essentially a children's book" find it emphatically double (much beyond the subtle doubleness Shavit finds in all canonical children's fiction) as "a book written for children *and* one written for adults, and its author can never make up his mind which" (301). The substantial difficulty of *Kim* for young readers (and those not so young) should not be underestimated.[4] It takes a highly trained reader to penetrate the sheer density of this novel. Said's recent Penguin edition, for example, includes 545 endnotes to assist the reader in negotiating its range of political and historical references; the diversity of religious orders, castes, and ranks; the multiple dialects and idiolects; the allusive epigraphs, puns, and proverbs; the satiric mockery of unfamiliar social types from Bengali babus to quixotic idealists; the variations rung on the picaresque novel. Such demands on the reader not only far exceed those of contemporary young adult fiction (and all but the most exigent adult fiction) but even those of other highly literary Victorian and Edwardian children's texts.

The mere difficulty of *Kim*, however, does not negate its character as a children's book. Kipling wrote quite consciously for children who would read and reread the same book at different ages with increasing powers of comprehension. The modern age-specific, vocabulary-controlled text is a deceptive model for such a work as *Kim*, which is in fact coded "for children" in several politically resonant ways.

In *Something of Myself*, Kipling characterized his Edenic Indian childhood as a period of free movement belonging to a doted-upon child "below the age of caste." Free but beloved, casteless but not outcast, Kim reproduces this paradoxical childhood condition as "the Little Friend of all the World" and son of "half Hind" who is free to come and go everywhere. As children's text *Kim* too offers readers the freedom of private and public spaces and concerns far beyond their conscious understanding.

What further stamps *Kim* as a children's book is its evasion of definitive adult commitment to both love and work. Despite his age, despite the presence of sexual temptation all around him, Kim repudiates genital sexuality. Depicted at once as knowing ("he had known all evil since he could speak" [6]), as immensely attractive

both to such men as Creighton, the lama, and Lurgan (and indeed
"the other male characters in the book" [Seymour-Smith 303]) and
to such women as the nautch girl, the Sahiba, and the sexually and
politically powerful Woman of Shamlegh, Kim at seventeen keeps
up the demeanor of latency: sexual activity is for him a curiosity
among other curiosities, a bizarre, amusing, compromising pastime
for other people, boring and distasteful for himself.

Furthermore, the conclusion of the novel also pulls Kim back
from any definitive commitment to a specific choice of life and
a lifework. The ending is as inconclusive as Huckleberry Finn's
escape into the territories. It is inconclusive because Kim breaks
down under a double burden of antithetical possibilities and only
reconstitutes himself to uncertain purpose.

Kim, like many of the worn-out heroes of Kipling's Indian tales,
takes sick with "Punjab head," the "breakdown from overwork"
common among civil and military officers serving in northern India
in the mid–nineteenth century (Wurgaft 37). This boy falls prey to
a sickness of *men* because he has been the bearer of the unbearable;
he has broken under the unendurable burden of two cultures that
cannot be reconciled, the divide that runs through his head.

The *kilta* of letters weighs Kim down with his obligations to the
British way, to the Great Game; the heavy body of the old lama
weighs Kim down with his obligation to personal ties. The imperial
professional duty is written, formal, abstract; the Asian childhood
duty is embodied in a beloved person. Together they are too much.
Kim's strength suddenly gives out under this double burden of
equally imperative, equally heavy duties. The closest Kim has come
to being both a perfect Indian and a perfect Briton is in being a
perfect spy; but it is this state of cross-cultural double-cross that
breaks him down. The boy temporarily in adolescent flux had it
both ways, but if he is to be a man he must choose.

Though Kim recovers, the recovery promises no synthesis.
Rather, it opens up the choice of life with a "click" that puts Kim
back on the roads he had walked throughout his youth:

> All that while he felt, though he could not put it into words, that
> his soul was out of gear with its surroundings—a cog-wheel un-
> connected with any machinery, just like the idle cog-wheel of
> a cheap Beheea sugar-crusher laid by in a corner. The breezes
> fanned over him, the parrots shrieked at him, the noises of the
> populated houses behind—squabbles, orders, and reproofs—

> hit on deaf ears. . . . He did not want to cry,—had never felt less like crying in his life,—but of a sudden easy, stupid tears trickled down his nose, and with an almost audible click he felt the wheels of his being lock up anew on the world without. Things that rode meaningless on the eyeball an instant before slid into proper proportion. Roads were meant to be walked upon, houses to be lived in, cattle to be driven, fields to be tilled, and men and women to be talked to. They were all real and true— solidly planted upon the feet—perfectly comprehensible—clay of his clay, neither more nor less. [462–63]

This restorative "almost audible click" that releases Kim from self-rending introspection into "the world without" makes no promises for Kim's future. It is the final assertions of Mahbub Ali ("the boy, sure of Paradise, can yet enter Government service") and the lama ("Just is the Wheel! Certain is our deliverance! Come!" [474]) that point the direction about which Kim himself remains silent. Indeed, the novel stops abruptly—"it" stopped, Kipling told his father of the almost audible click of his own daimon (*Something of Myself* 137)—as if to cut off any vision of an *adult* Kim living successfully in two worlds, as if such a prospect were unimaginable.[5]

I began this paper with a comparison of *Kim* to *A Passage to India*. Indeed, Forster's work is in one respect a rewriting for adults of Kipling's book for children. There is little doubt that Forster bases his Mrs. Moore partly on Kipling's lama. As an older wisdom figure leading a questing youth through India, Mrs. Moore echoes the lama's praise of the "broad smiling river of life" that is India, "a great and a terrible world" (*Kim* 110). "What a terrible river!" she says of the Ganges, "what a wonderful river!" (26). But while Kipling's lama never abandons his paternal care of the "Son of my Soul" (473), Mrs. Moore cuts herself loose from Adela. Making meaning and finding love in the great, terrible land prove too much for both guru and chela in *A Passage to India*: Mrs. Moore refuses to attend any longer to the world and retreats into death in the manner of a *sanyassi* at the highest, most ascetic level of Hindu spirituality; Adela Quested finds that the complexity of being an Englishwoman in India leads her first to injustice and then to a self-defining limitation that is at once maturity and humiliation. Adela's decent choice of self-limiting, self-incriminating truth cuts her off from a world of possibilities even as it fixes her character, even as it foretells the novel's final rejection of private love and friendship under empire—"No, not yet. . . . "No, not there." For Kim, however, there is no such maturing choice demanded by the narrative. He is still left with the possibility of everything before him, still with multiple "roads to be walked on," still a boy with multiple fathers and illimitable futures as "little friend" and "perfect spy."[6]

Notes

1. "Isabella-colored" garb is yellow-gray. According to a traditional though false etymology, the Isabella who gave her name to this shade was the daughter of Phillip II of Spain. According to Isaac D'Israeli's *Curiosities of Literature* (1791–1823), "Isabella, daughter of Phillip II and wife of the Archduke Albert, vowed not to change her linen till Ostend was taken; this siege, unluckily for her comfort, lasted three years; and the supposed colour of the archduchess's linen gave rise to a fashionable colour, and hence called d'Isabeau or Isabella, a kind of whitish-yellow-dingy." Kipling certainly had read D'Israeli's *Curiosities*, for Beetle of *Stalky & Co.* is depicted as reading the volume rapturously in "The Propagation of Knowledge" (1897). With his taste for curiosities of language, Kipling is likely to have noted "Isabella-colored" and added it to his trove. That the legendary dirty underwear of a seventeenth-century Spanish princess should be associated with the clothes of a street urchin in Victorian Lahore is at the very least an instance of the kind of cultural mixing pervasive in the book, an interassimilation of high and low, male and female, East and West, past and present.

2. In *All About H. Hatterr*, one of H. Hatterr's seven quests—each inspired or supervised by a different fraudulent guru—is to find a buried treasure in the Western Ghats. Lest his treasure-seeking goal be guessed and preempted by others, H. Hatterr conceals his practical mercenary ends under a religious pilgrimage disguised as a holy beggar much as Kim disguises his Secret Service mission as a Buddhist pilgrimage. The connection is not lost on H. Hatterr, who has gleaned this tactic ("This is romance for you! The Orient, damme!") from "R. Kipling's autobiographical *Kim*," which he has picked up in "a crooked lending library." In *Kim* "this self-appointed whiteman's burden-bearing sherpa feller's stated how, in the Orient, blokes hit the road and think nothing of walking a thousand miles in search of something." With the glamour of *Kim* upon him, Hatterr observes: "I used to hate walks out East. But I enjoyed this one" (199). *Kim* has imparted "romance for you" to "the Orient" and "walks out East" (a phrase mocking *and* borrowing the romance of "out West"). Though such an attitude, Desani makes clear, may well have been borrowed at exorbitant cost ("2½ chips deposit on the volume, 1½ chips on the volume, if you lose it, deposit forfeit and 5 chips fine for the volume" [199]), *Kim* does manage to serve H. Hatterr as a model for embarking on his all-India quest for totality. In Rushdie's *Midnight's Children* too, the quest is for a principle of unification. Thus Saleem Sinai shares Kim's habit of collecting surrogate parents, with "more mothers than most mothers have children, giving birth to parents has been one of my stranger talents" (243). Just as Kim deems himself the child of the totality of "this great and beautiful land" (222), so Saleem Sinai is born with the map of India imprinted on his face (231); like Kim, Saleem is an eavesdropper on the multitudes of India's voices: "The voices babbled in everything from Malayalam to Naga dialects, from the purity of Lucknow Urdu to the Southern slurrings of Tamil voices" (168). In the "fissiparousness" (399) of an India which he identifies as a country "which, although it had five thousand years of history, although it had invented the game of chess and traded with Middle Kingdom Egypt, was nevertheless quite imaginary . . . a mythical

land . . . a dream we all agreed to dream . . . a mass fantasy" (112), Saleem partakes of Kim's questioning, "Who what am I? My answer: I am the sum total of everything that went before me. I am everyone whose being-in-the-world was affected by mine. . . . [To] understand me, you'll have to swallow a world" (383).

The appeal of *Kim* to contemporary Indo-Anglican writers is in proportion to the fissiparousness of their visions of India. *Kim*'s seeming synthesis of all India hints at a model for representing the whole during an increasingly divisive time. Besides Rushdie's great synoptic account of postindependence India in *Midnight's Children*, there have been a number of other recent attempts at novelistic synthesis of great tracts of Indian historical and cultural experience. In the past few years alone there have been I. Allen Sealy's *The Trotter-Nama* (1988), Khushwant Singh's *Delhi* (1989), and Shashi Tharoor's *The Great Indian Novel* (1989). In *The Trotter-Nama*, the country-born Kim figure is called "Mik" (for Mikhail) and is trained by a Tibetan monk as a *Russian* spy.

3. Our contemporary master of the fiction of betrayal, John Le Carré, is fascinated with *Kim*. References, muted and ironic, to the "Great Game" are frequent within his novels of the Circus. Le Carré's principal hero-villains, both double agents, Bill Haydon of *Tinker, Tailor, Soldier, Spy* and Magnus Pym of *A Perfect Spy*, are both based in part on the notorious British traitor and spy Harold Adrian Russell "Kim" Philby. Kim Philby himself was in turn constructed (self-constructed?) along the lines of Kipling's Kim. Born in Ambala in the Punjab, one of Kim's haunts, of British parents, Kim Philby earned his nickname from his baby fluency in Punjabi (Knightley 24). Philby's "eminently distasteful father" (as Le Carré called him [Page et al. 4]), St. John Philby, was a role-playing, self-dramatizing Indian Civil Service officer who later operated in Middle Eastern desert kingdoms as an Arabist adventurer—simultaneously an empire-builder, intelligence gatherer, oil-rights agent, and Cadillac salesman. According to Le Carré's extended analysis of Kim and St. John Philby in his introduction to *The Philby Case*:

> Duplicity for Kim Philby was something of a family tradition. . . . From his father, Kim acquired the neo-Fascist instincts of a slightly berserk English gentleman; from his father, the Establishment's easy trick of rationalizing selfish decisions and dressing them in the clothes of a higher cause; from his father the cartographer's memory; for he no more forgot a word or a gesture than another man forgot the way home; from his father the scholar's perceptions which enabled him to keep track of his own complicated treachery. And he could hardly fail, when his father delivered him over to the Establishment for his education to feel already that he was being trained in the enemy camp. Like Kipling's boy, one feels, he was already waiting for the call: *"It was intrigue, of course—he knew that much, he had known all evil since he could speak—but what he loved was the game for its own sake—the stealthy prowl through the dark gullies and lanes. . . ."* [Page et al. 4–5; italics in original].

The affinity between Kipling's Kim and Kim Philby is a leitmotiv of *The Philby Conspiracy* by Bruce Page, David Leitch, and Phillip Knightley, a book which takes as its epigraph Kipling's verses in praise of "Allah, Who gave me two / Separate sides to my head."

4. My own experience in teaching *Kim* to intelligent undergraduates in both children's literature classes and an Anglo-Indian/Indo-Anglican literature class suggests that the book is very hard reading for all but experienced readers of Kipling and/or inhabitants and residents of India. Students in the children's literature class, mostly junior and senior English majors, found *Kim* difficult in the multiplicity of its language codes, the difficulty of its idioms, the subtlety of its plotting, and the range of its political, historical, and social references. They regarded it as vastly more dif-

ficult than any other text in the course, even the two *Alice* books. Students in the Indian literature course considered *Kim* more difficult than *A Passage to India* and comparable in complexity to *Midnight's Children*.

5. Indeed, any imagining of a grown-up Kim is a dubious enterprise. Timeri Murari has recently ventured a two-novel sequel to *Kim* in his *The Imperial Agent* (1989) and *The Last Victory* (1990). The books are dogged works of period reconstruction, half swashbuckling romance and half political revisionism. A radicalized Kim idealistically repudiates his imperial service on behalf of an independent India and the love of fair Parvati. Murari's Kim is a man not a boy, and a good man at that; but sadly without the duplicity of either adolescence or spycraft. Murari's hero is a flat pasteboard figure.

6. An abbreviated and undeveloped version of this paper was presented as "Crossing and Double-Crossing Cultural Barriers in Kipling's *Kim*" at the Children's Literature Association Conference at Carleton University, Ottawa, in May 1987 and later printed in *Cross Culturalism in Children's Literature: Selected Papers from the 1987 International Conference of the Children's Literature Association* (1988), ed. Susan Gannon and Ruth A. Thompson, 61–65. I am especially grateful to Barbara Rosen for her comments on subsequent drafts of the essay.

Works Cited

Chaudhuri, Nirad. "The Finest Story About India—in English." *Encounter* 13 (April 1957): 47–53.

Davis, Boyd H. "Childe Reader and the Sausserian Paradox." *Children's Literature Association Quarterly* 7 (Fall 1982): 36–38.

Desani, G. V. *All About H. Hatterr*. 1948. New Paltz, N.Y.: McPherson and Co., 1986.

Forster, E. M. *A Passage to India*. 1924. New York: Harcourt Brace Jovanovich, 1984.

Hutchins, Francis G. *The Illusion of Permanence: British Imperialism in India*. Princeton: Princeton University Press, 1967.

JanMohamed, Abdul R. "The Economy of Manichean Allegory: The Function of Racial Difference in Colonialist Literature." *Critical Inquiry* 12 (Autumn 1985): 59–87.

Kettle, Arnold. "What is Kim?" In *The Morality of Art*, ed. D. W. Jefferson. New York: Barnes and Noble, 1969. 210–21.

Kinkead-Weekes, Mark. "Vision in Kipling's Novels." In *Kipling's Mind and Art: Selected Critical Essays*, ed. Andrew Rutherford. Stanford: Stanford University Press, 1964. 197–234.

Kipling, Rudyard. *Kim*. Vol. 19 of *The Writings in Prose and Verse of Rudyard Kipling*. 1901. New York: Charles Scribner's Sons, 1916.

———. *Something of Myself*. Vol. 24 of *The Collected Works of Rudyard Kipling*. 1941. New York: AMS Press, 1970.

Knightley, Phillip. *The Master Spy: The Story of Kim Philby*. New York: Alfred A. Knopf, 1989.

Le Carré, John. *A Perfect Spy*. Harmondsworth: Penguin, 1986.

McClure, John. "Problematic Presence: The Colonial Other in Kipling and Conrad." In *The Black Presence in English Literature*, ed. David Dubydeen. Manchester: Manchester University Press, 1985. 154–67.

Murari, Timeri. *The Imperial Agent*. New York: St. Martin's Press, 1989.

———. *The Last Victory*. New York: St. Martin's Press, 1990.

Page, Bruce, David Leitch, and Phillip Knightley. Intro. John Le Carré. *The Philby Conspiracy*. Garden City, N.Y.: Doubleday, 1968.

Parry, Benita. *Delusions and Discoveries: Studies on India in the British Imagination 1880–1930*. Berkeley and Los Angeles: University of California Press, 1972.

Rushdie, Salman. *Midnight's Children*. 1981. London: Picador, 1982.

Said, Edward, intro. *Kim*. Harmondsworth: Penguin Books, 1987. 7–46.

Seymour-Smith, Martin. *Rudyard Kipling*. New York: St. Martin's Press, 1990.

Shavit, Zohar. *Poetics of Children's Literature*. Athens and London: University of Georgia Press, 1986.

Stewart, David H. "Aspects of Language in *Kim*." *Kipling Journal* 57 (June 1983): 25–39.

Tompkins, J. M. S. *The Art of Rudyard Kipling*. Lincoln: University of Nebraska Press, 1959.

Trilling, Lionel. "Kipling." In *The Liberal Imagination*. 1950. Garden City, N.Y.: Doubleday, 1953. 120–29.

Williams, Patrick. "*Kim* and Orientalism." In *Kipling Considered*, ed. Phillip Mallett. New York: St. Martin's Press, 1989. 33–55.

Wurgaft, Lewis D. *The Imperial Imagination: Magic and Myth in Kipling's India*. Middletown, Conn.: Wesleyan University Press, 1983.

The Socratic Pilgrimage of the Elephant's Child

Howard R. Cell

At his trial, Socrates suggests that it was the question put by his friend Chaerephon to the priestess at Delphi, "whether there was anyone wiser than Socrates," which compelled him to devote his life to philosophical inquiry (*Apology* 7 [21a]).[1] The oracle's response, "that there was no one" (ibid.), had to be true, of course, since it would be improper for the god to lie. But what, precisely, did the god mean? "After puzzling about this for some time, Socrates reluctantly began to interview everyone who had a reputation for wisdom—politicians, poets, skilled craftspeople; and he urges the jury to think of these interviews as a sort of pilgrimage" (7–8 [21a–22a]).

Even though this pilgrimage was undertaken as a matter of religious duty, "it aroused against Socrates a great deal of hostility, and hostility of a particularly bitter and persistent kind" (9 [23a]), which eventually led to his indictment and trial. After the jury had determined that he was indeed guilty and had sentenced him to death, Socrates offered the following prophecy to those who voted against him:

> You have brought about my death in the belief that through it you will be delivered from submitting your conduct to criticism: but I say that the result will be just the opposite. You will have more critics . . . and being younger they will be harsher to you and will cause you more annoyance. [24 (39c, d)]

Now, in my view, one of Socrates' more important youthful successors is the Elephant's Child. I do not assume that Kipling had Socrates, or a Socratic pilgrimage, in mind when he wrote "The Elephant's Child." Perhaps, as Socrates claims, "it is not wisdom that enables authors to write their works, but a kind of instinct or inspiration, such as you find in seers and prophets who deliver all their sublime messages without knowing in the least what they

Children's Literature 20, ed. Francelia Butler, Barbara Rosen, and Judith A. Plotz (Yale University Press, © 1992 by The Children's Literature Foundation, Inc.).

mean" (8 [22c]). But since the concept of pilgrimage is ubiquitous in human experience and in the literary tradition, it is hardly surprising that Kipling would utilize this concept at some point. What may seem surprising are the parallels between a Socratic pilgrimage and the journey of the Elephant's Child to the banks of the Limpopo River. Yet, as I shall argue, the Elephant's Child does replicate the principal features of a Socratic pilgrimage, and she even fulfills Socrates' most preposterous wish.[2]

One Elephant, but a New Elephant

In the *Republic*, Socrates—with the concurrence of his interlocutor—claims that one "who is finical about his studies, especially when he is young and cannot yet know . . . what is useful and what is not, is not a lover of learning or a lover of wisdom. But the one who feels no distaste in sampling every study, and who attacks his task of learning gladly and cannot get enough of it, him we shall justly pronounce the lover of wisdom, the philosopher" (714 [475b, c]). Now, this claim provides the three essential characteristics of a genuine philosopher: openness to every sort of knowledge, enjoyment in the process of study, and an insatiable appetite for learning. Certainly, the Elephant's Child fits this description.

Most obvious is the fact that the Elephant's Child too is "full of 'satiable curtiosity, and that means [she] asked ever so many questions" (Kipling 63). But since the scope of her usual questions encompasses the whole of her immediate sense experience, while her "new fine question . . . 'What does the crocodile have for dinner?' " (64) extends into the unknown, the Elephant's Child also evidences an extraordinary willingness to taste every kind of learning. Extraordinary, that is, because she is never deterred by the predictable reaction of her "dear families" to any of her questions, but especially to this one. Rather, this 'satiable Elephant's Child proceeds undaunted until she encounters the object of her quest. And when the Crocodile confirms his identity, by a distinctive act as well as by an express statement,

> the Elephant's Child grew all breathless, and panted, and kneeled down on the bank and said, "You are the very person I have been looking for all these long days. Will you please tell me what you have for dinner?" [68]

Such excitement at the prospect of learning the answer to her question surely indicates that she "attacks the task of learning gladly." I take it as established, then, that the Elephant's Child fulfills the three defining characteristics of a genuine philosopher, as stipulated by Socrates.

A Sort of Pilgrimage, to the Limpopo River

Now to become a philosopher, at least in Socrates' sense, requires that one undertake "a sort of pilgrimage" with certain specifiable characteristics and an uncertain, yet supremely desirable, outcome. The pilgrim must first provision herself with skill in the art of questioning. In the *Phaedo* (78–81 [96a–99c]), Socrates supplies an account of his own philosophical development which exhibits that skill, while noting a shift from questions about causation in the natural order to questions about meaning and purpose in the human order. Thus, when the oracle's claim was brought to his attention, Socrates became appropriately perplexed:

> What does the god mean? Why does he not use plain language? I am only too conscious that I have no claim to wisdom, great or small, so what can he mean by asserting that I am the wisest man in the world? [*Apology* 7 (21b)]

The capacity for such well-focused and fecund perplexity surely equipped Socrates most suitably for his sort of pilgrimage. So too, the Elephant's Child, having first become perplexed about everything in the scope of her immediate environment, then proceeds to ask a question which falls outside that scope and which, for that very reason, is "new and fine." Like Socrates, she has honed her questioning skill on what is observable but then shifts the focus of her perplexity to what is not (or at least not immediately) observable. This skill, then, should be added to the bananas, sugarcane, and melons as provisions for her journey.

The occurrence of a particular focal concern or question is itself a distinct, second characteristic of the Socratic pilgrimage, for such a question supplies both a goal and a method for achieving that goal. Again, the focal question for Socrates himself is, "What does the god mean [by asserting that there is no one wiser than Socrates]?" As already suggested, Socrates' perplexities in natural science led him "to the conclusion that he was uniquely unfitted for this form of inquiry—indeed, he was so befogged by these speculations that he unlearned even what he thought he knew" (*Phaedo* 78 [96c]). The oracle's claim was peculiarly providential, then, since it offered Socrates the opportunity to begin a new form of inquiry, and one for which it seems he was uniquely fitted. That inquiry, furthermore, turned his "unlearning" to account, by compelling him to compare himself with "everyone who had a reputation for wisdom." For the logic of "wiser than" requires a comparative judgment, and Socrates realized that the relevant kind of wisdom to be compared was precisely the willingness to acknowledge one's ignorance, and even to engage in unlearning in order to achieve authentic ignorance.

But to what end? Socrates states that by exposing the pretentiousness of others he is "helping the cause of God"—as well as furnishing his followers with considerable amusement on the side (*Apology* 9 [23b, c]). Is the god's purpose merely to use Socrates to bring pretentious folk down a peg? Rather, it seems to me, the purpose of the god—and it is Apollo whose oracle is at issue—is so well known to Socrates and to his immediate audience that it is quite unnecessary to identify that intention any further. For it is the principle very briefly, though by no means simply, expressed in the motto of the Delphic oracle: Know thyself! Thus Socrates' pilgrimage, his series of interviews, has as its goal the acquisition of self-knowledge, and it employs the one method which is most likely to enable Everyperson to achieve that goal: namely, to bring each pilgrim into a condition of perplexity about what it means to be a self. This usually requires the removal of a major obstacle—the pretentious assumption that one already has this knowledge—by means of interpersonal comparisons.[3]

Though the Elephant's Child's focal question, "What does the Crocodile have for dinner?" may seem altogether unlike that of Socrates, it turns out to be remarkably similar, if not precisely equivalent. In the first place, the raising of the question is equally providential and timely. Though she had already "asked questions about everything that [she] saw, or heard, or felt, or smelt, or touched, still [she] was full of 'satiable curtiosity" (64). Given the exhaustive nature of her questioning, at least as to type, what more could she ask? Or rather, where could she go but up? to a question that she had never asked before, one she may have been enticed to ask by the precession of the equinoxes, or, in other words, the peregrinations of Apollo. At any rate, up to a different type of question: a question which seems to involve a simple matter of empirical discovery, about food chains and all that, but which turns out to be self-referential and indeed to require a transformation of the very own self of the Elephant's Child.

To be sure, this transformation was, from the initial perspective of the Elephant's Child, an unintended consequence. But it was the goal implicit in her pilgrimage, just as the goal of Socrates' own pilgrimage was more assumed than stated. And, just as Socrates derived, from the oracle's claim, the one method most likely to enable him to reach the goal of self-knowledge (in accordance with the oracle's motto), the Elephant's Child receives crucial procedural instructions from the Kolokolo Bird: "Go to the banks of the great grey-green, greasy Limpopo River, all set about with fever-trees, and find out" (65). So the Elephant's Child now knows where to go, if not precisely what to do when she gets there. Even though Socrates seems to realize the dangers that a persistent quest for the answer to his focal question will involve, as his reluctance to begin his pilgrimage implies, while the Elephant's Child displays no such awareness, at least until the Crocodile gives his answer, the goals and methods entailed by their respective focal questions do seem to have much in common.

In addition to ensuring that she is equipped with skill in the art of questioning and that her focal question supplies both goal and method for her journey, the Socratic pilgrim must be fully committed to "go the distance," though dangers of many kinds will surely be encountered along the way. Socrates does acknowledge that he began his pilgrimage "with considerable reluctance," and he "had not gone very far before he realized with distress and alarm that he was making himself unpopular; but he felt compelled to put his religious duty first . . . [and] to interview everyone who had a reputation for wisdom" (*Apology* 8 [21e]). As Socrates subsequently remarks to the jury,

> it would be shocking inconsistency on my part, gentlemen, if, when the officers whom you chose to command me assigned me my position at Potidaea and Amphipolis and Delium [the sites of three critical battles during the Peloponnesian War], I remained at my post like anyone else and faced death, and yet afterwards, when God appointed me, as I supposed and believed, to the duty of leading the philosophic life, examining

myself and others, I were then through fear of death or of any other danger to desert my post [that is, to refuse to undertake that sort of pilgrimage]. [15 (28d–29a)]

Thus, not even the threat of death deters Socrates from his pilgrimage.

Likewise, the Elephant's Child, though seemingly unaware of the potential risks to her life, remarks to the Kolokolo Bird,

"My father has spanked me, and my mother has spanked me; all my aunts and uncles have spanked me for my 'satiable curtiosity; and *still* I want to know what the Crocodile has for dinner!" [64–65; Kipling's emphasis]

Moreover, she follows the advice of the Kolokolo Bird, despite the fact that it was given with a "mournful cry." Though still a child, she journeys ever so far and very much alone—"from Graham's Town to Kimberly to Khama's country, and then, east by north, to the banks of the great grey-green, greasy Limpopo River, all set about with fever-trees" (65–66). Finally, she receives from the Bi-Coloured-Python-Rock-Snake the most severe and painful spanking ever. But—after "politely saying good-bye and helping to coil him up on the rock again—[she] went on" (67). I thus find no evidence that the Elephant's Child was ever the least bit hesitant, or even reluctant, to continue her pilgrimage. Nor, when she encountered the Crocodile at last, did she flinch—as he winked one eye, and then the other, or wept crocodile tears, or said, "Come hither, Little One . . . and I'll whisper" (67–68). How seductive could he get? And yet, she proceeds to "put [her] head down close to the Crocodile's musky, tusky mouth" (68). Now that's real dedication!

On the other hand, and no less remarkable, is the fact that the Socratic pilgrim can expect helpers to come forward when help is needed.[4] Acceptance of this help is really a special form of nonpretentiousness: namely, the recognition that one needs the assistance of others in order to reach one's goal, and that such assistance must be graciously accepted. In order to answer his own new fine question regarding the god's meaning, Socrates is helped by all those he encounters, and examines, along the way. They did not necessarily intend to help him, of course, but he couldn't have made all those comparative judgments without them. In order to determine the dietary inclinations of the Crocodile, the Elephant's Child first

receives procedural advice from the Kolokolo Bird and then substantial assistance from the Bi-Coloured-Python-Rock-Snake. And
finally, the Crocodile is himself a helper, though unwittingly; he
does suggest one possible answer to the dietary question after all.

Now, the aid supplied by the Bi-Coloured-Python-Rock-Snake is
given before, during, and after the encounter of the Elephant Child
with the Crocodile. Before, he obliquely confirms the validity of the
Kolokolo Bird's advice; in response to the first question that the
Elephant's Child asks him, he says, " '*Have* I seen a Crocodile?' in a
tone of dretful scorn. 'What will you ask me next?' " (66; Kipling's
emphasis). How reassuring to know that she is in the right place
to find an answer to her focal question! But when she proceeds
to put that question to the Bi-Coloured-Python-Rock-Snake, she
misinterprets his response. That is, given her prior experience, in
which all her "dear families" have spanked her for her curiosity
she assumes that his spanking her "with his scalesome, flailsome
tail" is "the same thing" (66–67). But in fact it's quite a different
thing: his scornful response to her first question had implied that
he was qualified to answer the second; yet he spanks her instead. To
her credit, the Elephant's Child initially recognizes that this is odd,
but she quickly dismisses her perplexity and conflates his spanking
with all the others. The Bi-Coloured-Python-Rock-Snake doesn't
set her straight about this, for he understands the difference between an answer supplied by an apparent authority such as himself
and one based on personal experience with the Crocodile. And so,
like an even more famous reptile, he beguiles the Elephant's Child
(albeit with a spanking instead of an apple); but, unlike his ancestor,
he stays close by and offers direct assistance when the Crocodile's
answer becomes "too butch for be," as the Elephant's Child so aptly
puts it. Afterward, though obliquely and patiently, he helps the Elephant's Child understand what that answer could mean, even if it
isn't quite what the Crocodile meant. But I shall return later to the
ways in which the answer is "good for [her]" (71).

Finally, while the Socratic pilgrim can expect help from some,
she must also expect misunderstanding and hostility from others.
This is but one of the dangers to be encountered on such a journey, though it was especially prominent in Socrates' case. Thus, he
observes that his young associates

> take me as their model, and go on to try to question other
> persons. Whereupon, I suppose, they find an unlimited num-

ber of people who think that they know something, but really know little or nothing. Consequently their victims become annoyed, not with themselves but with me, and they complain that there is a pestilential busybody called Socrates who fills young people's heads with wrong ideas. If you ask them what he does, and what he teaches that has this effect, they have no answer, not knowing what to say. But as they do not want to admit their confusion, they fall back on the stock charges against any philosopher. . . . They would be very loath, I fancy, to admit the truth—which is that they are being convicted of pretending to knowledge when they are entirely ignorant. [9 (23c, d)]

Socrates organizes his remarks to the jury by considering first the accusations that have been made against him for at least a generation, and then the specific charges brought against him by Meletus (with the connivance of two others, Anytus and Lycon). But these turn out to be essentially equivalent to "the stock charges against any philosopher," to which Socrates alludes in the above passage. Thus, even before he cross-examines Meletus he convicts this accuser of entire ignorance regarding what he, Socrates, actually does and what he teaches his young followers to do. Meletus, that is, misunderstands the goal and method of a Socratic pilgrimage. But since in Socrates' own case, this had included interviews with poets, who were unable to explain what their poems meant even when they contained profound insights, and since Meletus was "aggrieved on behalf of the poets" (10 [23e]), Meletus' only recourse was to "fall back on the stock charges against *any* philosopher" (emphasis mine). As a result, it might be more correct to say that philosophy itself is on trial, with Socrates serving merely as its contemporary representative.[5]

Well, much the same could be said about the reaction of "her family" to the Elephant's Child. To be sure, when she first posed her new fine question, "Everybody said, 'Hush!' in a loud and dretful tone, and they spanked [her] immediately and directly, without stopping, for a long time" (65). But this response does not mean that any of them really know the answer. In the first place, the Elephant's Child observes to the Kolokolo Bird that she has been spanked for her 'satiable curtiosity—that is, merely for being inquisitive. And even the fact that they hushed her reflects the desire, so common among adults, not to have to admit ignorance. For, in the second place, when the Elephant's Child announces her intention to follow the path recommended by the Kolokolo Bird, they spank her once more, but this time "for luck" (65). Wouldn't that have been a strange thing to do if they had actually understood the sort of risk her pilgrimage entailed? Finally, their lack of understanding is exhibited by their behavior when the Elephant's Child returns. Initially, "they were very glad to see [her], and immediately said, 'Come here and be spanked for your 'satiable curtiosity'" (77). Though seemingly unlike Socrates' accusers, insofar as they are "glad" to see the Elephant's Child again, they derive pleasure from the renewed opportunity to spank her. *Plus ça change* . . . ? Not at all; for things really have changed, and to such an extent that "at last [her] dear families [go] off one by one *in a hurry*" (81; Kipling's emphasis) to replicate her pilgrimage. This lack of hesitancy surely bespeaks a lack of awareness as to the dangers involved in such a pilgrimage. Consequently, I take it as established that the family of the Elephant's Child, no less than Meletus, misunderstands the import of a Socratic pilgrimage and falls back on a stock response toward the pilgrim.

Until, that is, they encounter an extremely powerful motive for setting off, one by one, on their own Socratic pilgrimages. In my concluding section, I shall consider how this situation constitutes a fulfillment of Socrates' most preposterous wish: that power and wisdom might be combined in the rulers of a just political order.

'Vantages

In the *Republic*, Socrates stipulates three necessary conditions for the realization of his model of a well-ordered state. So preposterous are these three "waves," as he calls them, that he "shrinks from touching on the matter lest the theory be regarded as nothing but a 'wish-thought'" (689 [450d])—that is, lest the theory be "engulfed" by ridicule. The first wave is that women and men (at least, those who are to serve in the governing class) are to have the same form of life, are to be entirely equal. A second, somewhat larger wave is that there is to be one community of wives, husbands, and their children—in the sense that private cohabitation of men and women and also family relationships are to be forbidden (again, so far as the governing or guardian class is concerned). But the largest, most preposterous wave of all is the third:

> unless . . . either philosophers become kings in our states or
> those whom we now call our kings and rulers take to the pursuit

of philosophy seriously and adequately, and there is a conjunction of these two things, political power and philosophical intelligence, while the motley horde of the natures who at present pursue either apart from the other are compulsorily excluded, there can be no cessation of troubles . . . for our states, nor, I fancy, for the human race either. [712–13 (473c–e)]

Socrates proceeds to recommend, and his interlocutor to accept, the threefold characterization of the genuine philosopher, which, as I suggested earlier, might be as justly asserted of the Elephant's Child as of Socrates himself.

One rather poignant aspect of the situation to which Socrates alludes in the above passage is its self-referential or reflexive import. For since Socrates began his philosophical pilgrimage in obedience to a divine command yet was "debarred from entering public life and from engaging in politics" by another divine command (*Apology* 17 [31d]), he implies that he must himself be included in the "motley horde" of those who pursue either philosophy or political power "apart from the other." Notwithstanding this, his dearest wish-thought is for these two things to be combined in someone else at least; and that person, O Best Beloved, is none other than the Elephant's Child. How so?

In reply, it may be helpful to recall two observations made by the Bi-Coloured-Python-Rock-Snake: first, that the Elephant's Child was a "rash and inexperienced traveler whose future career was in danger of being permanently vitiated" by the Crocodile's answer to her new fine question; and second, after that outcome was happily forestalled, that "some people do not know what is good for them" (70, 71). Though the Snake recognizes that the Elephant's Child is rash and inexperienced, he also seems to recognize her potential and so assists in releasing her from the Crocodile. Then, in true Socratic fashion—that is, by skillful intellectual midwifery—he assists her in the process delineated by Diotima in the *Symposium* of "conceiving and bearing the things of the spirit, namely, wisdom and all her sister virtues" (560 [209a]). In other words, once the Elephant's Child has demonstrated her readiness to learn how and why the elongation of her nose into "a really truly trunk" is good for her, the Bi-Coloured-Python-Rock-Snake proceeds, albeit obliquely, to teach her some of its "'vantages."

She first learns how to eliminate certain causes of discomfort (a stinging fly, for instance) and then how to enhance her comfort (by making "a cool schloopy-sloshy mud cap, all trickly behind the ears") and how to gather food more easily. In each case, she acted "before [she] knew what [she] was doing," (75) in the first instance without any prodding from the Bi-Coloured-Python-Rock-Snake. In all three cases, the latter simply remarks: " 'You couldn't have done that with a mere-smear nose' " (75). But, since she herself now realizes what she has done, and how her trunk made it possible, no elaboration is needed. The Snake does offer a brief lecture on an as yet unexperienced but most important advantage of her transformed condition, namely, its potential as a weapon. Her three previous lessons have prepared her for the lecture quite well. For these lessons have given her self-confidence, together with the beginnings of genuine self-knowledge.

Such, at least, is implied by the following circumstances. First, she promises to *remember* the teaching of the Bi-Coloured-Python-Rock-Snake regarding the usefulness of her new trunk as a potential weapon (76). But memory, as Saint Augustine aptly suggests, is the sine qua non of the self: "This force of my memory is incomprehensible to me, even though, without it, I should not be able to call myself myself" (*Confessions*, 226). Second, she explores new applications for her trunk: in particular, its potential uses as a musical instrument to overcome loneliness and as a tool to tidy up the environment (cf. 76–77). Such explorations, moreover, are undertaken autonomously, and this, to be sure, is another index of enhanced self-awareness and self-confidence. In the third place, when she returns home and is told to come and be spanked, she replies: "Pooh, I don't think you peoples know anything about spanking; but I do, and I'll show you" (77). Which she proceeds to do, of course; but more than that, she shows them what can happen when philosophical intelligence and political power are conjoined in a single individual.

How else is one to account for the subtlety with which she discounts the risks involved in her Socratic pilgrimage? When two of her dear brothers (whom she has just knocked "head over heels") ask, "What have you done to your nose?" she replies:

"I got a new one from the Crocodile on the banks of the great grey-green, greasy Limpopo River. . . . I asked him what he had for dinner, and he gave me this to keep." [77]

Disingenuous? Perhaps; but it isn't easy to overturn such a well-established practice as pursuing political power alone. And so she demonstrates the utility of her new trunk (or, as Socrates puts it, her knowledge of "what is useful and what is not") until

> at last things grew so exciting that [her] dear families went off one by one *in a hurry* to the banks of the great grey-green, greasy Limpopo River, all set about with fever-trees, to borrow new noses from the Crocodile. And when they came back nobody spanked anybody anymore. [81; Kipling's emphasis]

Thus, by dint of her acquisition of self-knowledge and of the confidence that should go with it, she is able to give not just an effective, but an utterly convincing, demonstration of her knowledge of spanking (that is, of her political power).[6] This provides her relatives with a sufficient motive to embark on their own Socratic pilgrimages. And when they return, and it becomes possible to replace the hitherto unquestioned hierarchical social order with a more egalitarian one, "nobody spanked anybody anymore." That is, there was a kind of equal empowerment of all the members of the social order. In this way, the Elephant's Child achieves Socrates' seemingly preposterous wish-thought: that our troubles might cease were political power and philosophical intelligence to become embodied in the same persons.

To which, I suppose, one can only say: Just so!

Notes

1. The Stephanus pagination has been supplied (in brackets) for citations from Plato to enable the reader to locate more precisely the passage from the text in question.

2. Though Kipling consistently utilizes the masculine pronoun to refer to the Elephant's Child, I shall assume that he was merely following the conventions of his time and that in fact the Elephant's Child is a female. One reason, and not the least, is that the "person small" to whom this, and the other *Just So Stories*, was addressed kept not just six (as in Kipling's own case), but ten million serving-men whom "*she* sends abroad on *her* own affairs, from the second *she* opens *her* eyes"—as the poem that follows "The Elephant's Child" notes. In other words, since Kipling's immediate audience was his daughter, Josephine, who was a most curious girl (as evidenced by "the one million Hows, the two million Wheres, and the seven million Whys!"), it seems likely that he had a female in mind, even if he followed the convention and used the masculine pronoun to refer to the Elephant's Child. In addition, one can find indications that Socrates expected at least some of his successors to be females: he suggests that he himself would like to be reincarnated as a female artisan; and he argues, as I shall note, that women and men should have the same form of life, and the same opportunity to participate in education and in political rule. Finally, curiosity, when personified, is feminine. And so, the assumption I have made in this article—viz., that the Elephant's Child is female—is entirely plausible.

3. In *Alcibiades I* (an illuminating, if probably spurious, dialogue), Socrates supplies his own version of "the meaning and lesson of the Delphic inscription, Know

thyself." By analogy, "if someone were to say to the eye, 'See thyself,' the meaning would be that the eye should look at that in which it would see itself." More specifically, "if the eye is to see itself, it must look at the eye [of another person] and at that part of the eye [viz., the pupil] where sight which is the virtue of the eye resides." In much the same way, "if the soul is ever to know herself, she too must look at the soul [of another person] and especially at that part of the soul [viz., reason] in which her virtue resides." But this analogical account of the meaning of the oracle's motto follows upon, and is intended to clarify, a discussion of Alcibiades' particular mode of pretentiousness. Thus, the linkage I've drawn between the oracle's motto and its claim about Socrates comes close to explicit development in this rather neglected dialogue. See Jowett, trans., *The Dialogues of Plato*, pp. 768–69 (132d–133c).

As for the claim that pretentiousness is the principal obstacle to acquiring knowledge (whether of the self or of something else), Socrates demonstrates precisely that point by working through a geometry problem with a slave boy for the benefit of Meno. Just after getting the boy to acknowledge that he doesn't know the answer to the problem, to which he has made two incorrect guesses, Socrates turns to Meno and makes the point of the lesson explicit.

> SOCRATES: Observe, Meno, the stage he has reached. . . . At the beginning he did not know. . . . Nor indeed does he know now, but then he thought he knew and answered boldly, as was appropriate—he felt no perplexity. Now, however, he does feel perplexed. Not only does he not know the answer; he doesn't even think he knows.
> MENO: Quite true.
> SOCRATES: Isn't he in a better position now in relation to what he didn't know?
> MENO: I admit that too. . . .
> SOCRATES: In fact we have helped him to some extent toward finding out the right answer, for now not only is he ignorant of it but he will be quite glad to look for it. . . .
> MENO: No doubt.
> SOCRATES: Do you suppose then that he would have attempted to look for, or learn, what he thought he knew, though he did not, before he was thrown into perplexity, became aware of his ignorance, and felt a desire to know?
> MENO: No.
>
> [*Meno* 368 (84a–c)]

4. See Luthi, *Fairytale as Art Form*, 137–38, for an illuminating account of the fairytale hero as deficient and of the role of helpers in compensating for such deficiency.

5. Like the poets, who seem unable to explain what their poems mean, Meletus has brought formal charges against Socrates without any clear notion of what they mean. Socrates' strategy in cross-examining Meletus seems to involve pushing the latter to assign to each charge a meaning that is either wildly implausible or just plain self-contradictory. But he leaves to the ingenuity of his auditors the task of comparing Meletus' charges against him with the stock charges against any philosopher.

6. Though I would much prefer that the exercise of political power as displayed in the penultimate scene of "The Elephant's Child" might involve moral persuasion— or at least symbolize such persuasion—rather than violence, even here Kipling is closer to Socrates' stated position than he was probably aware. Consider Socrates' proposal regarding the quickest and easiest way for true philosophers to establish a well-ordered society: "All those in the city who happen to be older than ten they will send out into the country; and taking over their children, they will rear them— far away from those dispositions they now have from their parents—in their own manners and laws that are such as we described" (*Republic*, 220 [540e–541a]). The

point, of course, is that both Socrates and the Elephant's Child use violence (force with the intent to harm); perhaps both also assume that it is impossible to change the social order in any other way.

Works Cited

Hamilton, Edith, and Huntington Cairns, eds. *The Collected Dialogues of Plato*. Princeton: Princeton University Press, 1961.

Jowett, Benjamin, trans. *The Dialogues of Plato*. New York: Random House, 1920.

Kipling, Rudyard. "The Elephant's Child." In *Just So Stories*. New York: Schocken Books, 1965, 63–81.

Luthi, Max. *The Fairytale as Art Form and Portrait of Man*. Bloomington: Indiana University Press, 1984.

Warner, Rex, trans. *The Confessions of St. Augustine*. New York: New American Library, 1963.

Varia

Just-So Pictures: *Illustrated Versions of* Just So Stories for Little Children

Brian Alderson

For Christmas 1897, the cover of *St. Nicholas* blazoned forth "Rud-yard Kipling's First 'Just-So Story.'" The words were given banner position, in red, at the top of the seasonal cover and then, be-yond the advertisements (which included "A Great Christmas Book for Children": L. Frank Baum's *Mother Goose in Prose*, with illustra-tions by Maxfield Parrish), there came a Christmassy frontispiece by Maud Humphrey and, in pole position, "The Just-So Stories. By Rudyard Kipling."

There was, at this stage, no other title, and the generic heading was followed by an explanatory introduction by the author. "Some stories," he wrote, "are meant to be read quietly and some stories are meant to be told aloud. Some stories are only proper for rainy mornings, and some for long, hot afternoons." Stories like these could be changed as much as the inventor pleased, "but in the eve-ning there were stories meant to put Effie to sleep, and you were not allowed to alter those by one single little word. They had to be told just so; or Effie would wake up and put back the missing sentence. . . ."

These bedtime stories for Effie were three in number and the first of them, Kipling said, "told how the whale got his tiny throat." He then began the story: "Once upon a time there was a whale, and he lived in the sea and he ate fishes . . ." And so, with all the

Children's Literature 20, ed. Francelia Butler, Barbara Rosen, and Judith A. Plotz (Yale University Press, © 1992 by The Children's Literature Foundation, Inc.).

casual address of the speaking storyteller, with all the asides ("*Have* you forgotten the suspenders?") and all the private jokes ("Change here for Winchester, Ashuelot, Nashua, Keene, and stations on the *Fitch*burg road!"), one of the masterpieces of children's literature got under way.

This beginning to the *Just So Stories* (the preliminary definite article, and sometimes the hyphen, have led an uncertain existence) is of considerable importance. Kipling's introduction confirms what could never really be in doubt: that these stories originated in the living—and private—exchange between a teller and a listener, and it claims not only to reflect the oral transaction as it took place, but also to give that transaction validity for more than the single child to whom the story was originally told ("but I think if you catch some Effie rather tired and rather sleepy at the end of the day, and if you begin in a low voice and tell the tales precisely as I have written them down, you will find that Effie will presently curl up and go to sleep").[1]

By thus emphasizing the voice of the storyteller and by setting down the texts "just so" as Effie heard them, Kipling is obviously concerned entirely with words and with their rhythmic alignment. No concession is made to geographical or biological niceties. To the distress of the literal-minded, these are not introductions to natural history. The catalog of the whale's diet is formed for the sake of its sound rather than its accuracy, and although we can imagine " 'stute fish" existing as a distinct species, we shall find them in no ichthyology. By the same token, there is no concession made to illustration. Whale, fish, and mariner subsist only in a flux of words, taking on their dramatic shape from the molding of the sentences. Any attempt to impose a fixed form upon them is bound to limit their freedom as performers in a kind of balletic poem. Moreover, if the design of the whole narrative enterprise is to get Effie to curl up and go to sleep, then observable pictures may sadly interfere with the process.

To the publishers of books and magazines, however, such concerns are deeply unpractical. Not even the sensitive Mary Mapes Dodge could allow "Rudyard Kipling's First Just-So Story" to appear garbed only in its own fine rhetoric. The readers expect something to look at as well as to hear. Pictures must be made. So the blithe Oliver Herford is co-opted, and at the start of the tale in *St. Nicholas* he supplies a decorative title piece and initial letter done in ink and pencil. As the story progresses over the next two page openings its text is fitted into several rectangular spaces, almost entirely surrounded by more pencil drawings by the same artist (fig. 1). These show seriatim the whale and the 'stute fish, the mariner hopping and dancing in the whale's "warm dark inside cupboards," the whale having hiccups, and the mariner making his way up his natal shore. Because Herford was an illustrator of taste and good humor, these large, fairly informal drawings have the right kind of breeziness to make them chime with Kipling's story, but the storyteller does not need them—and this irrelevance is exacerbated by the extent to which they dominate the pages, forming large, insistent frames around the modest patches of words. There was probably an editorial rather than an artistic reason for this, since the story is very short and the proprietors of *St. Nicholas* must have wanted to deck out their scoop as impressively as possible.

From the very beginning, therefore, the printed *Just So Stories* were inescapably married to printed pictures. What happened to the whale story was repeated for its two companions, which appeared in the issues of *St. Nicholas* for January and February 1898: "How the Camel Got His Hump"—so titled—and "how the Rhinoceros got his wrinkly skin," as stated in the opening paragraph. Oliver Herford was again the illustrator, and he adopted a broadly similar graphic style—giving a decorative title and initial letter to the stories and then supplying large surrounding pictorial frames. In "Rhinoceros" he made some play with framing the illustrations and having the frame broken by the Parsee's hat, from which, of course, "the rays of the sun were reflected in more-than-oriental splendour."[2]

Completion of the publication of these three stories in *St. Nicholas* coincided with the terrible events of Kipling's last visit to the United States: the long-running row with Beatty Balestier, Kipling's illness, and the illness and death of the stories' chief recipient, Effie. From the preface to the whale story it would seem that Kipling did not have it in mind to publish any more of the "Just So" stories at that time—although according to Angela Thirkell's recollection (see note 1) he may well have invented and told some of the others by then. With the calamities in America, however, and with the onset of the Boer War, which was to take Kipling to South Africa, there were large hiatuses in the publishing sequence,[3] and nothing happened until March 1900, when the following "Announcement

Figure 1. Oliver Herford's second page of drawings for the first printing of a "Just So" story, from *St. Nicholas*, December 1897. Note how two brief incidents in the story are pictured in a way that dominates the letterpress.

About Mr. Rudyard Kipling" appeared in the Philadelphia magazine *Ladies' Home Journal*:

> When he recovered from his serious illness, and his convalescence had become assured, he turned instinctively to a series of animal stories he had previously had in mind. He took up his long-cherished idea with keen zest and fresh eagerness. The happy result can well be imagined. It is Mr. Kipling at his best. He calls them the "Just So" stories, and they are designed for young and old. . . . The Entire Series will be Published in *The Ladies' Home Journal*. [39]

Editorial ebullience (or even plain ignorance) may have caused the *Journal* to overlook the fact that three of the tales which Mr. Kipling "previously had in mind" had already been published—and to say later, erroneously, that the stories "have been written specially for the *Ladies' Home Journal* and will not appear in any other periodical in the world" (April 1900, page 3). Nevertheless, between April 1900 and October 1902 all the rest of the staple "Just So" collection made their first appearance in the pages of the *Journal*, with the exception of "The Crab That Played with the Sea," which appeared in *Collier's* (as "The Crab That Made the Tides"), and "How the Alphabet Was Made," which, hauntingly framed by the two parts of "Merrow Down," appeared only when the stories were published as a book.[4]

Once again it must have been de rigueur that the stories be illustrated, and the opening announcement included the statement that there would be provided "A WEALTH OF PICTURES BY FRANK VER BECK," who more usually called himself Frank Verbeck. Verbeck had some reputation for drawing animals and for an easy and adaptable pen, very necessary for magazine artists and especially for those who worked for the *Ladies' Home Journal*. This magazine had much larger pages than *St. Nicholas*, and since Kipling's text was set, variably, in two or three columns, there was more need for a pragmatic approach to the pictures. For the first three numbers Verbeck adopted different strategies. "The Elephant's Child" (April 1900) had an almost cartoon-strip accompaniment, with sequences of events being put into squared-off boxes (fig. 2). "The Beginning of the Armadilloes" (May 1900) seems to have presented difficulties—exacerbated by a decision to use more tonal tints—and, with the exception of a surprised jaguar, the pictorial response is de-

"His Aunt, the Ostrich, spanked him with her hard, hard claw."   "His Uncle, the Giraffe, spanked him with his hard, hard hoof."

Figure 2. Two of Frank Verbeck's sequence of framed drawings for "The Elephant's Child," reproduced from the first printing in the *Windsor Magazine*.

cidedly muddy. The same strictures apply to "The Sing-Song of Old Man Kangaroo" (June 1900), where all five framed illustrations have been plonked down on the first page of the story.

After these three stories, another gap occurred, to be ended "as soon as Mr. Kipling resumes his work, upon his return from South Africa," which did not happen until October 1901. By this time there are signs that the *Ladies' Home Journal* was turning into a far more self-conscious, not to say trendy, magazine (Frank Lloyd Wright is to be found advising readers on how to knock up a little cottage in the country), and it treats the last four "Just So" stories rather casually. Frank Verbeck has more or less given in to the half-tone revolution, his line drawings made fuzzy by the use of tonal shading, and for the penultimate story, "The Cat That Walked by Himself" (July 1902), there is no illustration at all—apart from two photographic cats at either end of the title heading.[5] The series concludes with "The Butterfly That Stamped" (October 1902), which is given a single, graceless tone drawing zigzagging down the opening page with the text weaving its way alongside as best it can.

Probably all the arrangements for the publication of these stories in the *Journal* were handled by Kipling's agent, A. P. Watt, who also seems to have issued some stories as pamphlets in Great Britain in order to establish copyright.[6] Presumably A. P. Watt was also responsible (to the chagrin of the *Journal?*) for arranging publication of some stories in British magazines, and thus it comes about that we find some variant pictures and illustrators. "The Elephant's Child" (*Windsor Magazine*, February 1902) retained Verbeck's boxed drawings, but scattered them about more, and even turned two elongated drawings so that they ran vertically up the side of the page. The tone drawings for "How the Leopard Got His Spots" required less adaptation when the story appeared in *Pearson's Magazine* (April 1902) and the pictures benefited from being more evenly spaced.

Two other stories from the main collection were illustrated for the first time in their English printings. "The Cat That Walked by Himself" (*Windsor Magazine*, October 1902) was given four heavily toned pictures by Cecil Aldin, who at this time was making a name for himself as an animal artist. They were not impressive, partly because Aldin's near-photographic representational style ran counter to the hieratic tones of Kipling's fable and partly because the pictures themselves had no graphic consistency, veering from pencil-drawing to wash-drawing effects produced by halftone. Nor can much be said of Lawson Wood's skimpy contribution to "The Crab That Played with the Sea" (*Pearson's Magazine*, August 1902, appearing as "The Crab That Made the Tides"). There are a title headpiece and three sketches in the text, one of them, disconcertingly, a silhouette, and they make no attempt to reflect the force of this tale, which is the one "Just So" story that has its roots in a local myth. (Pau Amma, rising from the sea, looks a bit like a two-gun fortress on the Maginot Line.) The alternative pictures by F. M. Dumond that appeared in the American printing in *Collier's*—also in August 1902—are no improvement. They have a gloom that may suggest the "time of the Very Beginnings" but is more likely the result of the heavy use of mechanical tints printed on inferior paper.[7]

I do not know if Kipling was involved with, or expressed any views about, these ephemeral illustrative contributions to his work. With the emergence of the concept of the stories as a book, however, he conceived a plan whereby his own illustrations would accompany the text. (One drawing had actually done so in "How the First Letter Was Written" [*LHJ*, December 1901], where, between Frank Verbeck's pictures, there occurs the first draft of Taffy's pictorial message that eventually ended up on page 131 of the book itself.)

That Kipling had inherited the artistic flair of his father is well

known, and his decision to illustrate his own stories clearly carried
no dangers in a publishing scene where far less committed or professional standards were to be found in both books and periodicals.
What is of consequence, however, is the kind of illustration that he
chose to do. As Kipling's younger daughter, Elsie, recalled in her
epilogue to Charles Carrington's biography:

> The *Just So Stories* were first told to my brother and myself dur-
> ing those Cape winters [that is, 1900–02], and when written,
> were read aloud to us for such suggestions as could be expected
> from small children. The illustrating of the stories gave their
> author immense pleasure, and he worked at them (mostly in
> Indian ink) with meticulous care and was delighted when we
> approved of the results. [396]

In other words, not only did the stories achieve their final form
through a new bout of "telling," this time in conjunction with the
final manuscript,[8] but the pictorial embellishment was drawn into
the storytelling process. Kipling's "meticulous care" was not so much
a technical procedure as a narrative one; everything to do with the
pictures was designed to heighten the printed story's impact on its
readers or its listeners. Illustration of this kind burrows into the
narrative in order to create pictures as visual events parallel to the
events of the text. As such, they differ from the conventional work
of the magazine illustrators, who are content merely to reflect the
surface of the narrative, photographing what happens rather than
making visual interpretations.

The "immense pleasure" that Kipling took in making these illustrations is not difficult to discern. At its simplest it is to be seen in
the decorated initials that he prepared for each story. These were
not just thematic in the way that Oliver Herford's 'stute fish had
been for the whale story; they also contrived to give a flavor of
place or period in the style of drawing, such as the quasi-"African"
stylization in the "O" of "How the Rhinoceros Got His Skin" or the
runic blade bone for the "H" of "The Cat That Walked by Himself."
There are even private or recondite references built in: "H. Olfen.
Tromsoe. 1847" on the knife at the start of the whale story; "–NAS"
and "–NAW" on the side of the ark in "How the First Letter Was
Written."[9] (Arks figure in various guises through the book as a
punning signature for "R.K." [Fig. 3].)

With the full-page pictures Kipling unleashes an extraordinary

NCE

Figure 3. One of Kipling's arks in the decorated initial at the start of "How the First Letter Was Written." The letter on the pennant bears references to the original sailors on the craft.

array of illustrative devices which testify not only to the pleasure that the challenge was giving him but also to a manifold artistic ingenuity. This is most immediately apparent in his mastery of various graphic styles, of which the extremes can be seen in the two drawings for "How the Leopard Got His Spots." Here, in the picture of Wise Baviaan, is a diagrammatic simplicity of line, heightened only by the solid black of the plinth, while at the end of the story is the jungle scene, which has all the textural complexity of a heavily etched copperplate. Between these two extremes there are pictures that show simple line drawing with only modest shading, as with the Parsee in his palm tree; pictures where there is heavy narrative drawing, employing large quantities of that Indian ink, as with Henry Albert Bivvens going down the whale's throat; and pictures where the narrative line is subordinate to, or mixed with, symbolic patterning, as in the design of the whale looking for Pingle (Fig. 4).

Kipling's command of technique here is combined with a playful attitude toward the illustrations' content. He comments on this himself when he distinguishes between the "truly pictures" and those symbolic utterances like the one of Pau Amma and the Eldest Magician, which he calls "Big Medicine and Strong Magic." In both instances, though, the complete image may have all kinds of internal jokes going on within itself (at least four in so simple a scene as that where Yellow-Dog Dingo chases Old Man Kangaroo) [Fig. 5]). Moreover, Kipling also plays with pictorial potential itself: the map of the Turbid Amazon, which takes half an hour to decipher; the

Figure 4. Kipling's symbolic style: a drawing crammed with images that are explained in his accompanying description.

Figure 5. A seemingly straightforward illustration with a variety of references and jokes included: the three gods of the story in sequence, the third god under a fanciful clock, the Kangaroo with a label on his pouch saying "Patent Fed. Govt. Aust.," and another Kipling ark.

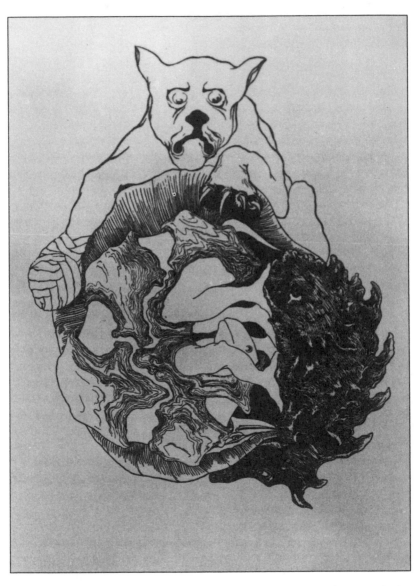

Figure 6. A playful drawing. Turn the page round and the main characters in the story reveal themselves in the concentrated ball.

composite narrative, such as "the whole story of the Jaguar and the Hedgehog and the Tortoise *and* the Armadillo all in a heap" (Fig. 6); and the "puzzle pictures" where the shading is used to camouflage hidden figures (did Maurice Sendak know Kipling's "Cave" when he made his drawings for Jarrell's *Animal Family*?).

But listing such a variety of graphic devices still does not exhaust the strength of the contribution that these illustrations made to the complete *Just So Stories*. There remains the most famous and most distinctive feature: Kipling's parallel commentary. Certainly, this does not exactly count as illustration, but it reinforces the presence of the picture as part of the story and then elaborates upon that presence in order to increase the communion between the storyteller and his audience.

The tone is set from the start, with "This is the picture of the Whale swallowing the Mariner," and the explanation goes on not merely to repeat phrases from the tale but also to add po-faced definitions: "The piece of wood is called the jaws-of-a-gaff." Information is given over and above what is written in the story (for example, the names of the whale and the mariner), and it is put into the same register as the voice of the story itself: "The reason that the sea looks so ooshy-skooshy is because the whale is sucking it all into his mouth."

From this point on there is an almost endless variety of jokes, ironies, and narrative extensions that serve brilliantly to enhance the impact of the stories (already heavily—and happily—re-edited from their magazine form, and also, of course, supplied for the first time with their framing poems).[10] You have only to read the artist's rueful comments on what he hasn't been able to include, or read his circumstantial accounts of the (fictitious) sources from which he derived details, or follow such running jokes as the instructions about not painting the pictures[11] to realize that what is happening here is an authorial game of a kind never played before. Telling readers to look at the illustrations is a traditional ploy ("Observe the *Merry Andrew*," says John Newbery in *The Fairing*; "Pray see them," he says of Margery and Tommy Meanwell, and of many other scenes in *The History of Little Goody Two-shoes*), but no one had ever elaborated it on the scale that Kipling did, or with his total commitment.

This peculiar integrity of the *Just So Stories*, this working of all the elements—diction, drawings, legends—toward the end of heightening the narrative impact, raises a challenging question about the role that illustrations play in imaginative literature for children. How far do they cohere with and enhance the words, how far are they decorative appendages with a more or less independent life? Nobody these days will see those Newbery comments as being much more than a typical editorial interjection, half joke and half puff, from the children's "old friend in St Paul's Church-yard." Even so, he is articulating a consciousness of the relationship between words and pictures that was to be developed in a variety of productive ways in the next century. Thackeray in "The Rose and the Ring" (1854) was one of the first great authors to supply his own illustrations and to try to make them help the dynamic of the story. Lewis Carroll famously supplied sketches of his own for the manuscript *Alice*, some of which were reworked by Tenniel, and then, as publication was planned, the author insisted on getting the pictures to relate exactly to the relevant portions of the text. Kate Greenaway, in *Under the Window* (1879), created one of the earliest examples of a designer picture book, wreathing her watercolors around her own verses for the profitable delectation of Edmund Evans.

All such experiments—and in their own time, they *were* experiments—sharpen our awareness of the potential of illustration to complement texts. The pictures do not, however, possess the same organic relationship to the text as do Kipling's for the *Just So Stories*, and they do not raise so acutely the question of irreplaceability. Certainly, Thackeray enhances the burlesque of his "fire-side pantomime" with inimitable characters; certainly, the Carroll and Tenniel partnership creates an unsurpassed suite of drawings for two of the most remarkable fantasies ever written for children; but neither of these has the same degree of referential playfulness as the *Just So Stories*—the running reciprocation of story, design, and commentary.

For this reason the *Just So Stories* confronts the assessors of children's books with a dilemma. A plausible case can be argued that Kipling's text with illustrations is so indissoluble a unity that any interference with it injures not only his final intentions for the book but also the book's impact on the child reader. To tell the story of, say, "The Beginning of the Armadilloes" without the wonderful, absorbing "inciting map of the Turbid Amazon done in Red and Black," or without the "whole story" design (and the attendant information that "the Jaguar's pet name with his Mummy was Doffles"), is first to eliminate bits of the author from his own book, and second to deprive the reader of half the fun of the story. Furthermore, one can also see these stories, with their accompanying narrative pictures, as forming a sum that is greater than the constituent parts. The book is not a lucrative recycling of stories brought together from a scatter of magazines, but a carefully planned progression from the simplicity of the opening invocation ("In the sea, once upon a time, O my Best Beloved . . .") to the Arabian grotesqueries of "The Butterfly That Stamped." As Kipling himself said, we are in the presence of "Big Medicine and Strong Magic."

But it is not in the nature of book publishing or, very often, of book criticism, to be content with such eternal verities. To go on reprinting ad infinitum the same text with the same pictures (albeit in different formats) smacks of lack of enterprise; and to go on appreciating an unchanging presentation, without allowing for the possibility of alternative interpretations, may seem like critical authoritarianism. And so it comes about, all too predictably, that Kipling's *Just So Stories* are perceived not as the composer's final statement of his subject but as the raw material for other people's themes and variations. Almost from the start Kipling's purpose for his book came to be distorted.

To begin with, the change was in the direction of amplification rather than abridgment. Kipling's taut black-and-white designs were clearly too austere for American tastes, and, in 1912, Doubleday (the firm of Kipling's great chum "Effendi") put out an edition in which the original illustrations were supplemented by twelve colored plates by Joseph M. Gleeson. These were unnecessary, but harmless, and for another thirty years they remained almost the only incursion into the standard presentation, apart from the curious conversion, by agreement, of four stories into painting books with pictures worked up by an artist thought to be Miss Day Hodgetts (see bibliography). There were, understandably, variations in format and some excerptings of stories for schoolbook editions and the like; there was also a replacement in the United States of the original two color dust jacket with a more garish one by Dorothy Lathrop, but these were of marginal critical consequence.

From 1942 onward, however, publishers began to make more dramatic incursions into the *Just So Stories*. The first to do so was Doubleday itself, through its Garden City Press, which in 1942 brought out individual picture-book versions of four of the stories, illustrated by Feodor Rojankovsky. These were very similar in format and illustrative style to the mass-market Little Golden Books, which also arrived on the scene in 1942. They were squarish picture books, 9 × 6½ inches, of thirty-two pages, with the endleaves used as pastedowns, and the illustrations were prepared in color and in black and white for long-run lithographic printing. The four titles were marketed separately on a grand scale (and in 1947 Rojankovsky added two more stories to the series), but as an initial publicity ploy copies were also sold as a set in a cardboard box, whose lid opened to form a pop-up—a composite scene made up from elements of all four books (Fig. 7).

This pop-up is the only feature of Rojankovsky's series to touch on the playfulness that was central to Kipling's originals. The books themselves were typical examples of the artist at his gaudiest and most vulgar, and they make clear at the start of *Just So* exploitation the fatal weaknesses of picture-book interpretations. Leaving aside the facts that each story is now separated from its fellows, that the bridging poems are omitted, and that Kipling's pictures are necessarily abandoned, such treatments cannot help but also distract attention from the fluency of the storytelling that is the essential feature of the collection. The imagery of language is displaced by the far more limited imagery of the series of pictures, some of which will, in the nature of things, be produced for no better reason than to spread the text through a given number of pages. Artificiality takes over.

Such a dismemberment of Kipling's original intentions does not have to be so brutally carried out as in the Rojankovsky series, but there is not much evidence in later picture-book versions to show illustrators bringing any greater sensitivity to bear. Certainly in all the titles listed (and occasionally annotated) in the bibliography that follows this essay there is a great diversity of styles. We find, for example, at one end of the scale the twenty-five-cent Disneyfications of the Rand-McNally Elf Books of 1955, which show an influence from both Rojankovsky and Little Golden Books. At the other end, however, there are the trendy studio productions of illustrators like Ulla Kampmann and Heinz Looser, whose collages or use of flat patterning suffocates all the life and movement of the text. (Both illustrate "The Elephant's Child," which proves to be the most frequently chosen text for one-off productions.) In between such excesses there are the fairly conventional, semirealistic interpretations

Figure 7. Rojankovsky's pop-up lid for the packaged *Just So Stories* series. (The books can be seen below.) The scene incorporates the chief characters from the four stories that have been used. Reproduced by permission of the Pierpont Morgan Library, New York. PML 84898-901.

of Leonard Weisgard or Lorinda Bryan Cauley, who concentrate so heavily on pictorialism that they overwhelm the texts with artistry. Only Don Madden, who employs a heavy cartoonist's pen, gives the impression that he has understood the need for vigorous visual comedy in the pictorial interpretations.

Just as these picture-book editions obtrude themselves between Kipling and his audience, so too do the illustrators who have set about producing complete or selected versions of the stories. Once again the potential for calamity was demonstrated at the very start with Nicolas Mordvinoff's *Just So Stories* of 1952: "All twelve immortal tales with 72 pictures in full color." This large album (11 × 9½ inches) is an example of the illustrative kitsch of its period, with offset-litho pictures intruding randomly into the text and with no respect paid to the nuances of the storytelling. Walt Disney casts his shadow over some of the images (see the cute Taffy and the blue-eyed son of a jaguar), while the transitional poems—almost always omitted from the single-story picture books—are omitted here too.

No improvement on Mordvinoff is discernible in the album selections illustrated by H. B. Vestal in 1957 and Victor Ambrus in 1982—the first a rather stolid, near-representational effort and the second a typically frenzied splurge. Much the oddest treatment, though, is Doubleday's seventy-fifth anniversary edition, which was illustrated by Etienne Delessert and introduced by Nelson Doubleday, "Effendi's" grandson:

> We believe Mr. Delessert's pictures capture the wry flavor of the stories and are ideally suited as a means of introducing another generation of readers to an ever-popular book.

Neither claim bears consideration (as you might expect from anyone who thinks that the stories have a "wry flavor"), but this over-sophisticated *livre d'artiste* once again shows the lengths to which publishers will go to circumvent an admission that Kipling himself is the man "ideally suited. . . ." Delessert applies semisurrealistic tricks—which have no narrative content—to the stories and, in one notable instance, where the crocodile draws red blood from the elephant's trunk, betrays the depth of his failure to comprehend what the tales require from him.

Of all the attempts to introduce "another generation of readers" to the *Just So Stories*, perhaps the most zealous is the one carried out by Macmillan of London between 1983 and 1985, just before

Kipling went out of copyright in 1987: a twelve-book series of all the stories with a different illustrator chosen for each. (The series was later reissued in paperback, with variant covers. The publishers were fairly cavalier over whether or not they included the poetry, and with some stories the related poem turns up in the paperback edition but not in its parent hardback.)

This series brought to Kipling some of the best-known names of British illustration in the early 1980s: Pauline Baynes, Quentin Blake, Michael Foreman, Charles Keeping, William Stobbs. By and large, though, their response to the project was lackluster—an effort to fill out Kipling's little stories so that they could be issued as a uniform series of thirty-two-page books.[12] Only with Alan Baker's treatment of that fairly complex late story "The Butterfly That Stamped" did one see, suddenly emergent, a picture-book style that went some way to matching the narrative qualities of its text. Baker's pastiche "Eastern" atmosphere, his use of elegant borders, his commitment to powerful, realistic draftsmanship as a substructure for his color work, and, finally, his use of elfin motifs all demonstrated a response to Kipling that was thought through rather than abjectly mechanical.

For all the intelligence of Alan Baker's interpretation of this one story, however, and for all the responsiveness to Kipling's text in Jonathan Langley's more recent *Just So* series (1988), and the two Warne Picture Classics by Krystyna Turska (1987–88), the conclusion remains inescapable: from Gleeson onward, the motivation behind the reillustration of the *Just So Stories* has been largely commercial, with only marginal consideration being given to the nature of Kipling's texts or to the most desirable way in which these may be presented to the child reader.

An argument in defense of publishers may be advanced along the lines of the so-called "unapproachability" or "austerity" of Kipling's original conception. In his article "When the Kipling Had to Stop," (see note 12), Nicholas Tucker complains that Kipling's "'dead black' technique . . . obscured important detail" and that these "densely written tales" really required more numerous pictures in order to become "far more approachable" (24). That is a view which I have also heard expressed by some teachers and children's librarians, and, as I have indicated, it was almost certainly the reason why Gleeson's illustrations were commissioned in 1912. The plates would bring a colorful glow to the stark black-and-white

pages of the original, but Gleeson could not work out a satisfactory
way of designing plates to match the author's draftsmanship, so he
simply produced a number of paintings in varied modes (realistic,
stylized, decorative) in the hope that their variability would mingle
tidily with Kipling's own variability.

In doing so he was, of course, only playing a supporting role to
Kipling himself. Those illustrators who came after stand out more
starkly as diminishers of their source material. Whether they were
working in the comic-book register of Rojankovsky or "Nicolas,"
whether they were trying out modish Continental designs like Delessert, Maestro, or Looser, or whether they were adapting natural
history, like Weisgard or Cauley, the impulse behind their work was
contractual rather than committed. As with so many "ever-popular
books" the *Just So Stories* are seen by publishers as ready material
for both mass-market enterprise and experimentation, and illustrators emerge who can be commissioned for or directed toward the
work. Can one really believe that twelve good artists and true were
burning to illustrate one "Just So" story apiece for the Macmillan
series of 1983–85? Was it pure coincidence that Michael Foreman,
Meg Rutherford, and Safaya Salter all found themselves illustrating
the complete stories against a publishing date of 1987? The spontaneous urge here was not to say something about Kipling but to
cash in on the market.

Despite suggestions that Kipling's stories need to be reillustrated
because they are "inaccessible," very few modifications are ever
made to his text. Occasionally words deemed to cause offense may
be removed, or, as in the privately printed "Rhinoceros," inexplicable small changes may be made, but the "Upside-Down" version
of "The Elephant's Child" is the only example to carry out a drastic—and disastrous—rewriting of the story. From this it follows that
the transformation that is sought by publishers is a transformation
of appearance, and in the majority of reillustrated editions, the
eye for which the appearance is altered is either that of the house
editor or of the artist himself. The interpretations by Rojankovsky
or "Nicolas" were not undertaken with either Kipling or the child
audience as "implied lookers," but with an awareness of the kind of
illustration that was expected in the mass market. The semisurreal-
ist articulations of Delessert were essentially solipsistic—an ego-trip
at the author's expense.

Certainly, some illustrators—most notably perhaps Don Madden, Jonathan Langley, and Krystyna Turska—bring to their work a sense of the vigorous movement and the sustained comedy of the *Just So Stories*. Some of their sportive ideas—Turska's "illuminated" framework for the camel poem, for instance—carry a sense of what the author might have done in their position. But the author would not have needed to, since he had already perfected the process. For him there was no implied reader other than his living audience. The stories were told as they were told in the High and Far-off Times; the pictures were drawn with an energy that was generated directly from the sound of that telling. Word and image fuse into a unity for teller and listener alike. To say that Kipling is the only illustrator of the *Just So Stories* whose work can be countenanced is not critical dogmatism but an acknowledgment of the privilege that we too may join his audience.

Notes

1. Success with Effie led Kipling to extend his audience—perforce, once Effie was beyond his speaking. Angela Thirkell (née Mackail) has put famously on record how "during long warm summers Cousin Ruddy used to try out the *Just So Stories* on a nursery audience" (i.e., herself and one or more of his own children). The passage is given in Carrington (220–21), and it includes the description of his ritual incantation of the phrases.

2. Few illustrators (including Kipling himself) have done justice to that hat, the "more-than-oriental-splendour" construction being so completely a verbal trope. No perfect solution has been found, but (surprisingly) one of the most attractive formulations is that by the otherwise pedestrian Erika Weihs, who provides a kind of Siamese coronet that she shows to be well adapted to the business of pouring sand.

3. Carrington notes that Kipling was working on "The Elephant's Child" when James came to see him in October 1899 (235).

4. Two other "Just So" stories exist and are noted in the bibliography at the end of this paper: "The Tabu Tale," first published in 1905, and "Ham and the Porcupine," which appeared, more or less sandwiched between Mickey Mouse and Pip, Squeak, and Wilfred, in *The Princess Elizabeth Gift Book* of 1935.

5. The story also suffers the indignity (reserved for lesser features) of being concluded in the back pages of the magazine, among the advertisements.

6. The Carpenter Kipling Collection at the Library of Congress includes copies of the pamphlet editions of "The Elephant's Child," "The Beginning of the Armadilloes," and "The Sing-Song of Old Man Kangaroo." These were printed by the *Ladies' Home Journal*, and, from correspondence in the collection, it appears that twenty-five copies of the first two were printed, but only twenty-two of the last, since the magazine ran out of paper for the wrappers. Ten copies of each booklet were sent to A. P. Watt and five to officials in the United States; the rest remained with W. V. Alexander, the managing editor of the *Journal*, who seems to have slowly eased copies out into the market.

7. Although these were the last of the "standard" group of "Just So" stories, *Collier's* also published the further tale about Taffimai Metallumai, "The Tabu Tale," which appeared after the 1902 collection had been published (see the bibliography).

This printing was murkily illustrated by Charles Livingston Bull, while the English reprint in the *Windsor Magazine* had clearer, but not very distinguished, pen drawings by L. Raven-Hill. Readers interested in symmetry may like to know that the issues of *Collier's* preceding and following that of "The Tabu Tale" contained work by two of Kipling's earlier illustrators. Oliver Herford was sending in comic verses with his own line cartoons, and Frank Verbeck was providing halftone pictures for a sequence of new Uncle Remus stories by Joel Chandler Harris. No other "Just So" stories were to appear except for the little Noah's Ark tale that Kipling supplied to the editors of the *Princess Elizabeth Gift Book* in 1935, illustrated with a sparse sketch by Paul Bloomfield.

8. Surviving proofs show Kipling prolonging his work on the stories until he got the rhythmic flow that he wanted.

9. R. E. H. Harbord in his *Readers Guide* devotes most of his space to listing or elucidating private references in the text and the illustrations. "-NAS" and "-NAW," he says, are Plimsoll abbreviations for "North American Summer" and "North American Winter." "Olfen," or perhaps "Olsen," remains obscure.

10. Since this essay deals primarily with the illustrations to the *Just So Stories*, I have not entered into any connected discussion of the poems with which Kipling characteristically punctuates the story sequence. I have, however, noted some of the occasions when the poems are omitted, for this supplies supporting evidence of the casual attitude of editors and publishers toward Kipling's final intentions.

11. One gets the impression that Kipling would have liked his readers to color the pictures, but a more practical and less destructive alternative was offered in 1922 when Hodder and Stoughton began to issue a Painting Book series (see bibliography).

12. For a sympathetic review of this series see Nicholas Tucker, "When the Kipling Had to Stop." *Books for Keeps* 44 (May 1987): 24–25.

Works Cited

Carrington, C. E. *The Life of Rudyard Kipling*. Garden City, N.Y.: Doubleday, 1955.

Bibliography: Some Editions of the Just So Stories

The following classified list attempts to note the *editiones principes* of all English-language versions of the *Just So Stories* down to 1990. Brief annotations supply additional information or make critical remarks about books not dealt with in the foregoing essay. The author would be glad to hear of any omissions or of the location of copies that he has not seen.

Abbreviations

JSSS	Rojankovsky's *Just So Stories* series
LHJ	*Ladies' Home Journal*
MS	The Macmillan Uniform Series of 1983–85
PBS	The Just So Stories Painting Books for Children
Pbk.	Paperback edition

I) Separate publication of individual stories, arranged according to the date of their earliest printing

1) "How the Whale Got His Throat"
   a) 1897 Illus. Oliver Herford. *St. Nicholas* 25.2 (December 1897): 89–93.
      Published under the title "Just-So Stories," with "how the whale got his tiny throat" in the body of the text.
   b) 1972 Illus. Don Madden. Reading, Mass.: Addison-Wesley, n.d. [1972]
      A free engagement with RK's text, with much raw vigor but missing many points of detail (e.g., no jackknife).
   c) 1983 Illus. Pauline Baynes. London: Macmillan, 1983 (MS), pbk. 1986; New York: Bedrick, 1987.
   d) 1988 Illus. Jonathan Langley. London: Methuen, 1988.
   e) 1988 Illus. Krystyna Turska (in 2f below).

2) "How the Camel Got His Hump"
   a) 1898 Illus. Oliver Herford. *St. Nicholas* 25.3 (January 1898): 185–89.
   b) 1942 Illus. F. Rojankovsky. New York: Garden City Press, 1942 (JSSS).
   c) 1955 Illus. Erika Weihs. Chicago: Rand McNally and Co., n.d. [1955] (Elf Books).
   d) 1984 Illus. Quentin Blake. London: Macmillan, 1984 (MS); pbk. 1986; New York: Bedrick, 1985.
   e) 1988 Illus. Jonathan Langley. London: Methuen, 1988.
   f) 1988 Illus. Krystyna Turska. London and New York: Frederick Warne, 1988 (Warne Classics Series).
      Bound with 1e, above in a uniform series of "Potter size" books, which includes reductions of picture books by Leslie Brooke and Randolph Caldecott.
   g) 1989 Illus. Tim Raglin. Saxonville, Mass.: Rabbit Ears Books, 1989.
      The third in a group of books that began with the Knopf edition of "The Elephant's Child" (4 l below), which I have not seen. The plan for these editions is to box up each book with a cassette so that the purchaser is supplied with a ready-made storyteller and a quasi-musical accompaniment. Here the story is told by Jack Nicholson and the "music" (that is, electronic sound effects) is by Bobby McFerrin. The detailed color illustrations are too lavish for the brief tale.

3) "How the Rhinoceros Got His Skin"
   a) 1898 Illus. Oliver Herford. *St. Nicholas* 25.4 (February 1898): 272–75.
      As 1a above, with "how the Rhinoceros got his wrinkly skin" in the body of the text.
   b) 1922 Illus. Day Hodgetts (?). London: Hodder and Stoughton, n.d. [1922]; New York: Doubleday, Page and Co., 1923 (PBS: see IV below).
   c) 1942 Illus. F. Rojankovsky. New York: Garden City Press, 1942 (JSSS).
      A "special edition" in library binding is recorded as published at Eau Claire, Wis., by Cadmus Books, 1955 (?).
   d) 1956 Illus. Erika Weihs. Chicago: Rand McNally and Co., 1956 (Elf Books).
   e) 1973 Illus. Leonard Weisgard. New York: Walker and Co., 1973; London: Macmillan, 1973.

f)   1976 Illus. Sarah Chamberlain (?). Easthampton, Mass.: The Chamberlain Press, 1976.
      The title is "How the Rhinoceros Got His Wrinkled Skin" and the colophon reads: "The second book printed at the Chamberlain Press . . . The paper is mulberry, the type is Goudy Oldstyle, and the illustrations are wood engravings. The binding is by E. G. Parrot II [!]." The edition was limited to seventy-five copies. The text, inexplicably paragraphed with thistles, has been slightly modified and has been given a coda after RK's "Anantarivo [sic]" list: ". . . where all small people, just beginning to breathe slowly and evenly, must inevitably also accompany him—in order to arrive early and unknowingly at the enormous battlements of the luxurious city of Uninterrupted Slumber."

g)   1985 Illus. Jenny Thorne. London: Macmillan, 1985; pbk. 1986; New York: Bedrick, 1987.

h)   1988 Illus. Jonathan Langley. London: Methuen, 1988.

i)   1988 Illus. Tim Raglin. Saxonville, Mass.: Rabbit Ears Books, 1988.
      This is the first of the Rabbit Ears productions. In the reading Nicholson adds an additional "Best Beloved" in the penultimate paragraph.

4) "The Elephant's Child" (EC), sometimes retitled "How the Elephant Got His Trunk" (HT)

a)   1900 Illus. Frank Ver Beck. *LHJ* 25.5 (April 1900): pp 3–4. EC: "Being the first of a series of Just So Stories . . ." U.K. reprint with rearranged illustrations: *Windsor Magazine* 15 (February 1902): 333–40.

b)   1922 Illus. Day Hodgetts (?). London: Hodder and Stoughton, n.d. [1922]; New York: Doubleday, Page and Co., 1923. (PBS).

c)   1942 Illus. F. Rojankovsky. New York: Garden City Press, 1942 (JSSS).

d)   1955 Illus. Katherine Evans. Chicago: Rand McNally and Co., 1955 (Elf Books).

e)   1968 Illus. Don Madden. N.p.: CBS Records, 1968.
      Not in series with 1b above but showing the same lively humor expressed through rough cartoon drawing.

f)   1969 Illus. Ulla Kampmann. Chicago: Follett Publishing Co., 1969.

g)   1970 Illus. Leonard Weisgard. New York: Walker and Co., 1970; London: Macmillan, 1970.

h)   1971 Illus. Heinz Looser. New York: Scroll Press, 1971.

i)   1983 Illus. Lorinda Bryan Cauley. San Diego: Harcourt Brace Jovanovich, 1983.

j)   1984 Illus. Louise Brierley. London: Macmillan, 1984 (MS); pbk. 1986; New York: Bedrick, 1985.

k)   1985 (HT) Illus. Elisabetto Ferrero (with Maurizio Bajetti). Tulsa, Okla.: EDC Publishing, 1985 (An Upside Down Book). First published in Italian. Milan: Fabbri, 1985.
      The imprint has the grace to acknowledge that this banal retelling is after a story by RK, but claims that the source is *The Jungle Book*.

l)   1986 Illus. Tim Raglin. New York: Alfred A. Knopf, 1986. Not seen. This is the first book/cassette production, later volumes being published by Rabbit Ears (see entries 2g, 3i, 7e).

m) 1986 Illus. Arlette Lavie. Swindon, Wiltshire: Child's Play (International), 1986.
The illustrations cover each page opening completely, in such swirls of color that they look more like designer wallpaper.

n) c. 1987 Illus. Edward Frascino. New York: Prentice-Hall, n.d. [1987?]. Not seen.

o) 1987 Illus. Krystyna Turska. London and New York: Frederick Warne, 1987 (Warne Classics Series).
Companion to 2f.

p) 1988 Illus. Linda Medley. [? place]: Platt and Munk, 1988. Not seen.

5) "The Beginning of the Armadilloes"

a) 1900 Illus. Frank Ver Beck. *LHJ* 17.6 (May 1900): 3–4.

b) 1970 Illus. Giulio Maestro. London: Macmillan, 1970; New York: St. Martin's Press, 1974.

c) 1982 Illus. Charles Keeping. London: Macmillan, 1982 (MS); pbk. 1985, restoring the verses omitted in 1982; New York: Bedrick, 1983.

d) 1985 Illus. Lorinda Bryan Cauley. San Diego: Harcourt Brace Jovanovich, 1985.

6) "The Sing-Song of Old Man Kangaroo"

a) 1900 Illus. Frank Ver Beck. *LHJ* 17.7 (June 1900): 1–2.

b) 1922 Illus. Day Hodgetts (?). London: Hodder and Stoughton, n.d. [1922]; New York: Doubleday, Page and Co., 1923 (PBS).

c) 1985 Illus. Michael C. Taylor. London: Macmillan, 1985 (MS); pbk. 1986; New York: Bedrick, 1985.

d) 1990 Illus. John Roue. Saxonville, Mass. and London: Picture Book Studio, 1990 (A Michael Neugebauer Book).

7) "How the Leopard Got His Spots"

a) 1900 Illus. Frank Verbeck (sic). *LHJ* 18.11 (October 1901): 1–2. U.K. reprint with rearranged illustrations: *Pearson's Magazine* 13.76 (April 1902): 446–50.

b) 1942 Illus. F. Rojankovsky. New York: Garden City Press, 1942 (JSSS). Special Cadmus ed. as 3c above.

c) 1972 Illus. Leonard Weisgard. London: Macmillan, 1972; New York: Walker and Co., 1973.

d) 1985 Illus. Caroline Ebborn. London: Macmillan, 1985 (MS); pbk. 1986; New York: Bedrick, 1986.

e) 1985 Illus. Lori Lohstoeter. Saxonville, Mass.: Rabbit Ears Books, 1989 (as 2g, but with the story read by Danny Glover and with African music by Ladysmith Black Mambazo).

8) "How the First Letter Was Written"

a) 1901 Illus. Frank Ver Beck. *LHJ* 19.1 (December 1901): 11–12. With a sketch labeled "This is the letter as drawn by Kipling himself."

b) 1985 Illus. Victor Ambrus. London: Macmillan, 1985 (MS); pbk. 1986; New York: Bedrick, 1987.

9) "The Cat That Walked by Himself"

a) 1902 Unillustrated. *LHJ* 19.8 (July 1902): 4, 32.

b) 1902 Illus. Cecil Aldin. *Windsor Magazine* 16.94 (October 1902): 483–90.

c) 1947 Illus. F. Rojankovsky. New York: Garden City Press, 1947 (JSSS).

    d)   1970 Illus. Rosemary Wells. New York: Hawthorne Books, 1970.
    e)   1982 Illus. William Stobbs. London: Macmillan, 1982 (MS); pbk.
              1985; New York: Bedrick, 1983 (verses lacking in all eds.).
    f)   1988 Illus. Teresa O'Brien. Swindon, Wiltshire, Child's Play (International), 1988.
              Another large-format, all-color production job. Much of the drawing is high-definition realism but laid out on the page in stylized compositions. The text finds what space it can in the pictorial layout.

10) "The Crab That Played with the Sea"
    a)   1902 Illus. F. M. Dumond. *Collier's Illustrated Weekly* 29.18 (August 2, 1902): 8–9 (as "The Crab That Made the Tides").
    b)   1902 Illus. Lawson Wood. *Pearson's Magazine* 14.14 (August 1902): 209–13 (as "The Crab That Made the Tides").
    c)   1982 Illus. Michael Foreman. London: Macmillan, 1982 (MS); pbk. 1985; New York: Bedrick 1983 (verses lacking in all eds.).

11) "The Butterfly That Stamped"
    a)   1902 Illus. Frank Verbeck (sic). *LHJ* 19.11 (October 1902): 3–4.
    b)   1947 Illus. F. Rojankovsky. New York: Garden City Press, n.d. [1947] (JSSS).
    c)   1982 Illus. Alan Baker. London: Macmillan, 1982 (MS); pbk. 1985, restoring the verses omitted in 1982; New York: Bedrick, 1982.

12) "The Tabu Tale"
    a)   1903 Illus. Charles Livingston Bull. *Collier's Household Number* 31.22 (August 29, 1903): 10–11.
    b)   1903 Illus. L. Raven-Hill. *Windsor Magazine* 17.105 (September 1903): 343–71.
              N.B. This third story about Taffimai Metallumai was not incorporated into the standard collection and was never separately reprinted. It did, however, appear as the penultimate tale in the "Outward Bound" volume of the stories (New York: Charles Scribner's Sons, 1903), and is included in the English Folio Society edition planned for 1991.

13) "How the Alphabet Was Made"
    a)   1923 Illus. Day Hodgetts (?). London: Hodder and Stoughton, n.d. [1923] (PBS); New York: Doubleday, Page and Co., 1923 (PBS).
    b)   1983 Illus. Chloe Cheese. London: Macmillan, 1983 (MS); pbk. 1986; New York: Bedrick, 1987.

14) "Ham and the Porcupine. A Just-So Story"
    a)   1935 Illus. Paul Bloomfield. In *The Princess Elizabeth Gift Book*, ed. Cynthia Asquith and Eileen Bigland. London: Hodder and Stoughton, n.d. [1935], 21–26.
              N.B. A late addition to the canon, not subsequently reprinted except for a copyright ed. issued in the United States by Doubleday in 1935. Paul Bloomfield's contribution is minimal: one small sketch of Porcupine and Hedgehog Brother.

II) Complete editions containing the twelve main stories
    1) *Just So Stories for Little Children*. Illus. RK. London: Macmillan, 1902.
        The U.S. ed. was set up from this and published by Doubleday, Page and Co., 1902. Innumerable British and American reprints have followed, together with a variety of "official" editions in different formats, with and without Kipling's illustrations.

2) (as above). Illus. RK and Joseph M. Gleeson. New York: Doubleday, Page and Co., 1912.

The English printing stated "coloured plates by Joseph M. Gleeson." London: Macmillan, 1913.

Gleeson's plates, sometimes augmented, have been used on and off down to the Children's Classics edition from dilithium Press (New York: 1987). There was also a collected edition (c. 1930) with a double-spread title page in color halftone (jungle animals) by Paul Bransom.

3) *Just So Stories*. Illus. Nicolas (i.e., Nicolas Mordvinoff) New York: Garden City Books, 1952.

The poems are omitted.

4) *Just So Stories*. Illus. Etienne Delessert; foreword by Nelson Doubleday. Garden City, N.Y.: Doubleday and Co., 1972. Anniversary Edition (of the publisher).

The poems are omitted.

5) *Just So Stories*. Illus. Michael Foreman. London: Viking Kestrel, 1987.

A complete edition, illustrated with eight color plates and many drawings in pen and wash, all of a quasi-realistic nature.

6) *Just So Stories*. Illus. Safaya Salter, foreword by Ronald King. London: Pavilion Books (and The National Trust), 1987.

A complete edition, illustrated with a pictorial title spread, twelve ornamental chapter headpieces, eleven full-page plates, and one double-page plate, all of a decorative nature.

III) Selections

1) *Kipling Stories and Poems Every Child Should Know*. Illus. Kurt Wiese, J.M. Gleeson, Charles Livingston Bull, and RK. New York: Garden City Publications Co., 1938.

Includes six "Just So" stories with assorted poems; some of RK's illustrations are used in conjunction with some from C. L. Bull. In an edition of the book published a year later (by Doubleday, Doran & Co. for the Parents Institute), the material has been more systematically arranged and the editors, now named as Mary E. Burt and W. T. Chapin, Ph.D., make it clear that the edition is intended for teachers to use in schools.

2) *Favorite Just So Stories*. Illus. H. B. Vestal. New York: Grosset and Dunlop, 1957.

Includes seven stories, but without their attendant poems. The illustrations are uninspired and mostly naturalistic. The cover shows an Eastern storyteller addressing three polite American children, very much class of '57.

3) *Just So Stories*. Illus. Victor G. Ambrus. Chicago: Rand McNally and Co., 1982.

Includes five stories, much battered by the tumultuous artwork.

4) *Just So Stories*. Illus. Meg Rutherford. Twickenham: Hamlyn, 1987.

Includes nine stories, illustrated with decorative chapter initials and a variety of color plates and drawings in sepia. A smooth production job that succeeds in getting across a number of dramatic effects. The poems are omitted.

IV) Miscellanea

1) *The Just So Song Book, Being the Songs from Rudyard Kipling's "Just So Stories" Set to Music by Edward German*. London: Macmillan, 1903.

A photographically reduced ed. was published in New York by Doubleday, Page (also 1903).

2) The Just-So Stories Painting Books for Children (1922–23). Since these

four books are, in effect, illustrated editions of the individual stories, they have been incorporated in Section I above. Each book is constructed on the same plan, with a page opening of text (occasionally illustrated) alternating with a page opening showing an outline picture and the same scene printed in colors to be copied. The suggested coloring is not ornate, consisting mostly of slate blue, pale green, yellow, orange, and brown. The books were published in the following order: "The Elephant's Child," "The Sing-Song of Old Man Kangaroo," "How the Rhinoceros Got His Skin," "How the Alphabet Was Made." An American edition was published in 1923. No illustrator is named, but the National Union Catalog records Day Hodgetts for the last book.

   3) I have not investigated Randall Thompson's one-act opera of "Solomon and Balkis" (Boston: Schirmer, c. 1942) or Patsy Rogers's ballet score for "How the Elephant Got His Trunk" (c. 1978).

 V) Some sources consulted

Carrington, Charles. *Rudyard Kipling: His Life and Work*. London: Macmillan, 1955.

Green, Roger Lancelyn. *Kipling and the Children*. London: Elek Books, 1965.

Grolier Club. *Catalogue [of works] Exhibited at the Grolier Club from February 21 to March 30, 1929*. New York: Grolier Club, 1930.

Harbord, Reginald E. H. *A Readers Guide to Rudyard Kipling's* Just So Stories. Stevenage, Hertfordshire: Spring Grange Private Press, 1955.

Livingston, Flora V. *Bibliography of the Works of Rudyard Kipling*. New York: Wells and Co., 1927.

With supp. Cambridge: Harvard University Press, 1938.

Stewart, James M. *Rudyard Kipling: A Bibliographical catalogue*, ed. A. W. Yeats. Toronto: Dalhousie University Press, 1959.

Note: As we go to press, the Folio Society and the British Library are issuing a new edition of *Just So Stories* with illustrations re-originated from Kipling's own drawings in the Manuscript Department of the British Library. This edition includes "The Tabu Tale," with two drawings, with commentary, which had previously only been published in Scribner's edition, New York, 1920.

Reviews

The Influence of Anxiety: Kipling's Hidden Narratives

William Blackburn

Kipling's Hidden Narratives, by Sandra Kemp. Oxford: Basil Blackwell, 1988.

Rudyard Kipling, edited by Harold Bloom. New York: Chelsea House, 1987.

Rudyard Kipling's Kim, edited by Harold Bloom. New York: Chelsea House, 1987.

If more literary critics had any sense of shame, we would have far less criticism of Kipling than we have at present, or at least we would have criticism of a different sort—a sort that did not so readily betray Kipling's infernal facility for getting under the skin of so many readers. In historical terms, one may observe that Kipling fell into critical disrepute around the time of the Boer War; political partisanship and Kipling's iron reticence about his own life combined to obscure Kipling the man, and lent apparent substance to Kipling the myth, Kipling the chauvinist dwarf of Max Beerbohm's caricatures, mafficking across Hempstead Heath with "Brittania 'is gurl" on his arm. This is the Kipling who in Robert Buchanan's words "in his single person adumbrates . . . all that is most deplorable, all that is most retrograde and savage, in the restless and uninstructed Hooliganism of the time" (Green 238). So persistent has this view of Kipling been—a view based on an imperfect apprehension both of Kipling's politics and of his writing—that he received little seri-

Children's Literature 20, ed. Francelia Butler, Barbara Rosen, and Judith A. Plotz (Yale University Press, © 1992 by The Children's Literature Foundation, Inc.).

ous critical attention during the first half of this century; indeed, with the exceptions of R. L. Green's *Kipling: The Critical Heritage* (1971), and the biographies by Carrington (1955), Lord Birkenhead (1978), and Angus Wilson (1977), the best work on Kipling in this century has been done by historians and sociologists rather than literary critics.

The critics eventually began slouching, if not toward Bethlehem, at least toward plausibility, with T. S. Eliot's introduction to *A Choice of Kipling's Verse* (1941) and Edmund Wilson's "The Kipling That Nobody Read" (in *The Wound and the Bow*, 1947). Earlier notices of Kipling's psychology had been largely depreciatory—one reviewer of Kipling's early stories, who wished "to hazard a guess that the writer is very young and that he will die before he has reached the age of thirty" (Green 4) will serve for illustration. T. S. Eliot was the first critic effectively to suggest that Kipling's psychology might be at least as interesting as Kipling's politics. Eliot's observations that "there is always something alien about Kipling, as of a visitor from another planet" (28) and that he is "the most inscrutable of authors" who "remains somehow alien and aloof from all with which he identifies himself" (22–23) signaled the most fruitful direction for future studies. Eliot's insight was confirmed by, among others, George Orwell, who begins his famous essay on Kipling (1946) by conceding that Kipling's view of life cannot "be accepted or even forgiven by any civilized person" and that "Kipling is a jingo imperialist, he is morally insensitive and aesthetically disgusting"— and then goes on to the genuinely interesting question of "why it is that he survives while the refined people who have sniggered at him seem to wear so badly" (215).

Happily, empires come and go; we have others—far less amiable than the one imagined by Kipling—to bemuse us today. Sennacherib and the King Emperor of India mingle in the dust, and we no longer need to admit, as Orwell did, that "Kipling is almost a shameful pleasure" (226). Now, no longer obliged to waste their energies in deploring what Orwell called the "snack-bar wisdom" (225) of Kipling's political thought, critics are free to do what they should have done long since: to assess Kipling not as a huckster of empire (which he never in fact was), but as a writer. That is the object of the three volumes under consideration here, and the diversity of their approaches augurs well for the future of Kipling studies.

The two volumes of the Chelsea House series, both edited by Harold Bloom, present a selection of the best Kipling criticism produced since the appearance of *Kipling: The Critical Heritage*. That these collections are largely free of the political obsessions which clouded the judgment of earlier writers on Kipling is adequately illustrated by Bloom's introduction (common to both volumes), which explores "what Kipling finally shares with Pater" (of all people!) and which advances the astonishing contention that "Kipling's art . . . is after all art for art's sake, in the dark predicate that there is nothing else" (7).

Those familiar with Bloom's criticism are unlikely to be much damaged by his portentous introduction, which may profitably be ignored. Ignored not because it is devoid of interest, but because it is not about Kipling at all; it is really about Harold Bloom, who is a far less interesting writer than Kipling. Instead of seeking to turn Kipling into a cleverly disguised aesthete, Bloom would have done better to seek the core of Kipling's art in his mythologizing of childhood. The first line of Kipling's autobiography, *Something of Myself* (1937), is "Give me the first six years of a child's life, and you can have the rest"—and the operative word in the title is "something." Kipling never tells all and never seeks to tell all—but the quest for the lost paradise of childhood is at the heart of Kipling's oeuvre, and that quest makes Kipling a genuine romantic in a way utterly unsuspected by Bloom.

Fortunately, Bloom's infatuation with his own rhetoric is not typical of the essays assembled in the Chelsea House collections. Neither collection is intended for the novice; both will best serve the scholar who already knows a good deal about the subject and who is in a position to appreciate their many toothsome details. *Rudyard Kipling* opens with a fine essay by Randall Jarrell, who finds it necessary to begin by arguing that "Kipling *was* a writer after all—people just didn't realize the sort of writer he was" (11). Jarrell's judicious and clear-sighted analysis is generally typical of the volume as a whole; other particularly noteworthy essays are those of Zohreh T. Sullivan (who contends rightly that the most persistent of Kipling's imagery is that of "a fundamentally divided world" ([69]), Irving Howe (whose brilliant "The Pleasures of Kim" is also reprinted in *Rudyard Kipling's* Kim), and Elliot L. Gilbert ("there was no aspect of his life and art . . . that was not presided over by the profoundest silence"). All of the essays in this volume have a good deal to offer, though it is much to be regretted that the Chelsea House series reprints them sans footnotes or other apparatus.

The selection of essays in *Rudyard Kipling's* Kim is not quite so happy. The best of them address the rich theme of the divided self, and approach the novel as a demonstration of "Kipling's innate quest for selfhood" (9). Perhaps the most outstanding piece in this collection is Margaret Peller Feeley's "The *Kim* That Nobody Reads," an essay exploring the long-unknown manuscript "Kim o' the 'Rishti," the only extant working draft of Kipling's masterpiece. (It was Kipling's meticulous practice to destroy his drafts and manuscripts after publication.) Her deft comparison of manuscript and novel convincingly demonstrates "Kipling's imagination struggling to transcend old prejudices and stereotypes . . . gestating the major style and theme of his later vision" (74).

To my mind, the most obvious weakness of this collection is its failure to provide an adequate understanding of Kipling's use of Buddhism in *Kim*—R. W. Moss and Philip Mason come closest—and its consequent failure to arrive at a just appraisal of Kipling's most comprehensive vision of empire. Understanding how and why Kipling can use the lama's sacred quest to figure Kim's allegiance to the concept of empire is the key to Kipling's novel—a key that this volume, despite the many talents of its contributors, never quite manages to produce.

I confess to a similar niggling discontent with Sandra Kemp's *Kipling's Hidden Narratives*. She has a commendable sense of what she calls the "modernist self-consciousness" of her subject, and a keen appreciation—an appreciation a long time coming—of how all Kipling's major fiction constitutes "a continuing exploration of the way narrative makes and remakes identity" (1). She confronts squarely the possibility that "Kipling decided at an early stage of composition not to allow his narratives any straightforward resolution" (71) and gleans many useful insights by arguing that in Kipling's work, "the process of reading, the relation between the reader and the text, involves an engagement with language and narrative structures which disguise rather than disclose their meaning" (53). Of these three volumes, this is the most contemporary in its employment of modern critical methodology—and manages to be so without falling into the trendy and glitzy emptiness that results from attempting to substitute style for substance. Kemp likewise deserves praise for her tenacious attempt to understand the relationship between the author's psychology and the author's work; and also for her recognition that this relationship is neither as clear nor as direct as many earlier writers confidently assumed it to be. I cannot, however, praise her tenacity without also lamenting its premature demise. Her book does not arrive at anything resembling a unified-field theory of Kipling; she serves up many interesting tidbits to the reader, but *Kipling's Hidden Narratives* suffers from its lack of a strong conclusion. What the book finally offers is not a complete banquet but a large heap of hors d'oeuvres.

But finally, all those who love Kipling will be both pleased and instructed by these three volumes. "Methods," as Camus says in *The Myth of Sisyphus*, "imply metaphysics" (18), and the methods brought to bear in these works show that we are finally ready to attempt a long-overdue assessment of Kipling as a serious writer. Kipling the caricature belongs to history, and these three works demonstrate a gratifying readiness to explore Kipling as an artist, a major artist whose craftsmanship deserves attention as something more than proof of neurotic compulsion or political intransigence. While not all will agree with the rich variety of opinion expressed in these volumes, we may at least say of these critics what one of Kipling's characters says of the lama in *Kim*: that perhaps their gods are not gods, but certainly their feet are on the Way.

Works Cited

Camus, Albert. *The Myth of Sisyphus*. Trans. Justin O'Brien. Harmondsworth: Penguin, 1975.

Eliot, Thomas Stearns, ed. *A Choice of Kipling's Verse*. London: Macmillan, 1941.

Green, Roger Lancelyn, ed. *Kipling: The Critical Heritage*. London: Routledge and Kegan Paul, 1971.

Kipling, Rudyard. *Something of Myself*. London: Macmillan, 1937.

Orwell, George. *Collected Essays, Journalism and Letters of George Orwell*. Vol. 2. Harmondsworth: Penguin, 1970.

Mowgli Man

Charles L. DeFanti

Rudyard Kipling: A Biography, by Martin Seymour-Smith. New York: St. Martin's Press, 1989.

Kipling: Storyteller of East and West, by Gloria Kamen. New York: Atheneum, 1985.

Since biography has emerged as the darling genre of the last few decades, it is no surprise that studying the lives of children's book authors has become embedded in school curricula. Books are assigned, students "become" the authors for a day, and their lives and works are discussed—perhaps as guides to worthy forms of behavior, surely to gain a greater understanding of the artist and his or her times. In his recent review of Jeffrey Meyers's biography of D. H. Lawrence (*The New York Review of Books*, January 27, 1991), Noel Annan reminds us of Sainte-Beuve's belief that to understand an artist's work you must know his life, and vice versa. Proust, on the other hand, disagreed, insisting that the writer becomes a different person the moment he begins to write: "While he writes out of his experience, his characters are never taken solely from one person and are heightened, altered, and enlarged in the course of creation" (12). Never mind that the New Critics later sided with Proust (as did Lawrence): "Never trust the artist. Trust the tale." We remain obsessed with biography, flawed and subjective as the form might be.

From Dr. Johnson, whose Enlightenment sensibility decided it was proper to concern ourselves with the details of individual existences, until the appearance of Lytton Strachey, originator of the debunking biography, the seamier sides of writers' characters were left unremarked. However, psychoanalytic techniques, with us for now more than a century, coupled with newer research technologies, have added teeth to Oscar Wilde's dictum "Biography lends to death a new terror." Gentle creatures such as A. A. Milne wither under the scholar's glare, while macho magnificos such as Rudyard

Children's Literature 20, ed. Francelia Butler, Barbara Rosen, and Judith A. Plotz (Yale University Press, © 1992 by The Children's Literature Foundation, Inc.).

Kipling and Ernest Hemingway suffer humiliating reappraisals under the weight of evidence gleaned in the computer age.

Kipling, whose grotesque and unthinking imperialism seems more quaint than horrifying nowadays, survives in reputation mainly as a children's writer and a master of the short story. Few children who enjoy the luxury of being read to miss knowing about Kim, or Mowgli in *The Jungle Book*, so curiosity about the man who was once England's most popular author must begin soon after the cradle. Gloria Kamen's *Kipling: Storyteller of East and West*, written several years before Martin Seymour-Smith's definitive life, is an attractively produced juvenile biography, with charming and unmawkish sepia ink-wash drawings that resemble snapshot montages. The text should engage, though not overwhelm, younger readers with the well-known "authorized" material about Kipling, whose reputation was shielded for decades after his death by Elsie, his one surviving daughter. As had long been suspected, she pushed many significant skeletons deep into the Kipling closet, items that one might like to clean up or discard before presenting this author to children.

After his magical early childhood in India, the most famous episode in Kipling's life concerned his "abandonment" by his parents with a Southsea couple, "Uncle" Harry and "Aunty" Rosa Holloway, who had advertised as caretakers in a newspaper. Alice and Lockwood Kipling simply departed, leaving Kipling and his sister, Trix, without informing them. Now elevated to the status of myth, this betrayal was the "shock" from which Kipling never recovered. This myth is largely accepted by Kamen, who echoes Kipling's account, largely by paraphrasing and quoting "Baa Baa, Black Sheep" regarding the neglect and cruelty suffered by Kipling at the hands of the narrow Holloways and their sadistic son (especially after the early death of the eccentric Uncle Harry). The story that Ruddy was punished by being forced to read the Bible—until they learned that he enjoyed it—is well known. But "Baa Baa, Black Sheep" is clearly a revenge story, as are later accounts in *The Light That Failed* and *Something of Myself*. Unquestionably, he suffered considerable punishment at the hands of Mrs. Holloway and her son, "the devil boy." But Kipling was a brilliant, hyperactive, and uncontrollably fractious boy. At the local day school (also attended by the Holloway boy), he refused to work at his lessons and learned to lie. (Kipling claimed that once, when he tried to conceal a bad report, he was

sent through the streets with a placard bearing on it the words
KIPLING THE LIAR.) That he might bring his talent for lying, and, by
extension, for fiction, to bear upon the incidents of his childhood
(and the Holloways themselves) is never suggested by Kamen. In
fact, Seymour-Smith examines surviving evidence to conclude, "It
is difficult not to suspect that Mrs. Holloway might even have been
as kind a woman, at times, as she was severe at others" (26). Oddly,
Kipling never mentioned the Holloways' cruelty to his relatives, and
is even known to have visited Mrs. Holloway after he had left the
household. "Would a boy as damaged as he claimed he had been by
this woman ('misused and forlorn' he later told his wife, who noted
it) have made, or been expected to make such a visit? . . . Clearly it
was this early shock that launched him into that form of lying that
is fiction."

Now, Seymour-Smith is a thoroughly psychoanalytic (though not
Freudian) biographer, who places much weight on trauma and psychic lesions in the formation of human character. But his case is
convincing, since he is the first biographer to have had full access
to the surviving Kipling archives since the death of Elsie Kipling
(Mrs. George Bambridge). It is his handling and interpretation
of these materials that caused the firestorm of controversy following the first publication of *Kipling: A Life* in 1979. Central to
that controversy was Seymour-Smith's handling of the apparently
crucial events in Kipling's life: his relationship with his American
publisher, Wolcott Balestier, and his marriage to Wolcott's sister,
Caroline ("Carrie"). Seymour-Smith relates that "tabloid-minded
people, when they were not pretending to have 'known all along'
that Kipling was 'queer,' tried to make out that I was simply attempting—in their own horribly false and simplistic manner—to
change the 'image' of Kipling from one of 'patriot' to one of 'sod-
omite'" (xiii). Kamen reduces this supposedly pivotal relationship
to a single paragraph:

> Wolcott's older sister, Caroline, came from Vermont to visit
> her brother in London while Rudyard and Wolcott were writ-
> ing a book together, *The Naulahka* (Jewel of India). It was a
> mystery that took place in both India and the United States.
> Kipling enjoyed the novelty of writing with someone else . . .
> and especially enjoyed his visits with the Balestiers. He spent
> more and more time with them. Caroline found her brother's

friend charming and attractive, and it wasn't long before they were married. [43]

Nothing more is heard about Wolcott in this biography, and little about the marriage, except for the fact that the townsfolk of Brattleboro, Vermont, where the Kiplings moved, "considered them unfriendly." An unfortunate dispute between the Kiplings and Beatty Balestier, another of Carrie's brothers, is outlined: Kamen recounts the nasty climax, which ultimately humiliated Kipling and drove the family from America: "A fresh argument between the two ended with Beatty threatening to shoot Rudyard. Rudyard had Beatty arrested. The next day forty newspaper reporters arrived in Brattleboro. Everyone who had ever been denied an interview came to see Kipling squirm in the witness chair" (52).

As presented by Kamen, the Kiplings are a solemn couple, publicity-shy though otherwise content. Kipling continues writing his children's books and his vicarious advocacy of the strenuous life. But are some fundamental facts being skirted? Central to Seymour-Smith's thesis is the contention that *Wolcott* was the true love of Kipling's life, information that was available to Kamen: "Carrington [author of a 1955 biography of Kipling] describes Rudyard and Carrie as 'lovers,' yet also refers to the 'Wolcott-Carrie-Rudyard triangle.'" (200). Seymour-Smith theorizes that Wolcott, who knew he was dying at the time and had nothing more to lose, told Carrie of the nature of Kipling's friendship for him. In this reading, Carrie became the romantic ghost of Wolcott:

> [Kipling] would have intended to change that. But can anyone make that sort of change? Doing his marital duty, was he not sodomising Wolcott? No wonder he was confused, and no wonder he became fanatical about his privacy. [201]

Seymour-Smith triangulates much of this data from internal evidence in Kipling's fiction (such as *Naulahka*), and the known facts about Kipling's life with his charmless and awkward wife: "Carrie was a depressed person, temperamentally inclined to look at everything in a gloomy light: she was depressing her husband even now. . . . Kipling most astonished everyone who knew him in two ways: consenting to collaborate with a literary trifler, and marrying a gloomy dragon" (203). Eventually detractors, resenting his aloofness as much as anything else, pegged him as "The Mowgli Man," a slap at his naive and self-defeating faith in the law of the jungle.

It is unfair to expect that a "first" biography such as Kamen's should approximate any of the complexities of Seymour-Smith's very dense opus, in which virtually every incident in Kipling's life takes on an ominous cast and the significance of his literature is radically altered. For example, Seymour-Smith maintains that the notoriously unathletic and nearsighted Kipling actually admired the hated Beatty Balestier, who humiliated Kipling so much as to drive him from his beloved Vermont, thus exacerbating Kipling's permanent need to prove himself as a man of action. Many of his soldier's tales, and the dreadful *Stalky & Co.* fantasies about a flagellating schoolmaster roughly based on Kipling's teacher Cormell Price, reflect the depression he was experiencing at this time.

Carrie responded, after their exodus from Vermont, by surrounding Kipling with the "protective crust" of her increasingly offensive personality. She managed Bateman's, their newly acquired mansion in Sussex, in her own brutal way, bullying, cheating, and otherwise intimidating the servants so that they became convinced that she liked to make people unhappy (329). Seymour-Smith, however, theorizes that Kipling was rescued from artistic suffocation by his "daemon," his creative spirit, "which could pluck inspiration from the air" (363). When in the throes of composition, Kipling became, according to his daughter, oblivious to anything else. The philosophical temper of this daemon, however, is more chilling than has heretofore been supposed. Kipling's thoughtless conservatism Seymour-Smith sees as "stiff with fear and tension" (108). The famous imperialist that Kipling became was the classic authoritarian, a fundamentally frightened man who emerged as an uncritical admirer of Mussolini, and "insensitive to man's ill-treatment of man on the flimsy grounds that life is nasty, brutish and short and that we all need licking into shape" (114). Kipling's perverse fascination with punishment becomes another unadmirable facet of his polemic.

To place yet another finger on Kipling's ideological pulse, Seymour-Smith reprints the strange poem "The Prayer of Miriam Cohen," which includes the following stanzas:

> From the wheel and the drift of Things
> Deliver us, Good Lord;

And we will face the wrath of Kings,
The faggot and the sword! . . .

Thy Path, Thy Purposes conceal
From our beleaguered realm,
Lest any shattering whisper steal
upon us and o'erwhelm.

A veil 'twixt us and Thee, Good Lord,
A veil 'twixt us and Thee—
Lest we should hear too clear, too clear,
And unto madness see!

In this awkward but striking poem, Kipling adopts as his spokesperson an "outcast" like himself, a Jewish woman, who reveals the world as a terrible place, and the afterlife a horrifying prospect. She prays to God to conceal the true nature of His labors, and to put a veil between us and true reality lest we understand that reality too well, and go mad (212).

Does this Gnostic morbidity color Kipling's writing for children? Not invariably: Seymour-Smith insists that when he was with children, "over whom he cast a loving spell," Kipling could suspend his experience of evil, "his sense of unworthiness, as he put it— and become an *aphorist,* safe in the assumption that, since he was a grown-up dispensing real pleasure and giving genuinely felt love, it would be understood by them as wisdom. Sometimes, however, it was not wisdom, but ugly and over-emotional authoritarian propaganda" (352).

Nonetheless, Kipling endures mainly as a children's writer: in *The Jungle Book,* for example, Kipling neither patronizes nor writes down to children, even though the action transpires in a world of near perfection. *Kim,* Kipling's most heartfelt homage to the India he had loved as a child, comes closest to realizing his ideal fictional world for children. "Its fault is that, paradoxically, it does successfully set up a conflict between values material and immaterial; but it then fails to illuminate this conflict. The well-known criticism of the book, that at the end Kim has failed to choose between the Lama and government service, holds good" (301). Seymour-Smith insists that "an almost paedophilic attractiveness is given to Kim himself" (303). His beauty is fully appreciated by all the other male characters in the book, though Kipling would never have suspected himself of pedophilic emotions. Beyond that, Seymour-Smith makes the following observation about the overall solipsism of Kipling's children's books, and their appropriateness for modern youth:

> The two Jungle Books deserve to live for their ease of language, for their reflection of the soul of a man who wishes to become a child again, but they are redolent, too, of authoritarianism and ersatz cosy wisdom. They by no means represent Kipling at the peak of his achievement. They are the work of a man who is having it both ways: relaxing in an innocent world, but also one who is entrenching himself in a thoughtless, self-defensive creed. Those who read it as children are not made wiser by it. [247]

Despite Seymour-Smith's reservations, at least some of Kipling's literature will continue to appeal to contemporary children, if we allow for changes in taste and values. But how should we introduce the man himself? If, as seems likely, interesting lives are the most seamy, should we present simplified accounts of them? Kamen's biography is a whitewash, as it must be for children, and, as a result, it is unremittingly bland. Seymour-Smith's Kipling, on the other hand, is simply not appropriate for the young. Though it also records the facts of his life, it is more a painstaking (and painful) reconsideration of all the possibilities suggested by that life, and these, for a host of reasons, are not useful fare for the classroom. In fact, Seymour-Smith's account may be overburdened with speculation, even to the degree that Kamen's lacks any at all. Coleridge warned us that "when a man is attempting to describe another's character, he may be right or he may be wrong—but in one thing he will always succeed—in describing himself." However, in teaching this subjective genre, it will not do simply to present dull and basic facts to children. No one biography is capable of presenting the basic "truth," so we must insist on interpretation, preferably using competing versions of the life.

Critical Acts of Imperialist Criticism

Ian Wojcik-Andrews

Imperialism and Juvenile Literature, edited by Jeffrey Richards. Manchester: Manchester University Press, 1989.

Arguing that "imperialism was more than a set of economic, political, and military phenomena" (vii), *Imperialism and Juvenile Literature* sees juvenile literature as a "reflector of the dominant ideas of an age" (vii). The essays in this collection examine a wide range of topics involving the connection between juvenile literature and the dissemination of imperialist ideas. A few examples will provide a sense of the scope of the volume: Patrick Dunae's essay offers us a general sociological background of nineteenth-century children's literature; Martin Green explores a single aspect of that background, showing how the Robinson Crusoe myth was appropriated for nineteenth-century imperialist ends. Jeffrey Richards discusses class and racial issues in G. A. Henty's African novels for children, Denis Butts considers pilots as imperialists in turn-of-the-century flying stories for boys, and J. S. Bratton surveys the girls' fiction that appeared between 1900 and 1930.

Patrick Dunae's opening essay, "New Grub Street for Boys," shows the "social, economic and technological" (43) forces at work in the relationship between imperialism and juvenile literature. Dunae outlines how "boys' literature during the New Imperialism was an industry" (13), an industry that grew out of a broad range of social, psychological, and economic conditions such as "the Victorians' discovery of adolescence, technological advances, and educational reforms" (13). According to Dunae, these discoveries opened up the terrain of the domestic market for writers and provided them with the kinds of ideologically discursive spaces in which to explore and to "maximize their production and profit" (32). For writers such as Dr. Gordon Stables, Robert Leighton, G. A. Henty, and many others who produced literary texts according to tight production schedules, "theirs was a business" (32). Dunae's indefatigable research and presentation of market-oriented statistics about publishing-

Children's Literature 20, ed. Francelia Butler, Barbara Rosen, and Judith A. Plotz (Yale University Press, © 1992 by The Children's Literature Foundation, Inc.).

house contracts and national and international sales show how "empire was merely a vehicle for [writers to] advanc[e] their trade" (13). Dunae's essay convincingly demonstrates how writers of juvenile literature consciously produced ideological texts that disseminated sound imperialist values. Reminding us how profit feeds ideology (and vice versa) and how writers often knowingly plunder culture to satisfy the demands of the publishing houses to which they contract themselves, Dunae's essay shows that nineteenth-century juvenile literature was never disinterested.

Other well-researched essays in this collection further explore, provocatively and informatively, the ways in which juvenile literature reflected imperialist ideas. For example, Stuart Hannabuss's "Ballantyne's Message of Empire" takes as axiomatic the problematic statement that "social issues . . . characterise much children's writing in previous ages" (54). Hannabuss argues that "it is useful to see . . . fictions as touchstones for their age, as lenses through which we can peer and see . . . the stances which the writers adopted" (54). He discusses such a stance in Ballantyne's "unoriginal [yet] large output of books [that] mediated many powerful ideals about heroism and Christian courage through stories like *The Coral Island* (1858) and *The Gorilla Hunters* (1861)" (54–55). Hannabuss's balanced essay also points out, however, Ballantyne's ambivalence toward the use of his fictional characters and settings for imperialist ends. For example, Hannabuss draws a credible portrait of Ballantyne as a writer who, caught in the "pervasive cross-currents of his age" (58) by attempting to deal in fiction with "manliness . . . faith and empire" (58), "had an eye for productive themes [of which] slavery and missions were two" (60), yet nonetheless refused to depict the savage as a mere "fictional device" (58). In a sense, Hannabuss's representation of Ballantyne's ambivalence serves as a corrective to Dunae's essay: nineteenth-century writers of juvenile fiction made profits—but often with some reservations.

Denis Butts's brief "Imperialists of the Air-flying Stories: 1900–1950" discusses the formulaic plots used by W. E. Johns, Major T. Gorman, Jack Heming, and others to show pilots as the embodiment of empire values: heroism, manliness, bravery. Butts argues that the flying stories validate the kinds of technological developments necessary for the global dissemination of imperial values. However, noting the autobiographical component of Johns's juvenile fiction, Butts also suggests that "much more work needs to be done on the still largely neglected area of flying stories" (141). Butts thoughtfully concludes that though social and biographical contexts demonstrate the importance to imperialism of children's fiction, and children's literature generally, we must continue today to open up the topic of imperialism for examination from a variety of literary and historical perspectives.

The editor of this collection, Jeffrey Richards, appears to agree: the remaining essays explore other, diverse ways in which imperialist ideas surface in children's fiction. For example, John M. MacKenzie investigates juvenile literature's representation of hunting activities. J. A. Mangan's "Noble Specimens of Manhood: Schoolboy Literature and the Creation of a Colonial Chivalric Code" considers how professional writers such as W. H. G. Kingston, under the influence of Hughes's *Tom Brown's Schooldays*, located the fight for empire in the playgrounds of British public schools. Mangan's essay is particularly useful in showing the international scope of imperialism in boys' fiction. He does this by comparing the characterization and narrative strategies of Australian and English schoolboy fiction, finding that in Australian novels such as *Max the Sport* (1916), "Manliness . . . owes almost everything to British ideals and models and above all, to its public school" (181). Comparative studies such as Mangan's remind us to continue uncovering those hidden but crucial connections that exist between the children's literature of different countries.

Unfortunately, in *Imperialism and Juvenile Literature*, only J. S. Bratton's concluding essay, "British Imperialism and the Reproduction of Femininity in Girls' Fiction, 1900–1930," focuses predominantly on the representation of girls rather than boys, on the feminine rather than the masculine. Bratton informatively and subtly tells how "the British Empire, however, had some use for girls" (196); for middle-class girls were "both the motive for fighting and striving . . . and the guardians and transmitters of a more abstract justification of ideals, a sense of purpose and rectitude. They were both the warrior's prize and the embodied ideal" (196). In short, Bratton's lucid, carefully researched essay demonstrates how the ideology of British imperialism, usually defined by male writers in terms of masculine traits, was defined by female writers in terms of feminine traits.

However, Bratton's essay also shows that imperialistic elements in children's literature, relatively clear-cut in the case of boys, are more problematic in the case of girls. According to Bratton, women were demanding participation in "masculine activities" (196) related to imperialism: muscular Christianity, self-reliance, the experience of camaraderie, of command, of rule. But, as Bratton points out, "feminism was anti-imperialist" (197). Bratton's essay then traces the way in which women writers, aware of women's contradictory role in nineteenth-century imperialist England—represented by a "spiritualised, disembodied femininity and vigorous pioneering motherhood" (197)—provided "narrative strategies" (198) for girls caught between a "clash of ideological designs" (201): domesticity on the one hand, empire on the other.

Of the many women writers and publications Bratton mentions, such as the Australian Louise Mack, "the prolific Evelyn Everett Green" (199), Grace Toplis, and *The Girls' Empire*, "very few writers managed to find a narrative formula that could cope; the only outstanding example is Bessie Marchant" (201). According to Bratton, Marchant almost completely ignored the conventional narrative lines and requisite sense of closure in women's romances—that the girl's destiny was to find a "permanent place of subordination in marriage" (202). In the three novels that Bratton discusses—*A Heroine of the Sea* (1904), *No Ordinary Girl* (1908), and *The Gold-marked Charm* (1918)—Marchant places her middle-class girls in exotic settings, such as the Canadian forests or South America. Through her manipulations of plot and setting, Marchant sets up her girls with fantastic adventures during which they learn how to handle "crisis situations with strength and diplomacy." They are represented as "women of unlimited potential, and indeed of present power" (204). Nonetheless, according to Bratton, the power of the heroines in the minds of the readers remains an essentially domestic power exercised in the name of empire. The girls rule over great houses, servants, and the like. The heroine of *The Gold-marked Charm*, Audrey Felsham, for example, presides over a fabulously wealthy house, "peopled and worked by whole tribes of loyal retainers and servants" (204). In the context of nineteenth-century imperialism and juvenile literature, this "nest becomes an empire" (205). The middle-class girls travel to exotic places and undergo strange journeys of adventure, yet are ultimately confronted by and must deal with quite ordinary areas of life: the terrain of domesticity. Emotionally and psychologically, they do not travel very far at all. As Bratton points out about the Girl Guide stories that emulate masculine "codes of honor" (214), the traditional sexual division of labor based upon an equally conventional psychology that associates women with only service, self-sacrifice, and nurturing remains the ideological structure that validates the adventures of the girls in strange places.

The placing of Bratton's essay last is only one example of the way *Imperialism and Juvenile Literature* consistently marginalizes women, women writers, and women's roles in its treatment of its subject. For example, Martin Green's essay begins with this comparison: "In the National Union Catalogue, fifty-four pages are given up to listing different editions of Defoe's book whereas only four go to . . . *Middlemarch*" (35). Though this is, of course, a statement of fact, one must wonder why Green chooses not to compare the printing history of Defoe's novel with that of another adventure story or children's book by another male author. For another instance, take Jeffrey Richards's essay, "With Henty to Africa," in which Richards discusses the relationship between Henty's novels and issues of class, race, and gender. Richards writes: "Women play little part in the Henty world, except in the supporting roles of wives, sisters, and mothers, their function chiefly domestic" (88). Regardless of Richards's intention, it is not clear if he means Henty's fictional world or the one in which he actually lived. Moreover, his sentence implies a contradiction. A female presence in a traditionally supportive role is obviously *central* to imperialist ends because the woman is seen to validate conventional, familial ideology built around correct gender relationships: the outgoing husband and the domesticated, dutiful, loving, and supportive wife. By the same token, the woman's admittedly ambiguous power could hardly be acknowledged fully; to do so (as to acknowledge the "savages" as the human beings they were) would undermine what J. S. Bratton also calls "ideological designs" (201).

Imperialism and Juvenile Literature is an important collection of essays because the "sub-genres" (127) discussed—Henty's African novels, flying stories, hunting stories, schoolboy literature, fiction for girls—show what Raymond Williams in *Marxism and Literature* called the "clear social and historical relations between literary forms and the societies and periods in which they were originated or practiced" (182). But as vividly and dramatically illustrated as these essays are, and as useful as the collection as a whole may seem to be for scholars, historians, and teachers of children's litera-

ture, *Imperialism and Juvenile Literature* thematically and aesthetically
provides through individual essays and the collection as a whole a
metanarrative about boys' rather than girls' history. Feminist and
Marxist literary criticism has demonstrated that women and women
writers were what Williams calls an emergent cultural group that
shaped nineteenth-century attitudes. But the collection seems to
ignore this important fact, failing to work past the thesis that imperialism equals masculinity, that history is *his story*. In reconstruct-
ing a (partially critical) history of the relationship between juvenile
literature and imperialism, it fails to talk about *herstory*. A politics
of gender is central to the relationship between imperialism and
children's literature; it is precisely this politics that is absent from
Imperialism and Juvenile Literature.

Children's Literature and the Politics of the Nation-State

J. D. Stahl

Zur Lage der Jugendbuchautoren. Eine Untersuchung über die soziale Situation der Kinder und Jugendschriftsteller in der Bundesrepublik Deutschland, by Helmut Müller. Weinheim and Basel: Beltz, 1980.

Der Deutsche Jugendliteraturpreis. Eine Wirkungsanalyse, by Klaus Doderer and Cornelia Riedel. Weinheim and Munich: Juventa Verlag, 1988.

Die Welt gehört den Kindern. Das moderne China und seine Kinderbücher, by Jean-Pierre Diény. Trans. Helmut Müller. Weinheim and Basel: Beltz, 1973.

These three works, with their very different foci, are all concerned with the problematic relationship between children's literature and the state, or, more specifically, with the position of the author of children's literature in society. They examine the political and economic positions that children's book authors occupy in nations as diverse as the Federal Republic of Germany and the People's Republic of China. Müller, Doderer, and Riedel probe these and related issues through the techniques of sociological investigation— questionnaires that quantify and categorize the social position of a more or less representative group of West German children's authors (Müller) or that examine the influence and social context of the Deutsche Jugendliteraturpreis, the only state-granted literary prize in West Germany (Doderer and Riedel). These two works appeared before German Unification, and reflect only the West German situation; Unification will naturally require new studies to meet the dynamics of the new situation. Diény's study examines a group of children's books purchased in China on the eve of the Cultural Revolution and uses this group of works as the basis for his analysis of the relationship between propaganda and art in Chinese society.

Children's Literature 20, ed. Francelia Butler, Barbara Rosen, and Judith A. Plotz (Yale University Press, © 1992 by The Children's Literature Foundation, Inc.).

As varied as their approaches and materials are, these three books each raise the difficult question of what the role of government should be in the support, development, and control of children's literature. Müller criticizes West German cultural policy for surrendering children's book publishing to market forces that reduce literature to the status of commodity. Doderer and Riedel provide a sophisticated critique of the influence of the national children's literature prize in the context of its historical goal of reaching a broad audience, its actual effects, which tend to be confined to the educated and relatively privileged, and the inescapable pressures of the popular media that are altering if not threatening the whole culture of literacy. Finally, Diény brings into focus the conflict between art and propaganda in a nation-state in which all forms of art have become politicized, but he wavers between endorsements of the goals of the Chinese revolution and critiques of revolutionary art from an aesthetic perspective. These books raise the question of whether children's literature is ultimately a means of social control (even when its goal is liberation) or of subversion. If the state has a responsibility for promoting children's literature, does it have any right to influence the forms that literature takes and the ideas it expresses? The paradoxical nature of art as a social function is brought to light by these very different discussions.

Ironically, even the idea of a scholarly (and thus presumably state-funded) investigation into the conditions of life for children's book authors elicited resentment among those approached in the study conducted by Helmut Müller and a team from the Institut für Jugendbuchforschung at the University of Frankfurt. The appearance of a long, detailed, complex questionnaire in the mail of children's writers evoked some cries of protest, some (pointed?) silence, and even a sarcastic commentary on Bavarian radio. In an era of sensitivity to state control through data collection and supervision, such questions seemed to some an invasion of privacy. Yet the study itself suggested that West German children's book authors belong to a group that is not only intent on preserving its sense of privacy and individuality, but also lacking in any collective sense of itself as a group with common problems and interests. This is reflected in the tendency of publishers to shortchange if not exploit writers in their financial arrangements.

Though Müller's approach is partly statistical, the results are far from being dry and impersonal. Through a combination of personal statements, statistical information intelligently presented, and informed analysis and speculation, he draws a number of conclusions that present a revealing picture of the conditions under which many West German children's authors wrote. Based on the responses to the questionnaire (a remarkably high 48.8% of those queried responded), Müller discovered that more men than women were children's book authors in the group surveyed: 55.7% compared to 44.3%. There was a predominance of older authors: the investigators came to "an alarming conclusion" that only 17 of 636 authors were under 30, 66.8% were over 50, and 21.2% were over 70—alarming to the researchers because of the large age difference between authors and audience. "Apparently many children's and young adult books in the Federal Republic of Germany are written by authors who have long left behind their childhood and adolescent years and whose own memories are likely to be nostalgically idealized" (21–22). Indeed, the image of German children's book authors that emerges from the survey is one of older, conservative, privileged, and socially retiring aesthetes. West German children's book authors formed a large group (the few exceptionally well-known authors of children's books were not included, or at any rate not named), but most of them wrote only part-time. Many women wrote for children (a larger proportion than among other authors, though still not a majority), but few made writing their main career. As indicated earlier, these conclusions apply only to what was formerly West Germany; the impact of Unification on children's book authors in what was East Germany will be a valuable subject of study, and a similar assessment of their age and status will add useful data for comparison.

Though writers for children and young people in West Germany were above average in education, only a very small percentage of them earned a living from writing. Of the individuals who returned the questionnaires, only five were able to support themselves on the royalties from their children's books alone. For most it was a welcome addition to their income, and 90 percent said that the money earned by writing for children was only part of their means of survival. The largest groups were married women working at home, retirees, journalists or other media-related professionals, educators, and scientists. Partly because they were not able to earn a living solely from writing books for children, authors frequently worked for other media such as film, television, newspapers, and magazines. Those authors who claimed writing as their main source of income also frequently supplemented their income with fees from lectures or readings, or wrote for other media. Müller and his co-authors observe that it appears practically impossible to achieve a full-time self-supporting career as a writer for children before the age of thirty. Though their entry into a career may resemble that of academics in some respects, writers have much less financial security and rarely the same health and old age protections. Stories of exploitation and abuse by publishers and editors abound, and a general pattern of underpayment emerges.

However, interviews with a selected number of the authors in their homes gave an impression of well-to-do environments. The interviewers noted that many authors live in "idyllic isolation" in single-family homes away from urban centers, with rather conservative if tasteful furnishings, with an inclination toward the playful Biedermeier style. Müller notes a tendency toward regarding writing for children as a hobby, a dilettante air that permeates some authors' statements about their work, and a lack of self-critical or objective awareness. A large proportion of the authors named a combination of a desire to entertain and to educate morally and socially as a motive for writing—a combination which, Müller points out, is not unlike the "oft-despised" aims of the prolific authors of the eighteenth and nineteenth centuries. The authors' statements about their motivation and intention "reveal a common apolitical attitude and the rather naive idea that pedagogical correctness and political wisdom naturally derive from the simple good intention to write a 'good' children's book" (56).

On the other hand, Müller finds that many children's book authors suffer from the condescension of a public that has insufficient respect for children's literature. Many authors desire to do away with the strict separation of children's and adult literature, and want greater recognition, especially from fellow authors who do not write for a youthful audience. Yet, according to Müller, many of the children's authors surveyed desire greater respect while placing relatively little emphasis on the literary merits of their own work.

Müller laments two forms of distance between the youthful audience and the authors who write for them: in addition to the age gap, he notes that almost all of the authors surveyed belong to the "gehobene Bürgerschicht," or upper middle class. Thus there is a difference between the social world of an audience that is almost half working class and a literature reflecting middle- and upper-class life.

Müller criticizes the society that fails to reward and support writers for children adequately. One young author ruefully remarked that children's books are produced and sold like cheese. Müller traces the dilettantism of much German children's literature to economic conditions: a competitive publishing market in which authors' fees are often the only variable (and thus exploitable) expense. But Müller also criticizes writers' "almost mythic exaggeration of their function" as ethical educators, which he finds seldom matched by literary skill or depth of content. In his interpretation of the responses, children's authors tend to see themselves as gifted loners and to reinforce willfully their isolation and ignorance of other contemporary children's books. Literary ambition, effort, and disciplined literary self-criticism are too little in evidence, Müller finds. Here again, Unification may lead to interesting changes.

Müller argues that the education of the young is a duty of the democratic state, anchored in the constitution of the Federal Republic, and that the regulation of schoolbooks is a similar (though, he argues, even less influential) means of promoting free democratic social values. He opposes state control but is in favor of state financial support for talented younger authors, which might take the form of a "Schmökergroschen" (a tax on cheap novels), analogous to an energy tax, to raise funds from the massive sales of trivial literature to subsidize more valuable literature. The book offers other precise and practical suggestions for improving the status of children's book authors in the Federal Republic of Germany.

The German Democratic Republic actively promoted children's book production and authorship, but also more closely controlled the content of children's literature. The GDR sought to develop a socialist children's literature, officially committed to high artistic standards, humanism, internationalism, and a sense of class duty in "young socialists." German Unification has already sparked debate about what—if anything—of the East German approach to children's literature should be preserved, and which authors will be able to make the transition.

Doderer and Riedel's analysis of the German Youth Literature Prize examines an institution that has sought to promote both the educational development of young people and the quality of their literature. The Deutsche Jugendliteraturpreis is the best known of the many German literary awards for children's and youth books; its dual goal of aesthetic and pedagogical development has been interpreted in various ways since the inception of the prize in 1955. The prize is awarded in the following categories: picture book, children's book, young adult book, nonfiction, special award, and premium. This exceptionally thorough study begins with a history of the prize, from its beginnings as a means of fighting trash literature (Schund- und Schmutzliteratur), to the promotion of ethical, moral, and cultural values—an "ethical-pedagogical functionalization of literature" (27)—in the 1960s, to the support of a socially critical, emancipatory, engaged children's and youth literature in the 1970s and 1980s. As Bundesfamilienministerin Rita Süssmuth stated in her address at the 1986 award ceremonies in Göttingen, the history of the prize can be regarded as "a piece of German literary and cultural history, in which the varied developments of those years in almost all social realms are reflected" (32). Doderer and Riedel realistically observe, however, on the basis of their own experience and of many discussions with librarians, educators, and parents, that young people are most often indifferent to literary prizes and may even be put off by the knowledge that a jury of adults awarded a prize to a certain book.

Doderer and Riedel and their team from the Institut für Jugendbuchforschung (which included Helmut Müller, Hildegard Schindler-Frankerl, and Winfred Kaminski) compare the award with other similar awards (both German and international) and examine the degree of awareness of the award in the public mind. They also look at the meanings and effects of the prize for children's book authors and publishers, the usefulness of the prize for librarians, booksellers, and teachers, and the visibility of the prize in the mass media and specialized journals. Though the prize is well known among teachers of German, and is used as a guide for selection by teachers and by editors of textbooks, it is most influential among booksellers, who rate it as an important consideration in their selection of books to recommend and promote. Not surprisingly, the prize is best known among the best educated and most economically privileged young people. It has a different function and greater national and international impact than similar prizes, such as the Buxtehuder Bulle or the Astrid Lindgren Prize. Because it is awarded without regard for the nationality of the author, it garners significant attention beyond the borders of

Germany, and it promotes internationalism in children's literature. Authors interviewed who have won the award report an increase in self-confidence and a sense of inner freedom. They find that the prize gives them the legitimacy that allows them to pursue artistic goals independently of market considerations, though they are also sometimes drawn into an " Öffentlichkeitsrummel," a media circus. Doderer and Riedel's work is a comprehensive analysis of the philosophy, reception, implementation, and effects of a national prize that is equivalent to but probably even more influential in its realm than the Newbery and Caldecott awards are in theirs. *Der Deutsche Jugendliteraturpreis: Eine Wirkungsanalyse* is exemplary in its inclusion of diverse and painstakingly researched perspectives, particularly criticisms of the methods of awarding and promoting the prize.

Die Welt gehört den Kindern (the world belongs to the children) is a saying of Chairman Mao's, and in the context of Jean-Pierre Diény's study it is an ironic pronouncement indeed. Diény demonstrates, on the one hand, just how thoroughly children's literature can serve the ideology of the state, indoctrinating children into the political beliefs of adults, while, on the other hand, he also acknowledges the conflict between generations that led the children of the Cultural Revolution to renounce, denounce, and abuse their elders. Diény's work needs to be regarded as a dated document: it first appeared in 1971 as *"Le monde est à vous": La Chine et les livres pour enfants* (Éditions Gallimard), and there is already visible in Diény's writing a troubled ambivalence about the outgrowths of the Cultural Revolution. However, Diény is remarkably uncritical of the ideology of the Chinese Communist Party. He accepts prima facie that children's literature, at least in China, is propaganda, and presents it neutrally or approvingly as such. His only real quarrel is aesthetic: he attacks banality and clichés, but he seems to accept grudgingly that these are frequently the necessary result of following a party line.

There is a second sense in which Diény's work is a work that belongs to a particular historical moment. It examines approximately 180 children's books purchased in China between 1964 and 1966. To begin with, Diény acknowledges that the selection of works he studies is somewhat random. However, it is easy to see that the books he analyzes are probably quite representative of children's literature in China on the eve of the Cultural Revolution, because they reflect dominant themes of Communist Chinese ideology. The method of approach, a focus on themes, appears to be quite comprehensive and accurate. So, for example, he discusses the "black and white" dichotomies of the books he collected: peasants versus landowners, workers versus factory owners, Communist solidarity in the face of aggression from abroad, and the simplistic portrayals of capitalism (which are not too different from the simplistic portrayals of Communism in Western texts for children from the same era).

China treats children like adults and adults like children, Diény states. Perhaps for that reason his discussion of books for young children—children in kindergarten or primary school—reads like a survey of political themes from a Party congress. He finds an unequivocally moralistic children's literature, whose goal is not social advancement and personal success, but rather service to society. Respect for property is taught in many of these stories, but it is collective property. Guarding or returning lost goods is one of the favorite themes of the literature of this period. Individual ambition is portrayed as the main hindrance to the virtue of humble selflessness. Together, these books convey a utopian vision of a world ruled by cooperative and collectively self-motivating children. Diény sees simplicity and care in design and artistry as two distinctive qualities that mark these books, although they are frequently printed on cheap paper.

One of the values of Diény's analysis is his knowledge of ancient Chinese traditions. Frequently he identifies themes and forms that echo or revive artistic motifs from prerevolutionary days. He attempts to sift the traditional elements from the modern propagandistic ones in fables and folktales. He explores the Maoist battle against superstition (as distinguished from religion): the main goal is to purify nature of divinities. He is somewhat critical of the strict positivism of the modern tales and their merciless rejection of folk customs, legends, proverbs, and beliefs. In the place of the old superstitions, new ones are being cultivated by the Party. Class consciousness is formed through fables concerning exploitation and oppression of the peasants by the landowners in imperial China; tales of the working conditions in factories chronicle the exploitative misdeeds of factory owners; and propagandistic accounts of child abuse by Catholic and American orphanages and missionaries display fictionalizing tendencies which Diény cautiously identifies as such. Portrayals of the Americans in Vietnam as bumblers and fools echo a tradition of enemy depiction that goes back to the Han Dynasty (3rd century A.D.). On the idealizing side, praise of modern China sometimes reveals positively bourgeois dreams, "but the temptation of comfort has its antidote: work" (41).

Diény notes the tendency to portray women as superior to men: "Previously a victim of the old society, like the poor farmer or laborer, woman seems especially suited for a special role in the class conflict. Whether on the stage, in films, or in novels, frequently it is an invincible heroine who sets the example for her comrades and plays a leading role in the struggle for the good" (45). He notes that though the role of the family in children's lives has diminished in postrevolutionary children's literature, parents are not maligned or attacked, and grandparents are given (true to reality) relative prominence and influence. However, there is a clear movement toward the substitution of extrafamilial collective life for the primacy of the family. In this connection, he observes that parents were often not able to protect or sustain their children in prerevolutionary China. Diény is more descriptive than critical in presenting the idolization of Chairman Mao and the concurrent idealization of the authority of the Communist Party. He frequently recognizes the distortions of propaganda with faint touches of irony, but largely seeks to account for the content of such works on their own terms. He is knowledgeable about Maoist thought as well as ancient Chinese traditions, and shows the relevance of both to the principles inherent in Chinese children's literature. So, for example, he links the glorification of heroes and heroines of the Revolution with the ritual gong beats intended to immortalize the old in traditional China.

In his footnotes, perhaps added later when the meaning of certain excesses of the Cultural Revolution began to sink in, Diény reveals an increasing ambivalence toward his subject in relation to social realities. His most acute analyses of the constraints of propaganda are contained in the chapter on issues of form. He appears quite willing to criticize the literature he treats on aesthetic grounds (banality, poverty of imagination) but not on political or moral grounds. Yet when the two intersect, Diény makes some of his most astutely ironic observations, as when he remarks that the figure of the missionary always appears with a Bible in his hand: "Until the 'Little Red Book' appeared, one may assume that this gesture was regarded as ridiculous" (70). Though Diény clearly wishes to support the goals of the Revolution, he cannot let pass without remark some of the results of a literature dedicated uncritically to an ideology, even when he agrees with it:

> The vision of the world as divided into good and evil, imposed upon literature by politics in China, has led to the creation of two opposite groups of characters. Among the villains the worst, the most striking embodiment of evil, is the landowner. . . . In order to convince their readers thoroughly of his villainy and powerlessness, the narrators create intrigues of unparalleled absurdity. [58]

Perhaps most troubling in Diény's ironic balancing act is his apparent attack on the subtle subversion of orthodox ideas by some of the most gifted creative artists. He indicts their covert manipulations of seemingly officially acceptable forms with an ironic tone that could be interpreted as critical of the Party line, but which could also serve (or have served) Party purists as ammunition for arraigning bold artists. It is possible that some subtlety of tone was lost in the translation from the French into the German, but in fact he appears to condemn the best of the artists he selects, precisely for their dedication to art. In a discussion of the work of He Yaurong, he states, "To the artist, only beauty, grace, or simply the structure of things are important. The object allows one to forget the slogan" (102). If indeed Diény's book was being read in China, his flirtation with what he seems to regard as aesthetic indulgence in the midst of preserving ideological purity may have meant condemnation or worse for the artists themselves living in China.

Finally, Diény acknowledges explicitly the tension he so often skirts with irony: "By demanding of its artists the realization of an impossible fusion of art and politics, China condemns its artists to the suspicion of treason when they conduct bold experiments" (103). Recent events in China have shown that the desire for freedom is not just a matter of Western influence. And one may well ask, what role does democracy play in the formation of children's literature, and vice versa? Müller, Doderer, Riedel, and Diény all demonstrate that the answers to that question remain complex and controversial. In the Western capitalist democracies, the state is expected to improve the conditions for the best of children's literature to emerge freely, but as the German scholars demonstrate, economic as well as social forces always impinge on the uses of literature as well as its creation. With German Unification, the issues of state control versus economic control are likely to be raised in new ways. As the French scholar's investigation reveals, Chinese children's literature from before the Cultural Revolution shows us just how acutely the tensions and aspirations of a society can be reflected in and shaped by literature and art for children. The world belongs to the children? Maybe. Maybe not.

Close Encounters of a Pictorial Kind

Jane Doonan

Words About Pictures: The Narrative Art of Children's Picture Books, by
  Perry Nodelman. Athens: University of Georgia Press, 1988.

In recent years there has been an increasing interest in picture
books, and it is generally accepted that this flourishing genre is
capable of sustaining pleasure and learning well beyond the years
of early childhood. Many parents and teachers suspect that picture books could be used for more than language development and
literacy but are at a loss to know how to expand on these basic
uses. Perry Nodelman's *Words About Pictures* provides an answer: we
should be teaching children about the structures and conventions of
how stories are told in words, in pictures, and in both together, thus
enabling children to engage the picture book with greater vitality
and consciousness.

Although Nodelman modestly offers "a number of words that can
interestingly and usefully be said about picture books" (xi), what
he attempts is a prodigious feat: to claim for the picture book the
status of a serious art form; to reveal the pictorial sign to be linguistic in its inner workings; to resolve the traditional power struggle
of text versus image both by tracing resemblances and by finding
differences between the two sign types as they function in picture-
book narrative; and to encourage adults who share picture books
with children to widen and deepen their pedagogical practice.

In *Words About Pictures*, primarily semiotic in its orientation, Nodelman discusses how the art and the Art of the picture book form
engage in the telling of stories, literal and metaphorical. After an
introduction that invites his readers to reflect upon the extraordinary learning capacity of young children, the book divides broadly
into two areas: exclusively visual information and aspects of the
relationships between words and pictures. His method is to draw
upon an eclectic selection of scholarship and criticism from literary theory, psychology, and art philosophy, which, together with
theories and process models of his own, he applies to examples

Children's Literature 20, ed. Francelia Butler, Barbara Rosen, and Judith A. Plotz
(Yale University Press, © 1992 by The Children's Literature Foundation, Inc.).

from well-known picture books. His presentation is something like a taxonomic classification. His prose style underlines his sense of mission; it insists that we need to understand the picture book better in order to recognize its potential. The picture book is so familiar that we take everything about it for granted. However, as Nodelman shows, it has many unusual features, including unique conventions of shape and structure, a succinct and undetailed text partnered with a series of pictures intended to be taken as a whole, special rhythms that result from reading these two texts at different speeds, and a distinctive body of narrative techniques.

There is so much to be praised in Nodelman's book that I feel it would be best if I air two reservations at this point and qualify them by admitting that whereas Nodelman speaks "with the prejudice of one steeped in language" (8), I have no trouble at all in being rendered speechless by pictures (yes, even in certain picture books). While Nodelman's study enables us to understand and appreciate many aspects of the narrative art of picture books, I wish that he had not sidestepped the notoriously difficult problem of discussing the function of feeling in the essentially cognitive process he describes. Is it not the case that what makes your heart knock with fright or delight also makes your brain go tick? That is worth saying in some detail to the implied reader of this book, for there are still too many people who think that there is a great divide between the affective and the cognitive processes. The sensual pleasure to be derived from pictures is not something apart, but has a special role in the making of pictorial meaning. The other disquiet I have is that since Nodelman limits his concern to that which can be put into words, one gains the impression that grasping what a picture means is only a matter of words. Because he makes such a strong and most welcome case for the symbolic eloquence of images and their abstract organization, some of his readers might mistakenly assume that everything on the picture plane is capable of being translated into words with precision and without loss.

On the whole, though, Nodelman's book presents a useful critical overview, and more importantly it raises key issues that need to be realized and incorporated in personal and pedagogical practice by those who share picture books with children. The first of these key issues is that the "innocent eye"—that is, one without knowledge of contextual significations—is merely an ignorant one, which cannot take advantage of all that a picture has to offer, and that the comprehending of pictures depends upon learned competences. The more knowledge a child has, the richer and more complex even very simple pictures come to be.

Secondly, children should be encouraged to develop a meaning-conscious mind-set, one which, as it scans a picture, is always conscious of, and in search of, possible meanings; a major source of pleasure in picture books is the joy of discovering a meaningful aspect of visual information, such as a visual joke or an insight into a character. In order to be able to do this, children need to be taught how much more there is to pictures than an exclusive focus on descriptive aspects. We should be providing children with both the information that symbols exist and specific information about the meanings of particular visual symbols, thus giving them the tools to appreciate the otherwise hidden subtleties of many picture books. An appreciation of visual symbolism is not a matter of age, as Nodelman irrefutably points out in relation to a picture book by Charles Keeping: "[N]o one of any age could understand the symbolism of Through the Window without first learning not just that there is such a thing as visual symbolism and how to look for it but also what any specific visual symbol means" (38).

Third, a child needs to have some knowledge of the visual codes that are concerned with how the artist organizes and disposes the abstract elements on the picture plane. Visual conventions allow meanings to be attached to objects by shape, size, position, color, and techniques that imply three-dimensional space. The artist's choice of media is crucial to the symbolic meanings of what he depicts. His very style communicates mood and atmosphere as well as bearing historical and contemporary cultural associations.

Fourth, the relationships between pictures and texts in picture books tend to be ironic—a point that I will discuss later. Fifth, pictures have the effect of interrupting the text, so that they act as punctuation, but in addition, they always add something more to what we already know about the events being described. Nodelman believes that we need to teach children that the information contained in pictures is not merely information about how things look but is a significant part of the story and something we need to know at this particular moment.

Finally, complex rhythms arise when reading a picture book. Reading its short text is a relatively speedy process, whereas reading the series of pictures that accompany the words is a lengthy one that involves the need for close attention, the search for clues, the putting together of apparently disparate pieces of information, the scanning, remembering, projecting, predicting, discriminating, and all the other activities that arise from the meaning-conscious mind-set. If we read the text to a young child we must allow sufficient time for a just perusal of the pictures as well, and by so doing, we establish the pattern for her or his future independent picture-book reading.

These key issues are embedded in a wealth of interesting discussions. In the section of the book concerning purely visual matters, for instance, Nodelman's reader is made aware of both graphic and iconographic codes, and thus is given a basic knowledge of how pictures "work" and a vocabulary in which to describe what is being seen. Thus, a feature such as color (or the lack of it) plays an important part in our reception of a picture book. By applying simplified color theory to examples from Maurice Sendak, Charles Keeping, William Steig, Raymond Briggs, and others, Nodelman explains how differences in hues, tones, and saturation affect us psychologically. The quality of an outline, an arrangement of forms, framed or unframed views of events, bird's-eye or worm's-eye levels, can evoke a wide range of impressions. Large-scale close-ups, middle-distance views, or long shots of characters and their situations draw the viewer in or distance him. Nodelman examines at length the narrative information that pictures provide from the specific objects depicted—not just what they are but how they relate to each other, within the actual text as well as through what Nodelman calls "a vast series of unspoken words that the pictures imply and depend on" (103). He offers a clear definition of intertextuality and demonstrates how we interpret pictures according to the kind of work in which they appear and the places in which we see them. He explains how pictures depict action and imply the passage of time.

If you have ever questioned the creative vision of a picture-book artist who, at the service of his text, comes close to plagiarizing the illustrations of another artist, or the style of another period, then you will be interested in Nodelman's justification in the chapter that discusses how meaning is carried in style. He also explains why caricaturing and cartooning are particularly suited to narrative art. Citing Nancy Ekholm Burkert's *Snow White*, Gerald McDermott's *Arrow to the Sun*, and Maurice Sendak's *Mr. Rabbit and the Lovely Present*, and intending no insult, he argues that they are all caricatures of style—high art, folk art, and impressionism.

Within a book that covers so many aspects of picture-book form,

Nodelman is only able to scratch the surface of the huge subject of the psychology of visual perception; but his frequent references, both implied and explicit, to the works of Rudolf Arnheim, Norman Bryson, and E. H. Gombrich are valuable markers for anyone intent upon further study.

Following the material that is largely concerned with visual codes and that requires the reader to do little more than absorb information, Nodelman offers three chapters that challenge our general understanding of what happens in the process of reading a picture book with a text. These demand more muscular mental feats. When one considers the complexity of that multisensory process, with the book as physical object requiring manipulation and, at the same time, allowing us control over viewing time, with the two sign systems each having a different way of telling a story and requiring a different way of reading, it is hardly surprising that Nodelman gives the impression that he's engaged in a Laocoönian struggle as he wrestles to formulate a coherent account of the expansion that takes place as words and pictures come together and the pages turn. Reversing the outcome of the classical close encounter, Nodelman (aided by the theories of Wolfgang Iser and Roland Barthes) emerges from the coils, in gradual stages, with three insights that he invites us to grasp: a definition of the nature of the relationship between words and pictures, a location for "the essence of picture-book story telling" (239), and a revelation of the rhythms of picture-book narration.

In his discussion of the relationship between pictures and words, Nodelman stresses that each communicates different kinds of information and contributes in different ways to the total effect of a picture-book narrative. The text is brief, and asserts in undecorated language; the illustrations contain a vast amount of information and are inherently unassertive. As we look at the pictures, the words direct our attention and tell us what matters and what does not. The paradoxical truth is that words without pictures can be vague and incomplete, incommunicative about important visual information, while pictures without words can also be vague and incomplete, lacking the focus, temporal relationships, and internal significances so easily communicated by words. Although commentators often say that the purpose of pictures in picture books is to "extend" the text, Nodelman explains in a particularly interesting discussion that it would be more accurate to say that pictures limit the text—and the text also limits the pictures. He writes: "Because they communicate different kinds of information, and because they work together by limiting each other's meanings, words and pictures necessarily have a combative relationship; their complementarity is a matter of opposites complementing each other by virtue of their differences. As a result, the relationships between pictures and texts in picture books tend to be ironic; each speaks about matters on which the other is silent" (221).

Nodelman develops an argument that all picture books are ironic to the extent that they express two specific sorts of irony that develop when words and pictures come together in narratives. The first lies in the distance between the relative subjectivity of words (which allows us to put ourselves in the place of the central character) and the relative objectivity of pictures (which demands that we stand back and look at that character); the second involves the distance between the temporal movement of stories and the fixed timelessness usual in pictures. The alternations between subjective involvement and objective distance experienced by the reader and the ironic relationship between the sequential storytelling of words and the series of stopped moments we see in a sequence of pictures make up what Nodelman believes to be the essence of picture-book storytelling. Nodelman leads his reader to an appreciation of the range of degrees of irony through convincing analyses of the relationships of words and pictures in *Rosie's Walk, Mr. Rabbit and the Lovely Present, Where the Wild Things Are,* and *Peter Rabbit.*

Nodelman focuses next upon the temporal dimensions of words, pictures, and the reading process itself in the chapter he calls "The Rhythm of the Picture-Book Narrative." He describes in some detail a possible pattern by which the reader looks at the text and the pictures, moving between one and the other, apprehending, interpreting, and reinterpreting. At the same time, of course, the reader is moving constantly between strong evocations of space that more weakly evoke time to strong evocations of temporal passage that more weakly evoke space. Furthermore, as he notes: "Both the words and the pictures have temporality—the words by their very nature and the pictures by their sequence. Consequently, both are capable of having rhythms, and the two create the third: the rhythmn of picture-book narrative" (244).

The rhythm of the pictures in sequence is that of a series of one strong beat following another that is equally strong. In contrast, the rhythm of verbal narrative is climactic. We want to keep the page turning, to hurry on to find out what is going to happen next. But the picture demands that we stop and look. The tension set up by the opposition of the two demands is a source of frustration; but in art as in life, frustration is the grit that makes the pearl. A good artist may take advantage of the opposition by reinforcing it so that the demands become a major feature; a skilled reader recognizes that close attention to the picture carries its own rewards, as Nodelman demonstrates when he takes us through *Where the Wild Things Are* for the pleasure of discovering the rhythms of the narrative.

Just as he showed that the degrees of irony vary, Nodelman goes on to discuss the many different kinds of rhythmic relationships that exist between words and pictures. In his analysis he considers the effects of the moments chosen for depiction, repeated actions, and the contrapuntal, forward-backward movements of some stories. In the end, Nodelman argues, it is "a story whose climax is at its middle rather than toward its end and whose plot is a matter of rhythmic counterpoints rather than intensifying suspense" that is typical of picture-book narrative (261).

Throughout this study, but particularly in these three chapters, Nodelman obliges us to focus on the hybrid form of the picture book itself and to test his words against specific examples under our eyes and in our hands. We may agree or not, to a greater or lesser degree, with Nodelman's process models and his findings, but undeniably he increases the ways in which picture books may be considered, both in their parts and as a whole. Jerome Bruner writes that "much of the process of education consists of being able to distance oneself in some way from what one knows by being able to reflect on one's own knowledge." *Words About Pictures* does this and much more, very successfully.

A Personal Book and a Tribute

C. W. Sullivan III

Tail Feathers from Mother Goose: The Opie Rhyme Book, by Iona and Peter Opie. Boston and Toronto: Little, Brown and Company, 1988.

Children and Their Books: A Celebration of the Work of Iona and Peter Opie, edited by Gillian Avery and Julia Briggs. Oxford: Clarendon Press, 1989.

Tail Feathers from Mother Goose is a delightful and unexpected variation for the Opies. Iona and her husband, the late Peter Opie, began collecting, studying, and writing about children's folklore in the 1940s, and over the ensuing years they published significant studies in the field, including that path-breaking work of scholarship, *The Lore and Language of Schoolchildren.* Along the way, they also ventured into the complex world of nursery rhymes, those short verses that come from both oral and literary traditions, and that can be about almost any subject, from politics to preferences of diet.

In 1951, *The Oxford Dictionary of Nursery Rhymes* appeared, with its more than 400 pages containing some 500 rhymes, and 1955 saw the publication of *The Oxford Nursery Rhyme Book,* a 250-page collection of over 800 rhymes. Both volumes received enthusiastic critical praise for their excellence as reference works. More recently, two of the Opies' other collections, *The Oxford Book of Children's Verse* (1973) and *The Oxford Book of Narrative Verse* (1983), have commented authoritatively on classic literary verse for children, while *A Nursery Companion* (1980) provided a historical view of early-nineteenth-century rhymes, fables, proverbs, and other works for children, accompanied by hundreds of period illustrations.

All of those nursery-rhyme books were labors of rigorous scholarship, however enjoyable they were for both the Opies and their readers. But *Tail Feathers from Mother Goose* is obviously and thoroughly a labor of love, a book much more for parents and children than for scholars. These "cordials and simples," writes Iona Opie in

Children's Literature 20, ed. Francelia Butler, Barbara Rosen, and Judith A. Plotz (Yale University Press, © 1992 by The Children's Literature Foundation, Inc.).

her foreword to the volume, "provide comfort for the heart or an antidote to melancholy, fit for adult and child." These small poems, she continues, can "cure moments of ennui and black desperation, or grace moments of exuberance or tranquility" (6). What she says is not only true of the poems in this book but also of the book itself, in its unique combination of largely unknown poems from the Mother Goose tradition and original pictures from many of the best illustrators working for children today. At a time when there are a number of fine collections of familiar rhymes (among them, the Opies'), the refreshing quality about *Tail Feathers from Mother Goose* is that it is a collection of unfamiliar rhymes only.

Nowhere in this book will the reader find "Mary Had a Little Lamb," "Little Jack Horner," "Peter, Peter, Pumpkin Eater," or any of the other rhymes one might expect in a typical nursery-rhyme book. "Ride a Cock Horse" is here, but not in its usual version. In *Tail Feathers* it is called "Riding to Market":

> Ride a cock-horse to Coventry Cross,
>   To see what Emma can buy;
> A penny white cake I'll buy for her sake,
>   And a twopenny apple pie.   [76]

Some traditional riddles have been included, like the following, whose answer is, "The Wind":

> I went to town,
> And *whooo* went with me?
> I went up and down
> But nobody could see.   [113]

But by and large, this is a highly idiosyncratic collection, as fresh and funny as the illustrations from "Dinner Table Rhymes" (86–87) that the illustrator Bob Graham spreads across two pages to show a family's table with all its crumbs and the family dog licking the pie-stained baby clean. The final ditty captures the lively, playful spirit of so many of the verses in the book:

> Here's good bread and cheese and porter,
>   Here's good bread and cheese and porter;
> You all may sing a better song
>   But you cannot sing a shorter!

Many of the poems that the Opies have included are personal favorites, collected over the years from their fieldwork or sent to

them by people who knew of the Opies' studies. Others sent the
Opies poems to be sure that rhymes handed down in their families would be preserved. Some of the poems appear with notes; we
learn, for example, that "The Eccentric" (who "kept six butterflies
in the yard" and "fed them on beer, tintacks and lard") was recited
to the Opies by Richard Warner, a descendant of Oliver Cromwell
who had learned it from his nurse around 1875 (20). A number
of the verses that the Opies include suggest some intriguing possibilities about the importance of such traditional rhymes to writers.
Take, for example, "Mrs. Burns' Lullaby," which was sung by Jean
Burns to her children and was, according to the note, a source for
Robert Burns's lyric "O Wert Thou in the Cauld Blast":

> The robin cam' to the wren's door,
>   And keekit in, and keekit in:
> O, blessings on your bonnie pow,
>   Wad ye be in, wad ye be in?
> I wadna let you lie thereout,
>   And I within, and I within,
> As lang's I hae a warm clout,
>   To row ye in, to row ye in.   [16]

Robert Graves, we are told, "triumphantly recalled" one of the
favorite nursery rhymes, "Welsh Rabbit," from his own childhood
when he visited the Opies in the early 1970s:

> The gallant Welsh of all degrees
>   Have one delightful habit:
> They cover toast with melted cheese
>   And call the thing a rabbit.
>
> And though no hair upon it grows,
> And though it has not horny toes,
>   No twinkling tail behind it,
>   As reputable rabbits should—
>   Yet take a piece and very good
>   I'm bound to say you'll find it.   [42]

And George Bernard Shaw sent the Opies a nursery rhyme of his
own invention, "George Bernard Shaw's Opus I," to be said while
petting the dog:

> Dumpitydoodledum big bow wow
>   Dumpitydoodledum dandy!   [109]

The illustrations for *Tail Feathers* are similarly refreshing and idiosyncratic, from Maurice Sendak's cover to Janet Ahlberg's endpapers. In between, all of the poems are embedded in double-page illustrations, each one by a separate English or American artist. Each of the sixty different artists provides an illustration lively enough to hold its own with the vital energy of the poem. Helen Craig's delicate illustrations for "Visiting" follow Anne Dalton's enormous plum-pudding picture for "Roistering." Jan Ormerod uses the format of a newspaper cartoon panel to tell the story of a milkmaid who rides her cow bareback to market, performing splendid tricks and gracefully spilling every drop of her buttermilk along the way. Quentin Blake uses both pages for a single watercolor of a stubbly tree; two of the many eccentrics that fill the pages of the book have perched in the branches, Uncle Jim in his frock coat and dark glasses, and Uncle Simon with his telescope, "to see what he could see" (32).

Tail Feathers from Mother Goose is an appropriate title for this collection. The poems it contains may not be the recognizable head or wings of Mother Goose, and the volume itself does not mean to be a comprehensive, scholarly study of a representative text. This one is for fun, and what a display of plumage it is!

The twenty essays in *Children and Their Books* form a very different display. They were "assembled as a tribute to the achievement of Iona and Peter Opie, as a memorial to Peter's work which Iona has carried on alone since his death in 1982, and as a celebration of the success of the Opie Appeal . . . which [secured] the Opies' incomparable collection of historical children's books for the Bodleian Library" (1). Although the Opies may be best known for their work in children's folklore, the wide spectrum of essays in this volume is a fitting tribute to their equally important work in children's literature.

Any collection of essays that is commemorative rather than issue-, author-, or topic-oriented runs the risk of being so diverse as to appeal to no special group other than those interested in the person or persons being commemorated. Such is the case here. The essays cover everything from the activity of book collecting itself to the largely undiscovered or ignored potential of children's diaries and self-produced magazines, with the various issue, author, and topic studies arranged in between. Once the reader recognizes this, however, he or she may then go on to enjoy a diverse group of scholars writing generally interesting essays in honor of the two unique people who assembled one of the remarkable collections of children's books.

The book opens with a delightful foreword by Iona Opie that encourages the reader to jump right into the book. Unfortunately, the lead essay, Brian Alderson's "Collecting Children's Books: Self-indulgence and Scholarship," is not able to settle on a subject, but seems, rather, to ramble from topic to topic with little in the way of transition or connection. Clive Hurst's "Selections from the Accessions Diaries of Peter Opie," which follows Alderson's article, makes all the points by example that Alderson tried to make by dictum. Where Alderson asserts that books and book collecting can be seductive, Hurst provides quotations from Opie's journals which illustrate that seductiveness. "I remember my wonder 20 yrs ago," Peter Opie writes, "at buying, near the British Museum, an abridged edition of Robinson Crusoe, 1737, for 25/-, and then going into the BM and finding they did not possess it" (25). In fact, the Opie excerpts will leave many readers wishing for more of his journal entries, with their love for and knowledge of children's books and their collecting.

The next three contributions are topical essays which, for the most part, build on previous scholarship and suggest some new ways of looking at children and children's literature. Keith Thomas's "Children in Early Modern England" discusses the play of seventeenth-century children in an attempt to refute the idea that there was no such thing as childhood before the early modern period. Gillian Avery's "The Puritans and Their Heirs" argues that the "Puritan influence on children's books lasted well beyond the seventeenth century" (114). Julia Briggs provides a historical survey, "Women Writers and Writing for Children: From Sarah Fielding to E. Nesbit."

Half of the essays in the book are on specific authors or books: James Fischer (*The Wise Virgin*), Lewis Carroll, Arthur Hughes, E. Nesbit, Beatrix Potter, Kenneth Grahame, Henry James, Walter de la Mare, J. R. R. Tolkien, and William Mayne. Some tread new ground. For example, Barbara Everett's "Henry James's Children" examines children as characters in James's fiction and suggests that they are keys to James's development as a person and as a writer. Alison Lurie's "William Mayne" builds from the thesis that "many of the most interesting children's books are little known" (369) to argue that Mayne's skillful use of dialogue, poetic descriptions of events and places, and insightful depictions of the interior lives of his characters, among his other talents, have been, for the most part, ignored.

Other essays cover more familiar ground. John Batchelor's "Dodgson, Carroll, and the Emancipation of Alice" takes up the much-debated question of the primary theme of the Alice books and asserts that they "are about learning, not about sexual growth" and that Alice "grows intellectually and socially" in the course of her adventures (182). In "*The Wind in the Willows*: The Vitality of a Classic," Neil Philip suggests that the continued popularity of the novel is due, in large part, to its appeal to both children and adults. And Hugh Brogan takes up the question of World War I and its effects on Tolkien's *The Lord of the Rings* in "Tolkien's Great War." Although he acknowledges very little of the Tolkien scholarship that has preceded him, Brogan is by no means the first to discuss Tolkien's Sauron and Mordor as evidence that the horrors of the war continued to inform Tolkien's creative impulses or that the hobbits and their part of Middle Earth represented a Britain threatened by that horror.

The last two articles, A. O. J. Cockshut's "Children's Diaries" and Olivia and Alan Bell's "Children's Magazine Manuscripts in the Bodleian Library," may contain materials with which the reader is much less familiar. Cockshut suggests that the discovery of a heretofore unknown Victorian novel would not appreciably change our attitudes toward the Victorian novel, but that the "best children's diaries have not been preserved, or if preserved, lie unread; and it is not a fantastic or absurd supposition that a new one discovered at any time might give us something better than we at present have" (381). We might, Cockshut suggests, know significantly more about Victorian children if even one new diary was found. The Bells point out another little-studied area of children's literature, the family magazines that children themselves produced in the nineteenth century and that children still produce today. Both articles focus on the writings of children and discuss characteristics common to diaries or magazines, and both point toward areas ripe with possibilities for future study.

There are two refrains in *Children and Their Books* that need some comment. The apologia that children's literature is indeed worthy of serious attention is first articulated in Alderson's article. "Protestations—however specious—about the virtue of buying Modern Firsts, or Old Bibles, or books on butterflies have an air of authority about them which the collector of children's books cannot so easily muster. These trivia [i.e., children's books], compiled for the immature, must surely only appeal to the immature" (8). Similar comments occur elsewhere in this collection and seem, at best, unnecessary, especially considering the projected audience for this book. Second, the concept of children's literature as "subversive," either the activity of writing it or the content within it, seems to have gotten out of hand. In spite of Humphrey Carpenter's comments in "Excessively Impertinent Bunnies: The Subversive Element in Beatrix Potter," I would argue that not every Alice, Peter Rabbit, or Huck Finn who deliberately breaks society's rules is a thinly disguised anarchist (or even democrat) trying to overthrow the adult oligarchy; some scamps may be, in fact, just scamps.

While not every reader will be interested in every article, virtually all those who buy *Children and Their Books* will be interested in most of the articles it contains. The authors are all scholars within the broad field of children's literature, and their articles attest to the rich land that it is. Gillian Avery and Julia Briggs deserve much credit for this timely volume and its act of commemoration.

To Establish a Canon

Gary D. Schmidt

Touchstones: Reflections on the Best in Children's Literature, edited by
  Perry Nodelman. 3 volumes. West Lafayette, Ind.: Children's Literature Association Publishers, 1985–89.

While living in Boston, I was once dragged by a coterie of art-loving
friends to an exhibition of Monet at the Museum of Fine Arts. I
had never liked the impressionists and thought their use of color
too indulgent, but I agreed to go "for the experience." Once there,
my friends emoted wildly. Gushing, they ran from room to room. It
was all so wonderful. It all said so much. There was so much color.

Left behind in the pell-mell enthusiasm of my friends, I sat in
a single, small gallery across from a painting of the Riviera. An
elderly woman with a great hat sloping toward her shoulders sat
down next to me, took out a sketch pad and chalk crayons, stared at
the Riviera, sighed, and sat back. "And it looks so much like that,"
she whispered. When I asked her how that spate of color could resemble anything in the real world, she smiled as if I had just given
her a reason for being. She explained how the light looks on a late,
late afternoon of a summer's day over the water, and how Monet
had caught the effect not only with color, but with texture. Hold-
ing her hand in the air, she demonstrated the kinds of strokes he
would have used to pile one pigment against another, to gain effects
from the grain of the canvas, to make transitions from one texture to another. She talked about the painting holistically, and how
the arrangement of shape, the balance of opposing objects, and the
blurring of line all contributed both to a certain vision of a certain
place at a certain time and to a larger statement of how we see and
how we interpret what we see.

That afternoon was for me one of my first experiences of what
criticism can do: cut through the mess of nebulous emotions and
mere opinion and examine why a work of art is excellent, what its
meaning(s) might be, how it means what it means, and how it both
defines and broadens its genre.

Children's Literature 20, ed. Francelia Butler, Barbara Rosen, and Judith A. Plotz
(Yale University Press, © 1992 by The Children's Literature Foundation, Inc.).

This vision of criticism informs the purpose of the three *Touch-stones* volumes published by the Children's Literature Association and edited by Perry Nodelman. The project actually began in 1980, when readers of the Association's *Quarterly* were asked to list their suggestions for the most significant children's books. This in turn led to the formation of the Children's Literature Association Canon Committee, which argued over the books to be included in a canon of classics. The list the committee eventually produced was meant to begin discussion of what should and should not be in that canon. The *Touchstones* volumes—the first on fiction, the second on folk literature and poetry, and the third on picture books—are meant to continue this discussion.

While many of the essays in these volumes do just that, using critical skills to examine closely how a text or illustration does what it does, others merely emote. The latter approach mars Patricia Dooley's article on contemporary illustrators: "Why put the gaudy, if plausible cart of opinion before the donkey's-work of scholarship in such a shameless fashion? Because it can't work any other way. . . . [W]e are still in a period when enthusiasm counts for more than research, when the attention paid to children's books leans more heavily on sensibility than on analysis" (III, 153). A cynic would suggest that this is simply a rationalization for not using critical skills, but one need not be a cynic to see that it is this kind of attitude toward the criticism of children's literature that muddies the field.

An example of this attitude appears in a comment by Nodelman; even a fine critic nods at times. Attacking the sentimentality of Barrie's *Peter and Wendy*, Nodelman cites the well-known explanation for the birth of fairies. Instead of examining what precisely it is that makes this passage sentimental—the manipulative imagery, the connotations of the verbs Barrie has chosen, the sentence structure that simulates skipping and light movement—Nodelman suggests that it is simply "icky poo" (6). This evasion is the stuff of mere emotion, mere opinion, and one would be hard pressed to find anything quite like it in any other field of literary criticism.

Other essays take this same approach, with the result that they seem not so much the work of scholars as of cheerleaders. But we are no longer in the vanguard of criticism for children's literature, depending on taste alone, as Dooley asserts. To insist that we are is to denigrate the entire field. These articles are not the first assessments of the authors under consideration; for the most part these are not even the first scholarly articles on these authors. The articles are not so much the beginning of a discussion, as they are part of an ongoing discussion, and some of the essayists seem not to be aware of this.

But the majority of these essays are indeed serious, scholarly efforts at donkey work, at explaining why a book should be considered a classic. Some clarify critical attitudes toward a work, such as Virginia L. Wolf's essay on Laura Ingalls Wilder (I). Others point to the role of contemporary traditions in the formation of a work, such as Malcolm Usrey's examination of *Heidi* (I). Some focus on language, like Norma Bagnall's essay on Walter de la Mare (II). And others find new insights in works on which critical fertility seemed to have been exhausted, as do Jon Stott's and Teresa Krier's critique of Virginia Lee Burton's *The Little House* (III) and Raymond Jones's analysis of *Where the Wild Things Are* (III). In their multifaceted approaches, the essays of these three volumes are a feast for the scholar, occasionally challenging opinions (though most often affirming them, since most of these texts would be canonized by most scholars) and establishing ground for discussion.

These essays have overcome, for the most part, one of the queries embedded in this collection which leads to mere opinion—that is, the central question itself: Why is this book a classic? Why is it a touchstone, a book so excellent that readers can use it to judge the excellence of other works within the same genre? This can lead—and does in some cases—to fluffy subjectivity, to assertions that something is great and masterful without explaining why. In Patricia Demers's essay on Walter Crane, for example, the reader is told that Crane is "a byword for elegance and design" (III, 46); that he "demonstrates that a book can be a work of art" (III, 47), as though Crane were the very first to show this; that his "fancy never disappoints a reader" (III, 48); that his work is marked by "a delightful ebullience" (III, 50). Now I don't mean to be Mr. Gradgrind here, demanding proof and analysis in the face of ebullience. But if I were to write that Dickens's language was delightfully ebullient, I would be writing nothing of worth.

Mary-Agnes Taylor's article on *Swimmy* (III) suggests a different kind of problem. The vast majority of these essayists assume that there is no question that the works with which they deal should be considered classics; almost all write without a demurral. But surely *Swimmy* is barely on the boundary. The fact that it is innovative in its technique is not enough to qualify it for the status of a classic.

If innovation alone were the sole criterion, then, I would assert, Marcia Brown and Blaise Cendrar's *Shadow* should be on the list, as well as Robert Cormier's *I Am the Cheese*, William Mayne's *Drift*, and Keizaburo Tejima's *Fox's Dream*. But Taylor seems to have no awareness that canonizing this work needs response to opinions which differ. By contrast, William Blackburn's examination of *A Wrinkle in Time* refuses to acquiesce in the assumption that this is a classic. Instead, he points out the failure of the novel to cope with evil in a way that is integral to the plot, and attacks its displacement of evil away from the human psyche. One wishes that more, many more, of the essays would have taken such a balanced view of the works under consideration.

But a larger problem in this collection is the very notion of the touchstone. In his introductory essay for the three volumes, Nodelman defines a touchstone as "a book beside which we may place other children's books in order to make judgments about their excellence" (I, 2). Most of the authors in these essays use the words *touchstone* and *classic* interchangeably, but in fact they need not be considered the same. For most of the critics in these three volumes, *classic* implies *not contemporary*, but when Matthew Arnold first used the notion of a touchstone, his reference to "great masters" was not meant to limit his sources to only classics, nor was it meant to preclude great contemporary writers. If by *classic* and *touchstone* the CLA Canon Committee means what Nodelman means, then we must assume that the committee believes that no book written within the last twenty-five years can be used as a standard of judgment.

Almost all of the writers in the three volumes are actually writing about why books are classics, and describing books that have stood the test of time and have been recognized by the scholarly community and by the books' primary audience as excellent in literary and artistic craftsmanship. Such books very well might be touchstones, but it is equally possible for a book that has not achieved classic status to work as a touchstone. One thinks of Rosemary Sutcliff's *Eagle of the Ninth*, Katherine Paterson's *Bridge to Terebithia*, Patricia Wrightson's *The Nargun and the Stars*, Virginia Hamilton's *The People Could Fly*, Mildred Taylor's *Roll of Thunder, Hear My Cry*. By equating *touchstone* with *classic,* the list prohibits all recent literature; indeed, the most recent work on the list is *Where the Wild Things Are*, which is now a quarter of a century old.

But the actual application of a touchstone as imagined by Nodelman is also problematic. When Arnold imagined such an application, he was thinking of comparing "lines and expressions"; Nodelman here is thinking of comparing whole texts. While this at first may seem an easy progression, in fact it is not. The great books in children's literature, or in mainstream literature, are not ones that passively adhere to the conventions of a genre. John Gough remarks in his essay on childhood growth and literature that "these exceptional books are actually different; that is why they are touchstones" (III, 142). And here precisely is the problem. A book that is "actually different," that purposefully strains against conventions, cannot in fairness be compared to books that are not like it in kind (unless we may say that a particular book does not push the same conventions that a comparable touchstone does, which is to say very little).

Which books are we to put up against *Heidi* or *The Secret Garden* for comparison? We could undoubtedly compare them with books that were contemporaries of those works, but critical opinion and the child audience has long since passed its opinion on those. Is it profitable to compare recent fantasy to the work of George MacDonald? Or recent historical fiction to the work of Robert Louis Stevenson? And what is one to do with those authors and illustrators whose unique vision and approach make all comparisons futile, authors such as A. A. Milne and Dr. Seuss and Kate Greenaway? Certainly here, at least, we have writers who handle their material so idiosyncratically that to use them as touchstones is to use them illegitimately. These basic tensions are never resolved in the essays; worse, they are not discussed.

There are some practical difficulties with these volumes as well. The organization of the essays seems odd. One skips from genre to genre with dizzying speed, since the order is alphabetical by the subject's name. In the second volume Nodelman justifies this order by arguing that it simulates a child's reading experience, since a child reader—actually any reader—will skip from genre to genre. While this might be true, it is irrelevant; there is no reason that a collection of scholarly articles should simulate a child's reading experience. For one who is to read straight through these volumes, it would have been more effective to organize the works by genre, collecting together some of the same kinds of concerns.

Other problems include the lack of illustrations in the third volume, which deals with picture books. Nodelman argues correctly that a publisher's or agent's permission is required to reproduce an illustration, and that this permission often brings with it a fee (though he exaggerates the potential cost). But it does seem curious that no essayist is able to point to an illustration to support an argument and have that illustration immediately available to the reader.

Finally, some of the essayists needed a firmer editorial hand guiding them toward a more focused discussion. In the third volume particularly, some writers do not discuss the single work under consideration as a touchstone, but rather an author's entire corpus, with the result that the single work is lost in the shuffle. One sees this in Patricia Demer's essay on Walter Crane, Patricia Dooley's on Kate Greenaway, and especially in Anthony Manna's on Robert McCloskey, where *Make Way for Ducklings*, the work to be considered, is accorded only three paragraphs.

The best of these essays are themselves touchstones of children's literature criticism, essays that probe beneath critical acclaim and examine craftsmanship. These include in the first volume Jon Stott's essay on Lloyd Alexander, Hamida Bosmajian on *Harriet the Spy*, Neil Philip on *The Wind in the Willows*, William Blackburn on *A Wrinkle in Time*, and Roderick McGillis on George MacDonald. From the second and third volumes they include John Cech's piece on Hans Christian Andersen, John Warren Stewig on Joseph Jacobs, Myra Cohn Livingston on David McCord, Perry Nodelman on Mother Goose, and Kenneth Marantz on *The Snowy Day*.

When one has considered and addressed the scholarly qualities of the essays in these volumes, one still goes on reacting to the choice of books to be considered for touchstones. So, to wrangle along with them, I will first assert that it seems very curious to have not a single work of nonfiction be considered a touchstone. Certainly Jean Fritz's *Homesick: My Own Story* must be a contender here, and possibly her *The Double Life of Pocahontas*. William Kurelek's lessknown *A Prairie Boy's Winter* and *A Prairie Boy's Summer* might also be included, as well as David Macaulay's *Cathedral* or *Pyramid*.

In an essay on American fiction at the end of the third volume, Nodelman argues for possibly canonizing, among others, Virginia Hamilton, Randall Jarrell, and Robert Cormier, and these seem obvious contenders. I would also add Jean George, Susan Cooper, Elizabeth George Speare, Mildred Taylor, and Paula Fox. In the field of British fiction, Roderick McGillis suggests authors such as Joan Aiken, Jill Paton Walsh, William Mayne, and Alan Garner; I would elevate to this illustrious company two authors to whom he only alludes: Rosemary Sutcliff and Leon Garfield. In picture books, I would argue for Barbara Cooney, Leo and Diane Dillon, Peter Spier, and, perhaps, Marcia Brown, who, despite her Caldecotts, seems rarely discussed. I am tempted also to add Tomie de Paola, whose earliest accomplishments in works like *The Clown of God* and *Fin M'Coul* should not be dismissed because of the repetitive and merely workmanlike quality of some of his later material.

Even as I form this list, I become engaged in precisely the kind of discussion that these books call for. In the end, that may be one of their chief values. In a time when mainstream literature is reevaluating its canon, calling into question the nature of the classic, recognizing that political and social forces as well as literary considerations work to form critical opinion, scholars in children's literature need to be engaged in the same process. The essays collected in three *Touchstones* volumes are not the beginning of this process, but they are up to now the most visible and overtly purposeful of these efforts.

A Feast of Fairy Tales

Jan Susina

The Victorian Fairy Tale Book, edited by Michael Patrick Hearn. New York: Pantheon, 1988.

Before Oz: Juvenile Fantasy Stories from Nineteenth-Century America, edited by Mark I. West. Hamden, Connecticut: Archon, 1989.

Victorian Fairy Tales: The Revolt of the Fairies and Elves, edited by Jack Zipes. New York: Methuen, 1987.

Something there is that does not love an anthology. Any collection reflects the editor's interests, conforms to publisher's economic constraints, and results in a compromise with which readers can always quibble. Nevertheless, each of these anthologies achieves what must surely be the goal of any good anthology: to direct the reader back to the original texts from which the selections have been made. In each case, the editor's judicious selections will whet the reader's appetite for books that probably have not left library shelves for fifty years or more.

The nineteenth century experienced an explosion of interest in folk and fairy tales. Through the publication and subsequent translations into English of the work of Charles Perrault, Jacob and Wilhelm Grimm, and Hans Christian Andersen, fairy tales and their literary offspring, the *kunstmärchen*, became arguably the most important form of children's literature. These three anthologies of Victorian kunstmärchen should deservedly be added to the bookshelf alongside Jonathan Cott's pioneering *Beyond the Looking Glass* (1973) and U. C. Knoepflmacher's *A Christmas Carol by Charles Dickens and Other Victorian Fairy Tales* (1983) as excellent sources for interested readers and scholars who wish to sample the rich array of this popular form.

Each of the editors approaches the genre in a somewhat different fashion. Since Hearn and Zipes both limit their selections to English authors, there is a healthy overlap of writers and specific tales: John Ruskin's *The King of the Golden River*, Charles Dickens's "The

Children's Literature 20, ed. Francelia Butler, Barbara Rosen, and Judith A. Plotz (Yale University Press, © 1992 by The Children's Literature Foundation, Inc.).

Magic Fishbone," and Kenneth Grahame's "The Reluctant Dragon" appear in both collections, along with different tales by Mary De Morgan, George MacDonald, Oscar Wilde, Laurence Housman, and Edith Nesbit. Since West's collection focuses solely on American authors, his selections make a fascinating companion volume to the other two. *Before Oz* provides a sense of the cross-fertilization that took place between English and American children's authors.

Hearn's collection begins with *The King of the Golden River* (written in 1841 but not published until 1851), which he argues was the first important Victorian fairy tale. Because of the significance of the tale in the development of the genre, it is ubiquitous with anthologizers, appearing in both Zipes's and Hearn's collections as well as in those edited by Cott and Knoepflmacher. But given the availability of the Dover edition with the full set of Richard Doyle's illustrations, its constant anthologizing seems redundant. The real value of these recent collections is their recovery of overlooked or more-difficult-to-obtain tales. Both editors have uncovered some underappreciated authors and interesting, if obscure, tales, such as Henry Morley's "Melilot" in Hearn, and Evelyn Sharp's "The Spell of the Magician's Daughter" in Zipes. Sharp's school story, *The Making of a Schoolgirl* (1897), has been recently reissued, and after reading her tale in Zipes, one wishes that the same could be done for her four collections of fairy tales. Hearn quotes the artist Charles Bennet, best known for his archetypally Victorian version of *The Fables of Aesop* (1857), who praises Morley's fairy tales as "fuller of notions, conceits, and good honest daring absurdity than anything modern I know." That Bennet was Morley's illustrator is simply another reason in favor of reprinting one of his own two fairy-tale collections.

While all three editors provide succinct introductory essays that discuss the development of the kunstmärchen, the real purpose of these volumes is to reprint primary texts. The scholarship in each of these volumes is intentionally brief, but it is certainly solid and directs the interested reader to additional primary and secondary material. Of the three, Zipes's bibliography is the most extensive and serves as a fine source of information for any reader wishing to familiarize himself with the field. Both West and Zipes provide headnotes for individual authors and detailed bibliographies of primary and secondary texts, while Hearn provides endnotes. Still, one might want to have a copy of Zipes's *Fairy Tales and the Art of Sub-*

version (1983) or Stephen Prickett's *Victorian Fantasy* (1979) in hand while reading through Hearn and Zipes; and Brian Attebery's *The Fantasy Tradition in American Literature* (1980) would be useful for extended analysis of particular authors or tales found in West.

Zipes's approach is basically chronological, beginning with the interpolated fairy tale "Uncle David's Nonsensical Story about Giants and Fairies," from Catherine Sinclair's family story *Holiday House* (1839), and ending with Evelyn Sharp's "The Spell of the Magician's Daughter" (1902). While literary fairy tales come in many lengths, Zipes's twenty-two selections tend to approximate the short story, and thus give a rather distorted feel to the collection. Within this preference, Zipes provides a varied group of works that mixes stories by well-known authors (such as Lewis Carroll, Rudyard Kipling, and Mary Louisa Molesworth) with those by lesser-known writers (such as Lucy Clifford and Edward Knatchbull-Hugessen). Hearn is more eclectic in his seventeen selections. Along with such standard, book-length tales as William Thackeray's *The Rose and the Ring* (1855) and Dinah Mulock Craik's *The Little Lame Prince and his Travelling-Cloak* (1875), he also includes poems like Robert Browning's "The Pied Piper of Hamelin" (1842), Christina Rossetti's "Goblin Market" (1862), and William Butler Yeats's "The Stolen Child" (1889). West strikes a balance between the poles established by Zipes and Hearn. He limits his twenty fantasy stories to prose; consequently, his anthology does not include a selection from Palmer Cox's charming Brownies series. He occasionally provides selections from book-length tales, such as chapters from Christopher Pearse Cranch's *The Last of the Huggermuggers* (1856) and Charles Carryl's *Davy and the Goblin* (1885).

The chief problem in all three anthologies is the limited use of illustrations from the original tales. Given the important role that illustrations play in children's books and the number of significant artists who chose to illustrate Victorian fairy tales, the selection and poor reproduction of many of the illustrations in these volumes is unfortunate. The cover of the Zipes volume is graced by Doyle's color illustration from *In Fairyland* (1870), but its version of Andrew Lang's "Princess Nobody" (1884)—the literary fairy tale that was inspired by and written around Lang's rearrangement of Doyle's illustrations—retains only a handful of the original pictures, and these appear in black and white. Most of the warm appeal and some of the sense of the tale is lost when Lang's story is separated from Doyle's magnificent color illustrations. Zipes has not been well served by the often fuzzy and blurred reproduction of many of the other illustrations in this volume.

Both Hearn and West are austere in their use of illustrations. While the number of pictures in the Hearn volume is few, they are carefully chosen and include George Cruikshank's illustration for "The Pied Piper of Hamelin"—published with the poem for the first time—and Doyle's original frontispiece for *The King of the Golden River*, showing South West Wind Esquire with the more phallic-shaped nose that Ruskin had Doyle redraw for later editions.

A less significant problem with each of the anthologies is that in attempting to provide a wide variety of authors, the one tale from each that has been included tends to become representative of an author's work in the genre. While Hearn and Zipes both concur with their choices of Charles Dickens's "The Magic Fishbone" (1868) and Kenneth Grahame's "The Reluctant Dragon" (1898), they differ when it comes to Oscar Wilde. Zipes—who stresses in his introduction that Victorian fairy tales had dual audiences of young, middle-class readers whom authors wished to influence and adult, middle-class readers whom they wanted to challenge and re-form—includes "The Happy Prince" (1888). While Hearn argues that the Victorian fairy tale declined rapidly after it reached its pinnacle with George MacDonald's work and then spawned more introspective and aesthetically concerned variations produced by the Pre-Raphaelites and the Decadents, he oddly chooses "The Selfish Giant" (1888), though he does note that the tale is "the most free of the excess of his aestheticism."

West is concerned with establishing the tradition of American fantasy literature for children prior to the publication of L. Frank Baum's *The Wonderful Wizard of Oz* (1900), and he has divided his twenty selections into four categories: fairy tales, didactic stories, tales about magical objects, and nonsense stories. Just as English authors drew inspiration for their literary fairy tales from earlier folk-tale collections, West shows how many American authors were influenced by the European kunstmärchen as well as by folktales in their attempts to create their own fairy-tale tradition. Attebery has argued, and West's selections confirm, that while there were many nineteenth-century attempts to create fairy tales with American settings, the two most successful authors of the genre, Frank Stockton and Howard Pyle, preferred to use European settings. In reading the anthology as a whole, one notices that most of these fantasy stories were promoted in the United States by children's magazines, *St. Nicholas* in particular. West has culled a quirky grouping of the lesser-known works of such well-known authors as Louisa May Alcott, Joel Chandler Harris, and Thomas Bailey Aldrich, and of more obscure writers like Jane Austin and George Parson Lathrop, but the quality of most of these fairy tales pales when compared to those found in Zipes or Hearn. While the selections in West's collections show that children's fantasy in America did not originate with Baum, the earlier work of his less imaginative and innovative compatriots does not make the arrival of his *Wizard of Oz* appear any less wonderful.

For scholars and students of children's literature, these volumes will function as stimulating appetizers to the great feast of Victorian fairy tales. These are volumes that help the reader to find tales that have been, in many cases, simply intriguing titles mentioned in passing in the standard histories of children's literature.

Other Voices

Phyllis Bixler

The Voice of the Narrator in Children's Literature: Insights from Writers and Critics, edited by Charlotte F. Otten and Gary D. Schmidt. Contributions to the Study of World Literature, Number 28. New York: Greenwood Press, 1989.

To focus attention on the voice of the narrator in children's literature, Charlotte F. Otten and Gary D. Schmidt have collected forty-one essays sectioned by genre: illustrated book, folk literature and myth, fantasy, realism, poetry, historical fiction, biography, and informational books. Each section has an introduction by Otten or Schmidt, one group of essays by authors or illustrators ("The Authorial Voice"), and another group by critics ("The Critical Voice"). In their preface, the editors acknowledge that "the growth of literary theory" has brought "an increasing awareness of the complexities of narration"; nevertheless, they "hoped not to impose a theory of narration" on their contributors but rather to "act as a stimulus to inquiry and discovery" (xvii). While the collection does not place theory at its foreground, an anatomy of its unifying subject can be used to survey some of its contents.

A distinction between the narrator and actual author is usually acknowledged, if tacitly, even though some essayists discuss the role of autobiographical experience in artistic creation (for example, Maurice Sendak, Barbara Cooney, Ray Bradbury; Patricia Morley on William Kurelek, Janice Alberghene on Jean Fritz). In addition, Jill Paton Walsh insists on the importance of this distinction. Describing narrative voice as a "mask," Walsh argues that it must never slip to reveal the "real author" and thus distract the reader from experiencing the subject "unpestered, unobstructed" by the real author's "own feelings" (170–71). Sometimes blurred, however, is a distinction between the narrator and what Wayne Booth, in *The Rhetoric of Fiction* (1961), called the "implied author," an intelligence perceivably creating and shaping the entire work, narrative voice included. In "The Designing Narrator," for example, Milton

Children's Literature 20, ed. Francelia Butler, Barbara Rosen, and Judith A. Plotz (Yale University Press, © 1992 by The Children's Literature Foundation, Inc.).

Meltzer illustrates, from his own experience, how a "biographer tries to give a form to flux, to impose a design upon chronology" (333); and, in a similarly substantive essay, "Singing the Blood Song: The Narrator's Choices in Retelling Norse Myth," Alice Mills discusses how ancient myths are reshaped to be made accessible for modern readers.

More clearly focusing on the narrator are essays that discuss books exhibiting various kinds of first- and third-person narration. Joan W. Blos and Janet Lunn discuss how their struggles to create both immediacy and authenticity in their historical fiction resulted in different choices of narrator. In writing *A Gathering of Days: A New England Girl's Journal, 1837–1838* (1985), Blos found that the paucity of dialogue and description typical in diaries allowed her to write a kind of first-person narrative that minimized her anxiety about including inauthentic details. Writing about an early-nineteenth-century Scotch immigrant to Canada in *Shadow in Hawthorn Bay* (1987), Lunn decided that she could neither tell Mary Urquhart's story as her own nor as an "impartial observer"; instead, she told the story from Mary's "point of view but not in her voice," becoming "a sort of doppelgänger attached to her as firmly as her own shadow" (276–77). This kind of third-person narration is discussed by Lois R. Kuznets in "Henry James and the Storyteller: The Development of a Central Consciousness in Realistic Fiction for Children." Illustrating her generalizations by discussions of eight children's books, Kuznets describes an "unintrusive third-person narrator" (187) often developing in enlightenment along with the protagonist, as in the narrator's adoption of Lambert Strether's point of view but not his voice in James' *The Ambassadors*. The enlightenment possible with this kind of narration, as well as the distinction between narrator and implied author, is beautifully illustrated by Ann Donovan's discussion of William Mayne's *Drift* (1985). Being narrated in third person but from two very different points of view, Mayne's historical novel invites the reader to re-create a third version of the story being shaped by the implied author.

The kind of third-person narration Kuznets describes presents an instructive alternative to the first-person narration found in many problem-oriented books associated with the "New Realism," as Kuznets observes. In the hands of an unskilled writer, first-person narration fails to incorporate in the text "any measures of

the narrator's reliability"; it encourages in the reader a "naive,"
"unquestioning identification with the protagonist" and thus often
provides only minimal enlightenment (189). Multiple first-person
narrators, of course, foster greater reader sophistication, as in Paul
Zindel's *The Pigman* (1968).

Essays by Ann Grifalconi and Peter Dickinson discuss why these
authors chose multiple narrators for their respective tales about
an African village in *Village of Round and Square Houses* (1986) and
Old Testament stories in *City of Gold* (1979). Another kind of first-
person narration is discussed by Ruth MacDonald in an essay on
Beatrix Potter. Potter's insertion of first-person comments by the
"author" into typically third-person narration has sometimes been
criticized, no doubt because it recalls the "intrusive, often didactic
narrator" of nineteenth-century fiction that Henry James and his
followers disparaged (Kuznets 187). MacDonald argues, however,
that these insertions create a narrator who, being both human and
knowledgeable about animal behavior, mediates between the two
worlds, creating "a credible animal universe that exists side by side
with the human" (55). James E. Higgins claims a similar mediating
role for the cowboy narrator in Will James's *Smoky the Cow Horse*
(1926). And Richard Adams suggests that the narrator in *Watership Down* (1972) mediates between story and audience as does the
chorus in Greek drama.

While some essays discuss modes of narration and the role of
the narrator, others focus on the more variable and elusive matter
of the narrator's voice—more variable because one narrator can
be said to use different voices at different points in a story, more
elusive because, as Walsh points out, to speak of voice in a text
printed for the eye is to speak metaphorically. Nevertheless, the primacy of the ear in a creative process that results in printed pages
is noted by several author-essayists. In "On Three Ways of Writing
for Children" (1952), C. S. Lewis said his fantasies came to him first
as pictures. Here, however, Lois Lowry says that two years before
she began writing *Rabble Starkey* (1987), she heard two sentences
spoken by the voice of Rabble Starkey. Jean Fritz says that her biographical subjects choose her when she hears their voices and has
"an intense desire to record them" (339). Nancy Willard similarly
says that narrators often choose writers and that when a writer's
idea arrives, it carries "on its back a dozen characters clamoring to
tell *their* side of the story" (229).

Voice as something heard rather than seen is obviously important in poetry and is accordingly stressed in the essays by poet Eve Merriam, by Joanne Lewis on Robert Louis Stevenson, and by Roderick McGillis on various children's poets. Lewis argues that Stevenson's poetry still "speaks" because, unlike many of his imitators, "he located a voice that could retrieve genuine childhood emotions" (240). This voice modulates into a variety of voices Lewis identifies in a careful, insightful analysis of *A Child's Garden of Verses*. In "Reactivating the Ear: Orality and Children's Poetry," McGillis argues that poetry written for young children "attempts to recreate the immediacy of oral speech" (253); like the nursery rhyme it echoes, this poetry invites us to sing and dance, to perform. Other essayists use performance metaphors to describe voice in both poetry and fiction. Lowry compares her adult writing of fiction to her childhood fascination with ventriloquism; Adams and Grifalconi use metaphors from drama; Walsh and Myra Cohn Livingston use the word *mask*.

Not surprisingly, discussions of orality are found also in essays by authors adapting stories originating in an oral tradition. In "The Storyteller's Voice: Reflections on the Rewriting of Uncle Remus," Julius Lester describes the voice found in these oral tales as "collective," as a perceptible "presence of all black people whose lives were shaped by the tales" (72). Reflecting about how he and Van Dyke Parks adapted Joel Chandler Harris in *Jump! The Adventures of Brer Rabbit* (1986), Malcolm Jones says that "something is lost" "when oral storytelling makes the transition to the printed page" (76). Most problematic in this transition is narrative voice, as is suggested not only by Jones but also by Dickinson, who adapted Old Testament stories in *City of Gold*. Rejecting both "high" and "low" styles traditionally used in translations and retellings, Dickinson instead portrayed specific tellers narrating the tales to specific audiences. The result he describes as frankly "literary," having its ancestry in Browning's dramatic monologues and Kipling's *Puck of Pook's Hill* and *Rewards and Fairies* (80). Dickinson does not find this "literary" result reason for apology—appropriately, for it is easy to romanticize the oral and to assume a simplistic opposition between speech and writing. Adams similarly claims a literary ancestry for the narrative voice in *Watership Down*—Dostoevsky, Jane Austen, the Bible, the Book of Common Prayer—though he claims that "the narrator's voice did not change" (116) when the story told to his daughters became a written story.

Adams joins several other essayists in inviting us to consider how an author's narrative voice is affected by an "implied audience" of children or young people—Adams describes his daughters' responses to his oral story and book—but most essays ignore or touch only very briefly the issue of how children as "actual audience" have responded to the texts in question. Walsh in "On Wearing Masks" and Lewis in her essay on Stevenson both discuss the traps of condescension and pretension that often snare adult writers who address an implied audience of children. Authors so often lack trust in that audience, says Walsh, and adds that she herself was surprised that *Unleaving* (1976), in which she used narrative "masks to play a deliberate game with the reader," was so widely read; the letters elicited by this novel, Walsh says, belie the idea that "children don't understand metafiction" (172). The assumption that child readers cannot or do not want to assume sufficient distance from a text to consider its narrative voice nevertheless has a long history, as is illustrated by Lionel Basney's excellent article on how *Gulliver's Travels* has been abridged for children since the eighteenth century. Though variously truncated, bowdlerized, and rewritten, the children's versions consistently change "the narrative voice by subtracting its ironies, making it blander, more transparent" (154); the focus is on the story's vivid images and experiences rather than on Gulliver as observer and narrator.

The difficulty of finding an appropriate narrative voice in books presenting for a young implied reader the darker aspects of human nature and experience is illustrated by Hamida Bosmajian's "Narrative Voice in Young Readers' Fictions about Nazism, the Holocaust, and Nuclear War." Through careful analysis of six narratives, Bosmajian examines the problems of both first- and third-person narration in portraying a "cruel, life-denying world" for an implied reader presumably needing to retain a "life-affirming trust in a future" (322, 308).

This survey by no means exhausts what is to be found in the over four hundred pages of *The Voice of the Narrator in Children's Literature*. The critical anatomy chosen for this review has precluded discussion of issues and essays well worth a reader's attention. For example, some essayists, such as Walsh and Lloyd Alexander, attempt to describe what we mean when we speak of an author's unique voice to be found in all of that author's works. Also, to include the illustrated book in a discussion of narrative voice, Otten posits much broader definitions than those used here.

Finally, the essays in this collection are markedly heterogeneous in quality as well as subject and focus; some are naive and superficial in dealing with the book's admittedly elusive unifying subject; others deal with it only tangentially, if at all. This variety is not surprising, though it can be disconcerting. Nevertheless, Otten and Schmidt are to be thanked for eliciting this polyphony of voices. Quite apart from what it suggests about "the voice of the narrator," the anthology makes an important contribution by its serious discussion of such an admirable array of illustrators, authors, and genres. Readers will discover in it other melodies than those traced in this review.

You've Come a Long Way, Beauty (and Beast)

Claire L. Malarte-Feldman

Beauties, Beasts and Enchantment: Classic French Fairy Tales. Translated and with an introduction by Jack Zipes. New York: New American Library, 1989.

Beauty and the Beast: Visions and Revisions of an Old Tale, by Betsy Hearne. With an essay by Larry DeVries. Chicago and London: University of Chicago Press, 1989.

Jacques Barchilon, to whom Zipes's book is dedicated, has called the story of Beauty and the Beast, with its origins in the ancient myth of Cupid and Psyche, an "immemorial adventure." By the second century of our era, Apuleius had incorporated a version of the tale as a central episode in his novel *The Golden Ass.* Since then, a multitude of versions in a variety of forms have been created to tell and retell this story about the power of love and its ability to transform a horrible creature into a handsome, noble prince. Jack Zipes's collection of thirty-six French fairy tales that are concerned with this theme and Betsy Hearne's investigation of the major variations of the story remind us just how lively this archetypal narrative has remained.

Zipes's volume provides new translations of thirty-six of the best French fairy tales, bringing together different types of beauties (the sleeping kind being, of course, one of the best known) and various species of beasts (leopards, ogres, serpents, frogs, and the like). The starting point for Zipes is two collections of fairy tales translated and published by John Robinson Planché: *Four-and-twenty Fairy Tales Selected from Those of Perrault, Etc.* (1858) and *Countess D'Aulnoy's Fairy Tales* (1885). To his selection from these tales, Zipes has added translations of ten others, including Perrault's "Little Red Riding Hood" and Leprince de Beaumont's "Beauty and the Beast," which do not appear in the Planché volumes. The result is an impressive collection of fairy tales by twelve French authors covering a period of roughly a hundred years. Only Iona and Peter Opie's

Children's Literature 20, ed. Francelia Butler, Barbara Rosen, and Judith A. Plotz (Yale University Press, © 1992 by The Children's Literature Foundation, Inc.).

The Classic Fairy Tales (1974), a collection of twenty-four of the most famous fairy tales, is comparable to Zipes's effort. But Zipes's volume is more comprehensive, particularly in its inclusion of all of Perrault's prose tales.

Zipes's translation successfully renders a style appropriate to the seventeenth-century French literary fairy tale. The language of these tales incorporated some typically *précieux* elements, characteristic of an aristocratic literary genre, into traditional narratives rooted in popular literature. Since a literary French fairy tale was essentially a kind of performance in style and wit by authors of good taste, this highly sophisticated form of language could present intricate traps for a translator. On the whole, Zipes captures the general tone of these fairy tales and gives the reader the flavor of an often outdated style in which hyperbole is the rule. The major difficulty for Zipes lies in translating into English the seventeenth-century rhymes—such as those in Perrault's *moralités* or Mme. d'Aulnoy's verses within or at the end of her tales. He describes his solution to this problem: "In most cases I sacrificed meter and style to meaning; in some cases, particularly in d'Aulnoy's tales, I endeavored to temper the bombastic and lavish tone and style" (14). At times Zipes even surpasses d'Aulnoy's style: in shortening her morals, he greatly improves them.

In his introduction to the volume, Zipes provides a short historical survey of the French folktale, tracing its origins from the oral tradition into the seventeenth century, when it entered the literary salons of the most aristocratic society and turned into one of the most popular genres: the literary fairy tale. In this form, the tale became an expression of the idealism ("*l'esprit précieux*") of an aristocratic elite that glorified heroism and worshiped love in all the fashionable literary genres of the time (for example, the novel, the letter, the courtly poem). It was no accident that in a predominantly male literary world, a majority of the French fairy-tale writers were female; they represented, Zipes explains, a movement of "resistance toward male rational precepts and patriarchal realms by conceiving pagan worlds in which the final say was determined by female fairies" (4). Zipes also notes that the beginning of the fairy-tale fashion corresponds more or less to France's political crisis after 1688, and accurately observes that the fairy tale became a way "to vent criticism" of Louis XIV's irrational policies and to express "a hope for a better world" (6).

In the early years of the eighteenth century, the salons stopped playing the fairy-tale game, and by the 1720s parodies of the genre, such as those by Claude-Philippe de Caylus, had begun to appear. The fairy tale had become an established genre in the French literary tradition, and therefore, Zipes points out, it "could convey standard notions of propriety and morality that reinforced the socialization process of France" (10). To illustrate this point, Zipes translates two of the most famous eighteenth-century versions of "Beauty and the Beast" published in France, those by Mmes. de Villeneuve and Leprince-Beaumont. De Villeneuve was "the first writer to develop the plot of 'Beauty and the Beast' as we generally know it today" (10), but, Zipes argues, she also provides us with a "narrative about the manners and social class attitudes that reveal how closely the fairy tale was bound to the development of civility in France and reflected questions of socialization" (151). The version of the tale by Mme. Leprince-Beaumont that appeared in 1757 obeys the didactic purpose of educating little girls and to that end "preaches domesticity and self-sacrifice for women" (11)—without destroying the magic of the tale, Zipes believes. More importantly, though, it was the first French fairy tale explicitly written for children and helped make the fairy tale an established genre of children's literature.

This attractive volume incorporates works by twelve French authors, each of whose tales is introduced by a bibliographical note that clearly and concisely sets the social context in which the tales appeared. Each story is prefaced by a delicate frontispiece, and the book contains a wide variety of illustrations in black and white. Oddly enough, there is no indication throughout the volume of the origins of such drawings and reproductions, nor is there mention of the illustrators' names; yet these artists are not anonymous. The version of "Beauty and the Beast" by Mme. Leprince-Beaumont is illustrated by Margaret Tarrant (1920), and the cover picture is by Eleanor Vere Boyle (1875), as indicated by Betsy Hearne in her book. But this is a minor criticism of an otherwise remarkable volume that finally makes available to English-speaking readers (whether fairy-tale scholars or children) a collection of the finest French fairy tales.

Whereas Zipes has done an intensive, scholarly compilation of French literary fairy tales from a particular century, Betsy Hearne presents a survey of versions of "Beauty and the Beast" spanning three centuries. She introduces her work as "a study of the art and artifice of the story rather than an analysis of its meaning" (xiv). She has isolated a corpus of twenty-two versions of this tale, ranging from the first printed version by de Villeneuve in 1740 to a 1985 picture book by Warwick Hutton. Though Hearne does not provide the reader with original texts (with the exception of the English translation of Mme. Leprince-Beaumont's "Beauty and the Beast," which is included in one of the book's appendixes), Hearne's detailed presentation of each version, her careful commentaries, and her liberal use of quotations give valuable insights into the respective works and their authors.

Hearne begins with de Villeneuve's 1740 tale, which is often regarded as the first French version of "Beauty and the Beast." However, it would be more accurate to attribute the French literary origins of the tale to seventeenth-century authors, among them Mme. d'Aulnoy, whose version *"Le Mouton"* ("The Ram"), mentioned by Hearne, was published between 1696 and 1698 in her collection *Contes des Fées*. Catherine Bernard's *"Riquet à la Houppe"* (1696) and Perrault's 1697 version of the tale (both translated in Zipes's anthology under the title "Riquet with the Tuft") are also variations of "Beauty and the Beast" from the late seventeenth century.

In her examination of the myth of "Beauty and the Beast" Hearne stresses the influence of innovations in the field of book production on the nineteenth-century versions, where the beauty of the illustrations (such as those by Walter Crane) amplifies the moral lesson of the tale. In the twentieth century, the tale was further shaped by the advent of new media for storytelling (such as those that we find in Jean Cocteau's film version of the story) and by the more complex psychological awareness evident in recent revisions of the tale by Phillipa Pearce and Robin McKinley. What unites such diverse retellings, from Hearne's perspective, are the "enduring" elements of the story: characters defined as archetypal patterns; a narrative structure articulated around the theme of the journey, and various images, objects, and symbols recurrent throughout the many versions of the tale, regardless of their epoch or author (for example, the cycle of seasons, the rose, the garden, the ring). The narrative voice, which changes with each new telling, Hearne considers ultimately "less important to a powerful, lasting version of the story than faithfulness to and skill at manipulating the other elements of the story" (129).

It is understandable that Hearne regrets the "compartmentalization" (153) of fairy-tale scholarship, since her point of view is not one of a specialist in folklore. She alerts us from the start that she is much more interested in the artistic aspect of the folktale than in its meaning (xii–xv). Although it would seem impossible to dissociate one from the other, we can assume this is why she remains, for the most part, descriptive in her approach to the subject. An important aspect of Hearne's study consists of the lengthy technical explanations and knowledgeable descriptions of the illustrators' works. In keeping with her own sensitivity to book production and aesthetic concerns, Hearne's own book is a work of art, with exceptional illustrations in black and white and even more valuable plates in color, all of which make it a visual pleasure to read, especially for the general audience of children's literature specialists and bibliophiles for whom the book is intended. Given this audience, it would have been better if Hearne had left out the first of her book's four appendixes—a highly technical essay by Larry DeVries that provides a Proppian analysis of "Beauty and the Beast," exposing the skeleton of the folktale reduced to its basic functions: unfortunately, it ends up turning "Beauty and the Beast" into a mere mathematical equation of $m1\ w2 - w1\ m2$. In the other three appendixes, she usefully includes a number of eighteenth- and nineteenth-century versions of the story, designed to help the reader to juxtapose various tales from the oral and the literary traditions. Finally, and importantly, Hearne includes an extensive bibliography of the story's sources and a well-documented list of predominantly American critical sources.

Zipes's and Hearne's books are indicative of the strong vitality of the fairy tale as a genre that has survived because of its extraordinary ability to adapt to new forms of expression. This is the power of fairy tales: narratives without fixed texts, stories without authors, their origins are impossible to trace with precision. Their sources can be found in our strongest emotions: love and hate, violence and jealousy, fear and courage. From the myth of Cupid and Psyche to the most recent (sub)versions of the tale, "Beauty and the Beast" is a constant in this world of fantasy, a symbolic expression of our need for love and of our belief in the power of love.

Dissertations of Note

Compiled by Rachel Fordyce

Ackerman, G. Tova. "Folktales for the ESL Elementary School Classroom." Ed.D. diss. New York University, 1989. 338 pp. DAI 50:1236A.

Ackerman promotes the learning of English as a second language "through the use of drama as a method of integrating physical action" with the language it represents. She has adapted forty rhymes, fairy tales or folktales specifically to be used with puppets and teaching modules for each.

Amitai, Raziel. "From Theatre of Children to Theatre for Children: The Development of Children's Theatre in Israel." Ph.D. diss. City University of New York, 1989. 365 pp. DAI 50:3795A.

Amitai describes the enthusiastic and "lively" development of amateur, professional, and commercial children's theatre in Israel and Palestine and the recent change in the nature of plays for children.

Austin, Susan R. "A Field Study Assessing the Role of Children's Literature in Linking Language Arts, Social Studies and Science as Interdisciplinary Units at the Third and Fourth-Grade Levels." Ph.D. diss. University of Pennsylvania, 1989. 172 pp. DAI 50:2782A.

This study, directed toward the elementary teacher and librarian, does not use literature as a "purely pedagogic tool." It stresses "the enjoyment of literary works and aesthetic values inherent in them" as well as the use of entire texts to stimulate "a more holistic learning situation."

Barchers, Suzanne Inez. "Hera Transformed: Female Heroes in Folk and Fairy Tales." Ed.D. diss. University of Colorado—Boulder, 1985. 185 pp. DAI 46:3124A.

Barchers poses the question: "Does our culture's folk literature primarily portray women in roles emphasizing beauty and passivity, rather than heroism?" She concludes that for the most part it does. Examples that deviate from the norm come from a variety of cultures but few are known widely.

Barlow, Diane Ledbetter. "The Communication of Science Information to Children Through Trade Books: The Nature of Authorship." Ph.D. diss. University of Maryland—College Park, 1989. 276 pp. DAI 50:1837A.

Barlow examines "data about personal characteristics, education, professional experience, and attitudes" of writers of children's science trade books to determine major differences among the fifty-two authors studied.

Bivona, Daniel Edward. "Desire and Contradiction: A Nineteenth-Century Imperial Mythos and Its Critics." Ph.D. diss. Brown University, 1987. 222 pp. DAI 48:1773A.

Bivona analyzes the various manifestations of the theme of imperialism in Victorian novels, drawing from the work of Disraeli, Conrad, Carroll, Kipling, and Hardy.

Bubbers, Lissa Paul. "Telling Stories for Children and Adults: The Writings of Ted Hughes." Ph.D. diss. York University (Canada), 1984. 282 pp. DAI 45:3134A.

While surveying scholarship about Ted Hughes, Bubbers shows that the ma-

Children's Literature 20, ed. Francelia Butler, Barbara Rosen, and Judith A. Plotz (Yale University Press, © 1992 by The Children's Literature Foundation, Inc.).

jority of it is linear and chronological. She focuses "on the story Hughes tells and how he tells it." Of particular significance is her thesis that Hughes's writing for and about children "illuminates the entire body of his writings and his theories of imaginative literature," because "in his critical writings Hughes stresses the importance of mythic stories for children. In his imaginative works, he writes fairy tales, anthropomorphic fantasies, and adventure stories, all genres that are usually categorized as children's literature."

Buchanan-Berrigan, Dawna Lisa. "Using Children's Books with Adults: Negotiating Literacy." Ph.D. diss. Ohio State University, 1989. 401 pp. DAI 50:3874A.

Basing her work on the assumption that "adults who have little experience with mainstream literacy practices may be at a disadvantage in the effort to achieve schooled literacy for themselves and for their children," Buchanan-Berrigan shows that using children's stories with them improved literacy.

Carruth, Lajean Purcell. "A Comparison of Contemporary East and West German Children's Literature on Three Themes." Ph.D. diss. University of Utah, 1988. 205 pp. DAI 49:2673A.

Using works published between 1970 and 1983, Carruth explores the "themes of National Socialism, work, and relations between children and adults." While both literatures treated similar themes, particularly the "wrongs of Nazism," East German books "reflect the uniform, authoritarian society of the GDR, and West German children's books reflect the greater variety of ideas that are accepted in the FRG."

Chadwick-Joshua, Jocelyn. "*Alice's Adventures in Wonderland* and *Through the Looking-Glass*: A Menippean Assessment and Rhetorical Analysis of Carroll's Alice Books." Ph.D. diss. Texas Woman's University, 1987. 190 pp. DAI 49:1461A.

Chadwick-Joshua attempts to identify "the literary expertise underlying" Carroll's texts. She notes that despite myriad analyses of Carroll's work, the fact that he "employs a classical satiric format has eluded many. When one reads these books as Menippean satires rather than as Juvenalian or Horatian and rather than child's simple nonsense . . . a deep-textured purpose and expertise and control evince themselves slowly, consciously, methodically."

Chapman, Susan Elizabeth. "A Study of the Genre of T. H. White's Arthurian Books." Ph.D. diss. University of Wales (United Kingdom), 1988. 420 pp. DAI 50:2903A.

Chapman notes the popularity, and critical neglect, of *The Once and Future King* and other works by White. The latter she attributes to "the books' failure to conform to the generic norms of the mainstream novel" and the "unusually large number of genres" represented in White's work and within single works.

Chaston, Joel Duane. "Reading as if for Life: The Quixotic Reader in the Nineteenth-Century British Novel." Ph.D. diss. University of Utah, 1988. 177 pp. DAI 49:3366A.

In a dissertation devoted to the study of Austen, Scott, Carroll, George Eliot, and Dickens, Chaston analyzes "quixotic readers, characters who mistakenly believe that written texts represent the world, [who] dramatize the act of interpreting the stories in which they appear, [while] at the same time arguing for their value" to show the complexity of this type of character and the authorial purposes to which it is put. He notes specifically that Carroll, Eliot, and Dickens are most sophisticated in the use of the quixotic reader because they connect "the books their characters read with the act of creating literature."

Clark, Rosalind Elizabeth. "Goddess, Fairy Mistress, and Sovereignty: Women of the Irish Supernatural." Ph.D. diss. University of Massachusetts, 1985. 571 pp. DAI 46:704A.

Clark recognizes that "supernatural women were important in Irish literature from earliest times to the present, but their literary portrayal altered with changing societal values and literary tastes." She shows that the image of women has degenerated somewhat from that of a powerful, fertile goddess to that of the destructive war goddess who is neither benevolent nor constructive.

Coleman, Sarah Ann. "The Late Victorian Era and the Flowering of Four Literary Types: A Study in the Sociology of Literature." Ph.D. diss. Syracuse University, 1988. 325 pp. DAI 49:3366A.

Coleman shows that concurrent with the rise of a leisured middle class between 1870 and 1900 was the development of four literary types that met its reading needs: science fiction, fantasy, detective fiction, and society fiction. "The theoretical work of Max Weber on ascetic Protestantism, instrumental rationality and modernization, as well as the related theoretical insights of Robert Merton, Georg Lukacs, and Ian Watt provide the theoretical underpinnings for this study."

Cooper, Barbara Rosemarie Latotzky. "Madame de Villeneuve: The Author of *La Belle et la Bete* [sic] and Her Literary Legacy." Ph.D. diss. University of Georgia, 1985. 300 pp. DAI 46:1961A.

Cooper offers a biography of the well-read eighteenth-century author Gabrielle-Suzanne Barbot Gallon, dame de Villeneuve (1695?–1755) and analyzes her works, her popularity, and her special "brand of feminism." The latter is "decidedly undogmatic" and pragmatic.

Daniels, Phyllis Jane Beene. "The Impact of Introducing the Writing to Read System into a Whole Language Approach to Teaching Reading and Writing in Kindergarten." Ph.D. diss. University of Colorado—Boulder, 1988. 229 pp. DAI 50:910A.

Daniels' ethnographic, computer-based literacy study shows that young children become competent through a "write-to-read" program but concludes that "neither the material nor program makes a difference in teaching and learning." It is the "knowledgeable teacher" who makes a difference.

Debaryshe, Barbara Diane. "Facilitating Language Development Through Picture-Book Reading: Evaluation of a Read-Aloud Package for Parents and Preschoolers." Ph.D. diss. University of New York—Stony Brook, 1987. 213 pp. DAI 50:2174A.

Using forty-one two-year-old children and their mothers, Debaryshe structured her study to try to increase "spontaneity and complexity of child language."

Degni, Suzanne M. "An Interpretive Inquiry into Using Adolescent Literature to Inform Preservice Teachers about Middle Grades Students." Ed.D. diss. University of North Carolina—Greensboro, 1989. 149 pp. DAI 50:2864A.

By analyzing preservice teachers' different perceptions of young adolescents before and after their experience with realistic fiction, Degni shows that the teachers' reading of realistic fiction written for middle-grade students deepens their awareness of young adolescent development and of the variety of situations in which adolescent students find themselves, and enriches their professional perception and their image of themselves as teachers.

Dibiasio, Becky Lynn McCan. "The Path of Metamorphosis: Patterns in the Literary Fairy Tale Tradition." Ph.D. diss. Purdue University, 1984. 289 pp. DAI 45:3125A.

Dibiasio analyzes narrative structures in the fairy tale and its use in contemporary fiction to show that it "is still a developing form."

Dietz, Jacqueline Kelsey. "A Rationale for Teaching Folklore in Secondary English

Classes of Agricultural Community Schools." Ph.D. diss. University of Illinois—
Urbana-Champaign, 1988. 215 pp. DAI 49:3122A.

Dietz expounds the idea that the close "connection between prior knowledge and new knowledge" should not be overlooked by educators, especially
those involved in agricultural community schools, and that relating students'
prior farm knowledge to new information positively enhances students' ability
to acquire new knowledge.

Domo, Marlene Anne. "Seventh and Eighth Graders' Response to a Moral Dilemma
Across Three Genres in a Classroom Setting." Ph.D. diss. Ohio State University,
1989. 273 pp. DAI 50:3874A.

Using works of fantasy, historical fiction, and picture books that have strong
moral implications, Domo finds that moral responses to the literature are "significantly influenced by the teacher, peer interactions and the classroom community" and that students are capable of a "high level [of] moral reasoning."

Dorfman, Marcy Halpert. "A Model for Understanding the Points of Stories: Evidence from Adult and Child Readers." Ph.D. diss. University of Illinois—Urbana-
Champaign, 1988. 191 pp. DAI 50:427A.

From the results of this study of both child and adult readers Dorfman finds
that the readers' ability to understand the morals of fables depends on "cognitive or moral knowledge" and the "'genre specific' knowledge necessary for
understanding the fable as a literary-discourse type."

Fuller, Miriam Delois Morris. "The Wordless Book: Its Relationship to Children's
Literature as Perceived by a Selected Group of Principal Informants." Ed.D. diss.
University of Missouri—Columbia, 1989. 202 pp. DAI 50:1969A.

The purpose of this study is to determine whether or not the wordless book
is literature. Fuller concludes that it "work[s] as literature through its aesthetic
and skills functions" because this type of picture book contains plots, characters,
themes, and a distinct style.

Graham, Merika Sonia. "Psychological Aspects of the Feminine in Ukrainian Folk
Tales: A Jungian Analysis with Implications for Psychotherapy." Ph.D. diss. The
Union for Experimenting Colleges and Universities, 1985. 448 pp. DAI 47:359A.

Graham is concerned with the "manifestations of the feminine psyche" in
four Ukrainian fairy tales. "Clinical implications for the use of the folk tale in
psychotherapy are offered, supported by some literature on the therapeutic use
of metaphor."

Hartle-Schutte, David. "Home Environment Characteristics of Successful Navajo
Readers." Ed.D. diss. University of Arizona, 1988. 319 pp. DAI 50:654A.

Hartle-Schutte's study indicates that the home, rather than the school, is the
greater predictor of reading success for young Navajo readers and that "social
conditions, such as single parent families, low income, alcoholism, and unem-
ployment did not prevent the development of literacy for these children nor did
linguistic differences and limited amounts of written material in the homes."
Further, he discovers that there is "a much higher success rate for Navajo children than is commonly reported with standardized achievement tests." His work
has implications for the treatment of other minority students.

Hastings, Albert Waller. "Social Myth and Fictional Reality: The Decline of Fairy
Tale Thinking in the Victorian Novel." Ph.D. diss. University of Wisconsin—
Madison, 1988. 266 pp. DAI 49:3368A.

Hastings notes that fairy tales, such as those written by George MacDonald,
"with their potentially revolutionary message that lower-class people can ascend
to power, helped to shape social attitudes during the Romantic and early Victorian periods. Victorian novelists used allusion to fairy tales to criticize their
society for its failure to fulfill the tales' ideals." By the end of the century writers

such as Oscar Wilde "became more disillusioned about . . . society's possibilities [and] altered the models, rewriting the tales to reflect . . . disbelief in the social myths these folk narratives embody."

Honig, Edith Lazaros. "A Quiet Rebellion: The Portrait of the Female in Victorian Children's Fantasy." Ph.D. diss. Fordham University, 1985. 235 pp. DAI 46:2300A.

In a dissertation that deals with the work of Lewis Carroll, George Mac-Donald, Mary Louisa Molesworth, James Matthew Barrie, and Edith Nesbit, Honig tries to show that the seeds of a liberated female in twentieth-century literature are buried in the children's literature of the Victorian era. Contrary to the norm of adult Victorian literature, "mothers [in children's literature] were often absent from the scene. Spinsters were admirable, useful women rather than embittered old maids. Girls were intelligent and assertive, not squeamish and subdued. And magical women were not witches, but positive figures of great power." Honig believes that this "quiet rebellion . . . held out great hope for equality of the sexes because it worked in a magical way on the minds and hearts of future generations."

Huang, Jui-Chin. "A Study of Prosocial Behavior in Selected Chinese Children's Literature." Ph.D. diss. University of Oregon, 1989. 153 pp. DAI 50:3503A.

The prosocial behaviors Huang found in the twelve books he studied were "rescuing . . . , helping, sharing, caring, devoting, transferring, comforting, and cooperating," in that order of relevance. Huang concludes that Chinese children's literature of the type he studied provides children "with an image of macro-ethics beyond the family, and a feminine view of prosocial behavior involving human feelings and needs."

Hurley, Angela Brookshire. "Children as Reader-Critics: Literary Heroes and Moral Education." Ed.D. diss. University of Kentucky, 1988. 259 pp. DAI 50:107A.

Hurley tries to identify what moral judgments make adults recommend literature to children. These range on a continuum from a desire for children to read only literature that has "all-virtuous heroes and all-evil villains," an attitude that currently predominates in this country, to an attitude that being able to read about people who have both good and bad qualities "provides children the opportunity to learn to make reflective evaluations" and moral choices. Bruno Bettelheim, C. S. Lewis, Phyllis Schlafly, and John Whitehead fit into the first category; Maurice Sendak, Madeleine L'Engle, and Maxine Greene into the latter. By analyzing the advantages and disadvantages of various arguments, Hurley attempts to emphasize the "importance of allowing children to function as reader-critics."

Jo, Yong-Hwan. "Understanding the Boundaries of Make-Believe: An Ethnographic Case Study of Pretend Play among Korean Children in a U.S. Community." Ph.D. diss. University of Illinois—Urbana-Champaign, 1989. 316 pp. DAI 50:3502A.

Jo concludes that "the boundaries of children's pretend play are framed [by] the 'reality basis' and the 'fantasy ceiling'"; that "gender and age constitute two important perceptual/behavioral constraints" probably dependent on adult Korean culture; that "the boundaries of make-believe are constituted and constantly negotiated"; and that "in contradiction to many play theories, which have emphasized the 'disorderly' nature of children's play," the children in Jo's study "were found to conform to clear rules of order, many of which they created and shared among themselves." This frequent "failure to discern order is attributed to the cognitive and phenomenological estrangement of adult observers from the cultural world of childhood."

Johnson, Diane Kjaer. "Maria Clara Machado and the Brazilian Theatre." Ph.D. diss. University of Iowa, 1985. 380 pp. DAI 46:1640A.

Johnson gives a biography of Machado and analyzes the comic, optimistic spirit in twenty of her plays, some of them written specifically for children, all intended for "people of all ages and backgrounds."

Kemp, Marilyn Rainey. "A Study of the Influence of Children's Literature on the Moral Development of Academically Talented Students." Ed.D. diss. Memphis State University, 1989. 100 pp. DAI 50:1919A.

Kemp's study indicates "no significant growth in moral development" when selected children's literature is used to effect moral growth.

Kim, Glenn John. "'This Mad *Instead*': Studies in Metaphor and Literature." Ph.D. diss. Harvard University, 1985. 197 pp. DAI 46:1928A.

Kim focuses "on one significant distinction between kinds of metaphor: those with two clearly articulated terms ('man is a wolf'), and those with but one term possessing a dual reference ('cosmos')," which he identifies as "the metaphoric reification." He analyzes examples from Swift, Carroll, and others.

Konrad, Elaine M. "Developing Thinking Skills with Folktale Variants from Several Cultures." Ed.D. diss. University of Massachusetts, 1989. 190 pp. DAI 50:1212A.

This dissertation in elementary education "explores the possibility of using folktale and fairy tale variants from a variety of cultures to foster the development of thinking skills and to support the use of higher level thought processes." Her results were positive.

Koske, Mary Susan. "Finnish and American Adolescent Fantasy and Humor: An Analysis of Personal and Social Folklore in Educational Contexts." Ph.D. diss. Indiana University, 1988. 603 pp. DAI 49:2769A.

Koske studies "personal folklore . . . in the form of teenagers' reported daydream fantasies" and the relationship of these dreams to social folklore. Her research took place in Finnish and American secondary schools, and her results are based on cultural and gender differences. The latter are "startling." Her "findings about girls' concerns are particularly significant in the light of contemporary feminist scholarship which has all but overlooked adolescent girls in studies of popular culture and literary forms."

Lehman, Harvey Allen. "Ageism and Gerontophobia in Children's Literature." D.A. diss. St. John's University, 1984. 115 pp. DAI 45:3342A.

Lehman believes that from their earliest exposure to literature children are indoctrinated through stereotypes of old age that create "a feeling of antipathy towards the aged." He identifies many types of ageism in writing for very young children and, "in order to ameliorate the ageistic bias," offers selections that "show elder protagonists in positive ways."

Lewis, Jayne Elizabeth. "The Voluble Body: Re-Inventing the Neoclassical Fable." Ph.D. diss. Princeton University, 1988. 560 pp. DAI 50:148A.

Lewis studies the use of Aesop's fables in England from 1651–1738. Of particular note is chapter Six, in which she shows how "Anne Finch's early eighteenth-century translations of La Fontaine illuminate the paradox in which autonomous bodies become significant only as they are shattered and incorporated into rigid forms that reinforce existing cultural orders."

MacCann, Donnarae C. "The White Supremacy Myth in Juvenile Books about Blacks, 1830–1900." Ph.D. diss. University of Iowa, 1988. 469 pp. DAI 50:1055A.

"Among the major findings of this study is the high correspondence between North and South in their perpetuation of a white supremacist ideology in the culture of childhood." MacCann's dissertation is an interdisciplinary study of history, politics, biography, and literature that indicates that repression, ridicule, and disregard for human rights were rife in "books, schools, churches, and branches of government" that influenced children in the nineteenth century.

Martins, Isis de Araujo. "A Study of Levels of Physical Activity in Selected Outstanding Children's Picture Books of the 1980s." Ph.D. diss. University of Iowa, 1988. 102 pp. DAI 49:2092A.

Martins investigates "the extent to which level of physical activity [is] associated with age and gender in contemporary outstanding [award-winning] picture books" for children. She identifies prominent differences in physical activity by gender in older characters in the books investigated. As children in the books become older they become less active. "One other association suggested by the analysis was that the moderate level of activity appeared to be more strongly associated with adults than with other age groups."

Mavor, Carol Jane. "Utopic Imagings of Difference within Victorian Culture: The Little Girl, The Sleeper, The Virgin Mother and 'The-Maid-of-All-Work.'" Ph.D. diss. University of California—Santa Cruz, 1989. 422 pp. DAI 50:3774A.

Mavor uses an interdisciplinary approach in dealing with the "hysteria" that is often associated with Victorian women's ambivalent attitudes toward women's rights and sexual differences: "drawing from literature, literary criticism, psychoanalysis, feminist theory, art history and social history." Of particular interest is her use of Charles Dodgson's photographs of girls.

Maxwell, Rhoda Jean. "Images of Mothers in Adolescent Literature." Ph.D. diss. Michigan State University, 1986. 162 pp. DAI 47:3428A.

"The purpose of this study was to discover if the images of mothers in realistic adolescent literature published since 1975 reflected real-life mothers." She concludes that recent images of mothers more closely reflect society than those published before 1975.

Meacham, Mary Ellen. "The Development of Children's Book Reviewing in Selected Journals from 1924–1984." Ph.D. diss. Texas Woman's University, 1989. 187 pp. DAI 50:3400A.

This dissertation in library science examines children's book reviews in *Booklist, Bulletin of the Center for Children's Books, Horn Book*, and *School Library Journal* and describes their typical reading audiences. "The results of this study should help librarians select the reviewing journal(s) that best suit their libraries' needs. It may also serve to make local collections less parochial by encouraging reliance on outside, disinterested opinion and to combat censorship attempts by providing a buttress of informed critical evaluation." The study assumes that reviews in these journals are impartial and evaluative.

Miller, Sara. "Evil and Fairy Tales: The Witch as Symbol of Evil in Fairy Tales." Ph.D. diss. California Institute of Integral Studies, 1984. 255 pp. DAI 45:3147A.

Miller's dissertation uses the vehicle of witches in fairy tales to examine current theories of evil and to define the term.

Montenyohl, Eric Lawrence. "Andrew Lang and the Fairy Tale." Ph.D. diss. Indiana University, 1986. 298 pp. DAI 47:4479A.

Montenyohl surveys Lang's prolific use of the folktale in his written and edited works, stressing how he comingles folklore and literary tales.

Noel, Roberta Christine. "The Borrowed Cup of Courage: A Descriptive Comparison of Archetypes Presented by Male and Female Authors in Fantasy for Adolescents." Ed.D. diss. Gonzaga University, 1987. 345 pp. DAI 49:2206A.

Noel analyzes 107 works of fantasy written between 1965 and 1985 and "discover[s] that rites of passage elements are present in all" she selected for in-depth analysis. The number of female heroines "has increased since 1965, and . . . the growing influence of women in modern American society is positively correlated with the number of female heroes in fantasy novels." Noel also finds no author gender "effect upon the choice of hero, nor upon the rites of passage experienced by that hero on the journey to adulthood."

Pallante, Martha Irene. "The Child and His Book: Children and Children's Moral and Religious Literature, 1700–1850." Ph.D. diss. University of Pennsylvania, 1988. 205 pp. DAI 49:2788A.

Noting how many writers of religious and theological literature presage or mirror shifts in intellectual and social attitudes, Pallante observes that "children's religious and moral works provide stripped down versions of the theological idea[s] that predominated" between 1700 and 1850.

Pennington, John B. "Thematic and Structural Subversion in the Fairy Tales and Fantasies of George MacDonald." Ph.D. diss. Purdue University, 1987. 412 pp. DAI 49:1152A.

Pennington "attempts to distinguish between the fairy tales and fantasies of George MacDonald." He finds that MacDonald followed the normal conventions of the fairy tale but that his fantasies "have no ordered structure." The dissertation is primarily devoted to analyzing the themes in MacDonald's work.

Powell, Kirsten Hoving. "Tradition and Transformation: The Fables of La Fontaine and Their Nineteenth-Century Illustrators and Caricaturists." Ph.D. diss. Columbia University, 1985. 581 pp. DAI 46:2111A.

Powell shows how nineteenth-century artists "merged past and present in fable imagery. . . . The fables of La Fontaine offered artists an established textual and visual vocabulary which they could transform for their own purposes. By playing on words and punning on pictures, they pushed the fables to the limits of socially and ethically acceptable moral didacticism."

Quan, Norma Ann. "Social Values in Popular Adolescent Literature, 1940–1980." Ph.D. diss. University of California—Berkeley, 1989. 179 pp. DAI 50:3172A.

Quan's thesis is that "the social values in popular adolescent literature reflect to a great extent the social values of society—that these values support rather than contradict those of society." The social values she examines relate to manners, honesty, marriage, family, loyalty, education, civic-mindedness, liberty, and freedom. Her conclusions confirm her hypothesis.

Ralph, Phyllis C. "Transformations: Fairy Tales, Adolescence, and the Novel of Female Development in Victorian Fiction." Ph.D. diss. University of Kansas, 1985. 240 pp. DAI 46:3042A.

Ralph states that "fairy tales of transformation depict in symbolic form the process of maturation and provide young readers with ways of exploring and coping with the mysteries of this process." She examines the maturation process in the works of Jane Austen, Charlotte and Emily Brontë, and George Eliot.

Rollin, Lucy Ellen. "The Uses of Enticement: Fantasy and Growth in English Nursery Rhymes." Ph.D. diss. Emory University, 1989. 326 pp. DAI 50:2042A.

Like Bettelheim, Rollin argues that "the violence and sexuality in [nursery] rhymes, as in the tales, acknowledge the presence of forbidden wishes and thus can comfort the child who is struggling with those wishes." Her approach is psychoanalytic, and she concludes that nursery rhymes encourage psychic growth.

Smoke, Leslee Bloomgarden. "The Effects of Fairy Tales on the Inner Experience of Young Adolescents." Ph.D. diss. City University of New York, 1984. 93 pp. DAI 45:2323A.

This dissertation in clinical psychology is predicated on Bettelheim's theories about the effects of fairy tales on young children. She finds that the reading of fairy tales does not affect the moral judgment of the children she worked with, but it does affect their drawing. "The implications of these findings for inner experience and individuation" are discussed.

Smolkin, Laura B. "The Neglected Genre in Children's Literature: Children's Interpretations of Play Scripts through Speech Act Predictions and Reader Response Modes." Ed.D. diss. University of Houston, 1989. 200 pp. DAI 50:2414A.

Smolkin's study is based on Aurand Harris's *The Arkansas Bear*, and because of its results she concludes that plays "represent a valid literary form for children's reading."

Standish, Leah Darlene Hanson. "Fairy Tale Versus Non-Fairy Tale Fictional Material as Presleep Suggestion in Stimulating Dreams and Dream Symbols." Ph.D. diss. Georgia State University, 1987. 186 pp. DAI 48:891A.

The purpose of Standish's study is to see if fairy tales "would stimulate dreams and symbolization differently than contemporary literature, namely mystery stories." While the results are inconclusive, she does find that the number of dreams reported by her subjects declined during the test period, but she speculates that the material may have produced longer and more complex dreams that are harder to remember.

Stickney-Bailey, Susan. "Tieck's *Märchen* and the Enlightenment: The Influence of Wieland and Musaus." Ph.D. diss. University of Massachusetts, 1985. 296 pp. DAI 46:3730A.

In Stickney-Bailey's study "the *Märchen* of Christoph Martin Wieland and Johann Karl August Musaus are particularly suited to provide the context for a study of what Ludwig Tieck inherited from the *Märchen* of the Enlightenment," although "Tieck's skepticism is deeper and finds a more radical expression" than the authors he followed.

Strong, Elizabeth Lee. "Nurturing Early Literacy: A Literature Based Program for At-Risk First Graders." Ph.D. diss. Ohio State University, 1988. 380 pp. DAI 49:2528A.

Strong believes that many at-risk children are "provided literacy interventional instructional programs which are contrary to present theoretical and practical perspectives regarding how literacy emerges and how children learn." She offers an alternative program based on reading from children's literature.

Syme, Margaret Ruth. "Tolkein as Gospel Writer." Ph.D. diss. McGill University (Canada), 1989. DAI 50:973A.

Syme believes that Tolkein's fantasy can be read as gospel literature because "he intended his work to be read as 'gospel,' and 'the good news of the Kingdom of God' is suggested by its allusions to biblical and classical mythology, its linear view of history, its presentation as a compilation of received tradition collected and translated by many hands from a wide variety of sources, by the location of Middle Earth in the distant past of our own world and by the author's attempt to create a world which conforms to familiar patterns of evolution."

Weedman, Judith Elvira. "Communication Patterns Among Cultural Gatekeepers: A Sociometric Analysis of Interactions Among Editors, Reviewers, and Critics of Children's Literature." Ph.D. diss. University of Michigan, 1989. 231 pp. DAI 50:1467A.

Weedman states that "the role of gatekeeper in the world of art" is significant and that "an understanding of the extent to which individuals with these intermediary roles draw from and contribute to a shared pool of ideas contributes to an understanding of culture and how it develops." She surveys this community and finds that communication between and among the groups is predominantly social-based. Information in journals and through professional ties, while important, is less conducive to sharing information and ideas.

Also of Note

Bach, Raymond E. "The Sacrificial Child: A Phenomenological Study of a Literary Theme." Ph.D. diss. Stanford University, 1988. 273 pp. DAI 49:3714A.

Barone, Diane Marie. "Young Children's Written Responses to Literature: Exploring the Relationship Between Written Response and Orthographic Knowledge." Ed.D. diss. University of Nevada—Reno. 1989. 185 pp. DAI 50:1612A.

Calder, James William. "The Effects of Story Structure Instruction on Third-Graders' Concept of Story, Reading Comprehension, Response to Literature, and Written Composition." Ph.D. diss. University of Washington, 1984. 238 pp. DAI 46:387A.

Diamant, Harry R. "The Assessment of Fairy Tales as an Innovative Technique in the Counseling Process." D.SW. diss. Adelphi University (School of Social Work), 1985. 146 pp. DAI 46:3861A.

Doubleday, Catherine Newell. "Children's Perceptions of Television, Real, and Ideal Families." Ph.D. diss. University of California—Los Angeles, 1986. 356 pp. DAI 47:125A.

Enemark, Richard D. "The Limits of David Copperfield's Retrospective Authority: The Many Voices of a 'Monologic' Fiction." Ph.D. diss. Columbia University, 1986. 218 pp. DAI 49:1808A.

Estrada, Anita. "An Exploratory Study of the Relationship Between Curiosity and Print Awareness of Four Year Old Children." Ph.D. diss. University of North Texas, 1988. 120 pp. DAI 50:400A.

Galvan, Dennis Bruce. "The Acquisition of Three Morphological Subsystems in American Sign Language by Deaf Children with Deaf or Hearing Parents." Ph.D. diss. University of California—Berkeley, 1988. 146 pp. DAI 50:1292-3A.

Gleeson, Margaret Mary. "The Effects of Allegory, Fable, and Didactic Presentations on Problem Solving and Memory in Children." Ph.D. diss. Fordham University, 1985. 241 pp. DAI 46:2834A.

Guthrie, Barbara Ann Bowman. "The Spiritual Quest and Health and C. S. Lewis." Ph.D. diss. University of North Texas, 1988. 132 pp. DAI 50:368A.

Hillier, Robert Irwin. "The South Seas Fiction of Robert Louis Stevenson." Ph.D. diss. University of New Hampshire, 1985. 216 pp. DAI 47:537A.

Kelly, David M. "The Treatment of Universalism in Anglican Thought from George MacDonald (1824–1905) to C. S. Lewis (1898–1963)." Ph.D. diss. University of Ottawa (Canada), 1989. ADD 1989.

Neulander, Marina. "The Parent-Child-Conflict in GDR Prose of the Seventies." Ph.D. diss. University of Toronto (Canada), 1989. DAI 50:1672A.

Petrini, Mark Julien. "Children and Heroes: A Study of Catullus and Vergil." Ph.D. diss. University of Michigan, 1987. 160 pp. DAI 49:3714A.

Schulz, Armin Richard. "A Content Analysis of the Developmental Bibliotherapeutic Implications of the Books Nominated for the California Young Reader Medal (1975–1986)." Ed.D. diss. University of the Pacific, 1987. 308 pp. DAI 49:2918A.

Sofoulis, (Sofia), Zoe. "Through the Lumen: *Frankenstein* and the Optics of Reorigination." Ph.D. diss. University of California—Santa Cruz, 1988. 421 pp. DAI 49:3755A.

Talley, Jody Elizabeth. "The Effect of Picture and Story Text Structure on Recall and Comprehension." Ed.D. diss. Auburn University, 1988. 134 pp. DAI 49:2604A.

Woodfield, Deborah L. "Mass Media Viewing Habits and Toleration of Real-Life Aggression." Ph.D. diss. Tulane University, 1987. 76 pp. DAI 49:2931A.

Contributors and Editors

BRIAN ALDERSON is Children's Books Editor of the London *Times* and a peripatetic children's book bibliographer. He recently collaborated with Felix de Marez Oyens on the exhibition "Be Merry and Wise" at the Pierpont Morgan Library. He is currently writing a critical study of Ezra Jack Keats, based on the Keats Papers at the University of Southern Mississippi.

PHYLLIS BIXLER, professor of English at Southwest Missouri State University, has published widely on Frances Hodgson Burnett. More recently, she has provided afterwords for the New American Library Signet editions of *Heidi, Little Lord Fauntleroy*, and *Rebecca of Sunnybrook Farm*.

WILLIAM BLACKBURN teaches in the department of English at the University of Calgary. His research and teaching specialties are children's literature, Renaissance drama, and East-West literary relations.

FRANCELIA BUTLER, founding editor of *Children's Literature*, has published many books on children's literature, including *Skipping Around the World: The Ritual Nature of Folk Rhymes*.

JOHN CECH is the book review editor of *Children's Literature*. He teaches in the English department at the University of Florida. He is the author of a book for children, *My Grandmother's Journey* (1991). He recently completed a book about the works of Maurice Sendak.

HOWARD R. CELL teaches philosophy, and occasionally a seminar on fairy tales, at Glassboro State College, New Jersey. Though most of his research and all of his previous publications deal with Rousseau's political theory, he is currently engaged in a project on eighteenth-century children's literature.

CHARLES L. DEFANTI is a professor of English at Kean College in Union, New Jersey. He is the author of *The Wages of Expectation: A Biography of Edward Dahlberg* (1978) and serves as book review editor of *Cover* magazine.

JANE DOONAN teaches English and visual communications in England and pursues a research interest in the aesthetics of picture-book form. She has published various essays, principally in *Signal: Approaches to Children's Literature*.

RACHEL FORDYCE, former executive of the Children's Literature Association, is the author of four books, the most recent of which is *Lewis Carroll: A Reference Guide*. She is the dean of humanities and social sciences at Indiana University of Pennsylvania.

CHRISTINE DOYLE FRANCIS, at the University of Connecticut, has recently completed curriculum guides on Gerald McDermott's and E. L. Konigsburg's books. Her research emphasizes the relation between feminist and myth criticism and children's literature.

U. C. KNOEPFLMACHER, professor of literature at Princeton University, has contributed to volumes 11, 13, and 18 of *CL*. He recently has co-edited *Forbidden Journeys: Fairy Tales and Fantasies by Victorian Women Writers* with Nina Auerbach and has written the introduction to Glenn Sadler's *Teaching Children's Literature: Issues, Pedagogy, Resources*.

CLAIRE L. MALARTE-FELDMAN is an associate professor of French at the University of New Hampshire. Her earlier research on Perrault has developed into an interest, which is reflected in her current research, on contemporary fairy tales written for children.

CORINNE MCCUTCHAN received her Ph.D. from the University of Virginia in 1991 with a dissertation titled "Joyous Ventures: Kipling's Experiments with Form and Genre." She is an assistant professor of English at Lander College in Greenwood, South Carolina.

JULIET MCMASTER is University Professor of English at the University of Alberta. She is the author of *Thackeray: The Major Novels, Jane Austen on Love, Trollope's Palliser Novels,* and *Dickens the Designer,* in addition to many articles on eighteenth- and nineteenth-century fiction. Her main teaching interests are the English novel and children's literature.

JOHN MURRAY is head of the department of English and communication studies at the Sydney branch of Australian Catholic University. He is completing a study of the Australian children's novelist Patricia Wrightson.

JULIE K. PFEIFFER is pursuing her doctorate at the University of Connecticut. Her work focuses on Milton and eighteenth- and nineteenth-century women novelists.

ANNE K. PHILLIPS, at the University of Connecticut, has contributed to a festschrift in honor of Charleton Laird and was co-author of the instructor's manual for *The Bedford Introduction to Literature.* Her research interests include popular literature of the late nineteenth and early twentieth centuries.

JUDITH A. PLOTZ is chair of the English department at George Washington University, where she teaches nineteenth-century British, Indo-Anglican, and children's literature. She is completing a book on Romanticism and the construction of childhood and has written on Romanticism, childhood, and nineteenth-century children's literature. Her essay on Hartley Coleridge appeared in *CL* 14.

BARBARA ROSEN, retired professor of English at the University of Connecticut, has published on witchcraft, children's literature, and Shakespeare in performance.

GARY D. SCHMIDT teaches medieval and children's literature at Calvin College, Michigan. He is the author of *Robert McCloskey* (Twayne, 1990) and *Hugh Lofting* (Twayne, forthcoming) and coeditor of *The Voice of the Narrator in Children's Literature* (1989).

CAROLE SCOTT is undergraduate dean at San Diego State University and a founding member of the Children's Literature Circle. She has published in children's literature and in pedagogy. She is currently working on the function of parallel worlds in literature for children.

J. D. STAHL, of the literature department at Virginia Polytechnic Institute and State University, recently was guest editor of a special issue of *Children's Literature Association Quarterly* on cross-cultural themes in children's literature. He is working on a book, *Mark Twain, Culture, and Gender: Envisioning America Through Europe.*

D. H. STEWART is professor of English at Texas A & M University and recently has taught at Deep Springs College, California. He is the author of *M. A. Sholokhov* and of several articles on Kipling.

C. W. SULLIVAN III is professor of English and director of graduate studies in English at East Carolina University, North Carolina. His recent book, *Welsh Celtic Myth in Modern Fantasy,* was published by Greenwood Press. He is the vice president of the International Association for the Fantastic in the Arts and the editor of *Children's Folklore Review.* His articles on mythology, folklore, fantasy, and science fiction have appeared in a variety of anthologies and journals.

JAN SUSINA teaches English at Kansas State University and is the editor of *Logic and Tea: The Letters of Charles Dodgson to Members of the G. J. Rowell Family.* He is currently working on a study of nineteenth-century literary fairy tales for children.

SAMANTHA JANE WILCOX is currently working toward a M.A. in American Literature at George Washington University.

IAN WOJCIK-ANDREWS, assistant professor at Eastern Michigan University, teaches literary theory and children's literature. Recent publications include "Notes toward a Marxist Critical Practice" and "The Family as Ideological Construct in the Fiction of Arthur Ransome." Two current research areas involve Marxist feminist readings of children's literature texts and the relationship among literary theory, children's literature, and pedagogical practice.

Award Applications

The article award committee of the Children's Literature Association publishes a bibliography of the year's work in children's literature in the *Children's Literature Association Quarterly* and selects the year's best critical articles. For pertinent articles that have appeared in a collection of essays or journal other than one devoted to children's literature, please send a photocopy or offprint with the correct citation and your address written on the first page to Dr. Gillian Adams, 4105 Ave. C, Austin, Texas, 78751. Papers will be acknowledged and returned if return postage is enclosed. Annual deadline is May 1.

The Phoenix Award is given for a book first published exactly twenty years earlier that did not win a major award but has passed the test of time and is deemed to be of high literary quality. Send nominations to Alethea Helbig, 3640 Eli Road, Ann Arbor, Michigan, 48104.

The Children's Literature Association offers three annual research grants. The Margaret P. Esmonde Memorial Scholarship offers $500 for criticism and original works in the areas of fantasy or science fiction for children or adolescents by beginning scholars, including graduate students, instructors, and assistant professors. Research Fellowships are awards ranging from $250 to $1000 (number and amount of awards based on number and needs of winning applicants) for criticism or original scholarship leading to a significant publication. Recipients must have postdoctoral or equivalent professional standing. Awards may be used for transportation, living expenses, materials, and supplies, but not for obtaining advanced degrees, for creative writing, textbook writing, or pedagogical purposes. The Weston Woods Media Scholarship awards $1000 and free use of the Weston Woods studios to encourage investigation of the elements and techniques that contribute to successful adaptation of children's literature to film or recording, or to developing materials for television and video. For full application guidelines on all three grants, write the Children's Literature Association, c/o Marianne Gessner, 22 Harvest Lane, Battle Creek, Michigan, 49015. Annual deadline for these awards is February 1.

Order Form   Yale University Press, 92A Yale Station, New Haven, CT 06520

Customers in the United States and Canada may photocopy this form and use it for ordering all volumes of **Children's Literature** available from Yale University Press. Individuals are asked to pay in advance. We honor both MasterCard and VISA. Checks should be made payable to Yale University Press.

The prices given are 1992 list prices for the United States and are subject to change. A shipping charge of $2.75 is to be added to each order, and Connecticut residents must pay a sales tax of 6 percent.

Qty.	Volume	Price	Total amount	Qty.	Volume	Price	Total amount
___	8 (cloth)	$45.00	_____	___	14 (cloth)	$45.00	_____
___	8 (paper)	$15.00	_____	___	14 (paper)	$15.00	_____
___	9 (cloth)	$45.00	_____	___	15 (cloth)	$45.00	_____
___	9 (paper)	$15.00	_____	___	15 (paper)	$15.00	_____
___	10 (cloth)	$45.00	_____	___	16 (paper)	$15.00	_____
___	10 (paper)	$15.00	_____	___	17 (cloth)	$45.00	_____
___	11 (cloth)	$45.00	_____	___	17 (paper)	$15.00	_____
___	11 (paper)	$15.00	_____	___	18 (cloth)	$45.00	_____
___	12 (cloth)	$45.00	_____	___	18 (paper)	$15.00	_____
___	12 (paper)	$15.00	_____	___	19 (cloth)	$45.00	_____
___	13 (cloth)	$45.00	_____	___	19 (paper)	$15.00	_____
___	13 (paper)	$15.00	_____	___	20 (cloth)	$45.00	_____
				___	20 (paper)	$15.00	_____

Payment of $ _____ is enclosed (including sales tax if applicable).

MasterCard no. _____

4-digit bank no. _____ Expiration date _____

VISA no. _____ Expiration date _____

Signature _____

SHIP TO: _____

_____

_____

See the next page for ordering issues from Yale University Press, London.

Volumes 1–7 of **Children's Literature** can be obtained directly from John C. Wandell, The Children's Literature Foundation, Box 370, Windham Center, Connecticut 06280.

Order Form   Yale University Press, 23 Pond Street, Hampstead, London NW3, 2 PN, England

Customers in the United Kingdom, Europe, and the British Commonwealth may photocopy this form and use it for ordering all volumes of **Children's Literature** available from Yale University Press. Individuals are asked to pay in advance. We honour Access, Visa, and American Express accounts. Cheques should be made payable to Yale University Press.

The prices given are 1992 list prices for the United Kingdom and are subject to change. A post and packing charge of £1.75 is to be added to each order.

Qty.	Volume	Price	Total amount	Qty.	Volume	Price	Total amount
____	8 (cloth)	£40.00	_____	____	14 (cloth)	£40.00	_____
____	8 (paper)	£13.95	_____	____	14 (paper)	£13.95	_____
____	9 (cloth)	£40.00	_____	____	15 (cloth)	£40.00	_____
____	9 (paper)	£13.95	_____	____	15 (paper)	£13.95	_____
____	10 (cloth)	£40.00	_____	____	16 (paper)	£13.95	_____
____	10 (paper)	£13.95	_____	____	17 (cloth)	£40.00	_____
____	11 (cloth)	£40.00	_____	____	17 (paper)	£13.95	_____
____	11 (paper)	£13.95	_____	____	18 (cloth)	£40.00	_____
____	12 (cloth)	£40.00	_____	____	18 (paper)	£13.95	_____
____	12 (paper)	£13.95	_____	____	19 (cloth)	£35.00	_____
____	13 (cloth)	£40.00	_____	____	19 (paper)	£10.95	_____
____	13 (paper)	£13.95	_____	____	20 (cloth)	£35.00	_____
				____	20 (paper)	£10.95	_____

Payment of £_____ is enclosed.

Please debit my Access/Visa/American Express account no. _____

Expiry date _____

Signature _____ Name _____

Address _____

Volumes 1–7 of **Children's Literature** can be obtained directly from John C. Wandell, The Children's Literature Foundation, Box 370, Windham Center, Connecticut 06280.